The Beat Book

THE BEAT BOOK

Writings from the
Beat Generation

||||||||||||||||||||||||||||||||||||||||||||||||||||||||||||||||||||||||||||||||||||||||||||||||||||||||||||||||||||

Edited by **Anne Waldman**

Foreword by **Allen Ginsberg**

SHAMBHALA
Boston
2007

With thanks for editorial assistance to Andrew Schelling, Erik Anderson, and Todd McCarty.

SHAMBHALA PUBLICATIONS, INC.
Horticultural Hall
300 Massachusetts Avenue
Boston, Massachusetts 02115
www.shambhala.com

9   8   7   6   5   4   3   2   1

Printed in the United States of America
♾ This edition is printed on acid-free paper that meets
the American National Standards Institute Z39.48 Standard.

Distributed in the United States by Random House, Inc.,
and in Canada by Random House of Canada Ltd

The Library of Congress catalogues the previous editions of this book as
follows:
The beat book/edited by Anne Waldman.
      p.   cm.
   Includes bibliographical references (p.   ).
   ISBN 978-1-57062-000-3 (hardcover)
   ISBN 978-1-57062-427-8 (pbk.)
   ISBN 978-1-59030-455-6 (pbk.; alk. paper)
   1. American poetry—20th century.   2. Beat generation—
Poetry.   I. Waldman, Anne, 1945–
PS614.B33   1995   95-5326
811'.5408—dc20   CIP

For

Ambrose Eyre Waldman Bye
Althea Rose Schelling
their friends and their generation

We seek to find new phrases; we try hard, we writhe and twist and blow; every now and then a clear harmonic cry gives new suggestions of a tune, a thought, that will someday be the only tune and thought in the world and which will raise men's souls to joy. We find it, we lose, we wrestle for it, we find it again, we laugh, we moan. Go moan for man. It's the pathos of people that gets us down, all the lovers in this dream.

—Jack Kerouac, ON THE ROAD

Contents

Foreword

||||||||||||||||||||||||||||||||||||||||||||||||||||||||||||||||||||||||||||||||||||||||||||||||||||||||||||||||||||||||||||||||||||||

THE PHRASE "Beat generation" arose out of a specific conversation between Jack Kerouac and John Clellon Holmes in 1948. They were discussing the nature of generations, recollecting the glamour of the Lost Generation, and Kerouac said, "Ah, this is nothing but a beat generation." They talked about whether it was a "found generation" (as Kerouac sometimes called it), an "angelic generation," or some other epithet. But Kerouac waved away the question and said beat generation—not meaning to name the generation, but to unname it.

John Clellon Holmes's celebrated article in late 1952 in the *New York Times Magazine* carried the headline title "This Is the Beat Generation." That caught the public eye. Then Kerouac anonymously published a fragment of *On the Road* called "Jazz of the Beat Generation," and that reinforced the curiously poetic phrase. So that's the early history of the term.

Herbert Huncke, author of *The Evening Sun Turned Crimson,* and friend of Kerouac, Burroughs, and others of that literary circle from the forties, introduced them to what was then known as "hip language." In that context, the word "beat" is a carnival, "subterranean" (subcultural) term—a term much used then in Times Square: "Man, I'm beat," meaning without money and without a place to stay. It could also refer to those "who walked all night with shoes full of blood on the snowbank docks waiting for a door in the East River to open to a room full of steam heat and opium" (*Howl*). Or the word would be used as in conversation: "Would you like to go to the Bronx Zoo?" "Nah, man, I'm too 'beat,' I was up all night." So, the original street usage meant exhausted, at the bottom of the world, looking up or out, sleepless, wide-eyed, perceptive, rejected by society, on your own, streetwise. Or, as it once implied, "beat" meant finished, completed, in the dark night of the soul or in the cloud of unknowing. It could mean open, as in the Whitmanesque sense of "openness," equivalent to humility. So "beat" was interpreted in various circles to mean emptied out, exhausted, and at the same time wide-open and receptive to vision.

A third meaning of "beat," as in beatific, was publicly articulated in 1959 by Kerouac, to counteract the abuse of the term in the media (where it was being interpreted as meaning "beaten completely," a "loser," without the aspect of humble intelligence, or of "beat" as "the beat of drums" and "the beat goes on"—all varying mistakes of interpretation or etymology). Kerouac (in various interviews and lectures) was trying to indicate the correct sense of the word by pointing out its connection to words like "beatitude" and "beatific"—the necessary beatness or darkness that precedes opening up to light, egolessness, giving room for religious illumination.

A fourth meaning that accumulated around the word is found in the phrase "Beat generation literary movement." This phrase referred to a group of friends who had worked together on poetry, prose, and cultural conscience from the mid-forties until the term became popular nationally in the late fifties. The group consisted of Kerouac, Neal Cassady (Kerouac's prototype hero of *On the Road*), William Burroughs, Herbert Huncke, John Clellon Holmes (author of *Go, The Horn,* and other books), and myself. We met Carl Solomon and Philip Lamantia in 1948, encountered Gregory Corso in 1950, and first saw Lawrence Ferlinghetti and Peter Orlovsky in 1954.

By the mid-fifties, this smaller circle—through natural affinity of modes of thought, literary style, or planetary perspective—was augmented in friendship and literary endeavor by a number of writers in San Francisco, including Michael Mc-

Clure, Gary Snyder, Philip Whalen, and by 1958 some other powerful but lesser-known poets, such as Bob Kaufman, Jack Micheline, and Ray Bremser, and the better-known black poet LeRoi Jones. All of us accepted the term "beat" at one time or another, humorously or seriously, but sympathetically, and were included in a survey of Beat manners, morals, and literature by *Life* magazine in a lead article in 1959 by Paul O'Neil, and by the journalist Alfred Aronowitz in a twelve-part series entitled "The Beat Generation" in the *New York Post.*

By the mid-fifties a sense of some mutual trust and interest was developed with Frank O'Hara and Kenneth Koch as well as with Robert Creeley and other alumni of Black Mountain College in North Carolina. Of that literary circle, Kerouac, Whalen, Snyder, poets Lew Welch, Diane di Prima, Joanne Kyger, and Orlovsky, as well as myself and others were interested in meditation and Buddhism. (A discussion of the relationship between Buddhism and the Beat generation can be found in a scholarly survey of the evolution of Buddhism in America, *How the Swans Came to the Lake,* by Rick Fields.)

The fifth meaning of the phrase "Beat generation" refers to the broader influence of literary and artistic activities of poets, filmmakers, painters, writers, and novelists who were working in concert in anthologies, publishing houses, independent filmmaking, and other media. These groups refreshed the long-lived bohemian cultural tradition in America. Among major interactive figures were: in film and still photography, Robert Frank and Alfred Leslie; in music, David Amram; in painting, Larry Rivers; in poetry and publishing, Cid Corman, Jonathan Williams, Don Allen, Barney Rosset, Lawrence Ferlinghetti. This energy fell out into the youth movement of the day, which was growing, and was absorbed by the mass and middle-class culture of the late fifties and early sixties.

Some essential ideals of the original artistic movement can be traced clearly in these poets' writings, and continued intergenerational interest decade after decade has been magnetized by a number of consistent themes which might be summarized as follows: An inquisitiveness into the nature of consciousness, leading to acquaintance with Eastern thought, meditation practice, art as extension or manifestation of exploration of the texture of consciousness, spiritual liberation as a result. This led toward sexual liberation, particularly gay liberation, which historically had a part in catalyzing women's lib and black lib. A tolerant nontheistic view developed out of exploring the texture of consciousness, thus cosmic anti-fascism, a peaceable nonviolent approach to politics, multiculturalism, the absorption of black culture into mainstream literature and music, as, for example, Kerouac's spontaneous "bop prosody" or the odd identity of the group of poets later called the Beat generation: Burroughs, white Protestant; Kerouac, American Indian and Breton; Corso, Italian Catholic; myself, Jewish radical; Orlovsky, White Russian; Gary Snyder, Scotch-German; Lawrence Ferlinghetti, Italian, Continental, Sorbonne-educated; Philip Lamentia, Italian authentic Surrealist; Michael McClure, Midwest U.S. Scotch; Bob Kaufman, Surrealistic African-American; LeRoi Jones, Black Powerful, among others. So art's viewed as sacred practice, with sacramental approach to each other as characters. The color of candor emerges with good humor and an inadvertent spontaneous frankness, unpremeditated directness in life and in art, the end of secrecy and paranoia that runs beneath macho sexual politics and demagoguery all the way up through CIA-KGB and nuclear machinations. There's further realization we can destroy the human residence on the planet if we don't trust and exercise our better natures, thus an end to nineteenth-century Marxist-Capitalist myth of progress with expansionist imperial rivalry.

Our interest in psychedelic substances as educational tools, particularly marijuana, mushrooms, and LSD, led to a more realistic approach to drug laws, recognizing that tobacco and alcohol are physically more destructive than all other drugs except cocaine. Thus the junk problem should be decriminalized and medicalized, and hemp, now a problem, should be transformed into an asset for the failing family farm to help reinhabit the countryside and provide some sustainable product (cloth, rope, et al.) as alternative to plastic consciousness.

And finally, appreciation of eros, sacramental approach to sexual joy. Those are the main themes that have run through the art and poetry and prose of the writers I mentioned from the very beginning in the forties through the public poetry readings that surfaced in the mid-fifties into common consciousness. Many of these values have entered mainstream thought—e.g., ecology, grass, gay lib, multiculturalism—but haven't seen fruition in government behavior, so that now we have more folk in our prisons or under government surveillance than any country West or East.

This "Beat generation" or "sixties" tolerant worldview provoked an intoxicated right wing to go into "Denial" (as in AA terminology) of reality, and reinforced its codependency with repressive laws, incipient police state, death-penalty demagoguery, sex demagoguery, art censorship, fundamentalist monotheist televangelist quasi-fascist wrath, racism, and homophobia. This counterreaction seems a by-product of the further gulf between the rich and poor classes, growth of a massive abused underclass, increased power and luxury for the rich who control politics and their minions in the media. Prescription: more art, meditation, lifestyles of relative penury, avoidance of conspicuous consumption that's burning down the planet.

I think younger generations have been attracted by the exuberance, libertarian optimism, erotic humor, frankness, continuous energy, invention, and collaborative amity of these poets and singers. We had a great job to do, and we're doing it, trying to save and heal the spirit of America.

ALLEN GINSBERG
1996

Editor's Introduction

||||||||||||||||||||||||||||||||||||||||||||||||||||||||||||||||||||||||||||||||||||||||||||||||||||||||||||||||||||||

AFTER OVER half a century since the first tremors of the Beat Movement, what makes the legacy of the Beat writers so fiercely durable, their image tenacious and provocative? What is the wisdom that this controversial literary generation imparts through its writings? I think the nominal "Beat literature canon" endures and has major force because it holds together, through communality, a discourse that manifests a visceral relationship to an imaginative language *in the world*. In a complex and troubled world, this active engagement continues with subsequent generations of readers and writers, especially in a new century already tormented by a weakening of ethics, a time of Orwellian dystopia, a new century with nuclear proliferation on the rise, and the sense of "eternal war." Any intelligent, creative person cries out for alternatives to the tabloid culture we live in, which is dominated by a corporate media that indulges in mindless burlesques, churning out lies and euphemism.

How refreshing these Beat writers and thinkers are, how original their *sound* and *sense*. They were extremely prescient and interactive within Western culture, and considered issues of ecology, war, racism, homosexuality, feminism, drugs and addiction, censorship, religion/spirituality, as well as the omnipresent mammon of the State. Many of them traveled outside the conveniences of American lifestyle and privilege. They spent time in India, Japan, Mexico, Morocco, France, England,

Cuba. They were international in their outlook and appeal, were widely translated, and continue to be read and honored abroad. Some were put on trial and harassed. Some have (and continue to have) CIA files on their activities, most particularly during the time of the civil rights movement and the Vietnam War. All of them carry "crazy wisdom" in their genes, a Buddhist term which describes a fearless and imaginative unpredictability of mind.

One wonders where is a Hieronymus Bosch-like writer such as William Burroughs now? Who could wrap a mind and imagination around the grotesqueries of Abu Ghraib, Guantanamo, and other charnel grounds of the war machine? Where is the *Howl* for the twenty-first century? What new group of writers is willing to embrace a spirituality or philosophy based on fearlessness, compassion, and community as the Beats did with Buddhism? What group of writers is willing to stand up to the media and cultural conventions for art?

Initially, one is engaged, entertained, and drawn in by the Beat myth—the lore, the cultural image—but finally one focuses on the writing itself and exults in finding that it still *breathes*. These writers were literary companions who not only championed each other's work but also spoke of and to one another *inside* their work. Witness, for example, Allen Ginsberg's paeans to Neal Cassady in "The Green Automobile" and "On Neal's Ashes"; Joanne Kyger's charming homage, "Philip Whalen's Hat"; Whalen's stark image of Amiri Baraka (LeRoi Jones) as political prisoner in "International Date Line, Monday/Monday 27:XI:67"; and Kerouac's characters based on his friends in *Visions of Cody* and *The Dharma Bums*—to name but a few instances. And as scattered, destructive, and blunted as some of these writers' lives may have been, their work is amazingly diverse, including autobiographical prose, epistolary riff, spontaneous poetry, pure lyric, polemic, satire, political manifesto, and memoir. There's an unabashed candor and generosity operating inside this literature. This candor, or straightforwardness, signifies its own recondite fears and aspiration: "I write this book because we're all gonna die," eulogized Jack Kerouac in one of his novels. This impulse to write is gathered and centered in magnanimity through language. Candid American speech rhythms, jazz rhythms, boxcar rhythms, industrial rhythms, rhapsody, skillful cut-up juxtapositions, and an expansiveness that mirrors the primordial chaos come into play constantly. This is writing that thumbs its nose at self-serving complacency.

The Beat literary aesthetic embraces a boisterous experimentation and pursues, in Gregory Corso's words, "the use of mixtures containing spontaneity, 'bop prosody,' surreal-real images, jumps, beats, cool measures, long rapid vowels, long long lines, and the main content, soul." Much of the work hums with tangibles, with minute particulars, with luminous details. It rages with hot emotion, eschatological rant, scintillating intellect, playful wit, and a homegrown, particularly American innocence and optimism. At root it accommodates the intrinsic nature of our suffering. These *poètes maudits* (a term popularized by French poet Paul Verlaine, meaning "outcast" or "accursed" poets) were possessed of something akin to the Buddhist notion of *bodhichitta*—tender heart—which carries with it not only a sense of aspiration and cutting through worldly veils, but also "getting down" emphatically, soulfully, with the suffering of others; soul = heart, essence, psyche, originality, *compassion.*

Beat literature sings against cynicism, apathy, injustice, deception, compromise, racism, consumerism, war, evils and cons of all kinds. No wonder many of these bards were, and still are, considered outrageous. Allen Ginsberg fought censorship issues until he died. William Burroughs credited the Beats with being the "real architects of change." "There's no doubt," Burroughs argued, "that we're living in a freer America as a result of the Beat literary movement, which is an important part of the larger picture of cultural and political change in this country during the last forty years, when a four-letter word couldn't appear on the printed page, and minority rights were ridiculous."

Historically, the Beat writers empowered themselves through their writing at a time when the rest of the culture was under a collective hallucinatory yoke. The post–World War II doldrums, the cold war, and the Korean debacle all contributed to, even created, a false sense of security even while economic and ethnic storms raged on the horizon. This was the first literary generation to come of age with the possibility of the complete nuclear annihilation of the world. Prophets, outlaws, outriders, misfits, anarchists, pacifists, drug addicts, homosexuals, cultural activists, spiritual seekers—these are only some of the handy tags. It is strange to note that Kerouac remained a conservative all his life and supported the war in Vietnam. Burroughs, also defying the labels, had been conservative on certain issues, such as the Gulf War of 1990. Philip Whalen became a Zen priest. Diane di Prima raised five children and founded a school of healing arts. Hard to exploit for anyone's agenda, the Beat writers were and are primarily *individuals*.

The word *beat* was specifically employed after World War II by jazz musicians and hipsters as a slang term meaning "down and out," or broke. In 1944, William Burroughs heard his pal, Times Square hustler Herbert Huncke, using the word *beat*, and passed it on to young Columbia College freshman Allen Ginsberg. Jack Kerouac, who heard the "melancholy sneer" in Huncke's use of the word, later stressed that *beat* "never meant juvenile delinquents" but rather meant "characters of a special spirituality." And Kerouac, in a conversation with John Clellon Holmes in 1948, as Holmes probed him to characterize the "new attitude," mused, "We were a generation of furtives. You know, with an inner knowledge there's no use flaunting on that level, the level of the 'public,' a kind of beatness—I mean being right down to it, to ourselves, because we all really know where we are—and a weariness with all the forms, all the conventions of the world." Ginsberg speaks of sharing with Kerouac "the idea of transience of phenomena—the poignant Kewpie doll dearness of personages vanishing in time. Not a morbid interest in death but the realization of the mortal turn."

The event that not only brought East and West Coast poetic impulses together but also unselfconsciously launched the Beat movement was the "Six Poets at the Six Gallery" in San Francisco in 1955. As Allen Ginsberg read his apocalyptic poem

Howl, everyone knew, according to Michael McClure, himself a participant in the reading, that "a barrier had been broken, a human voice and body had been hurled against the harsh wall of America and its supporting armies and navies and academies and institutions and ownership systems and power-support bases." Lawrence Ferlinghetti, in the audience that night, sent Ginsberg a telegram after the reading, offering to publish *Howl* in the Pocket Poets series published by City Lights. In May of 1957, several months after its publication, *Howl and Other Poems* was seized by customs officials, and Ferlinghetti and his employee Shigeyoshi Murao (who worked at his North Beach bookstore) were charged with publishing and selling an obscene book. The *Howl* trial brought national attention to Ginsberg and Ferlinghetti, and after obscenity charges were dropped, the sales of the book swelled to the tens of thousands. The Beat movement had arrived.

Editing this anthology has been rather like trying to wrestle a dragon into a matchbox. I wanted to include substantial pieces by the "prime movers" of the scene that I felt would carry the Beat *rasa*—flavor or taste—in a distinctive, historical way. Thus, I chose to be focused rather than all-inclusive. I wanted to more fully represent Diane di Prima and Joanne Kyger—important writers who also happen to be women. I wanted to include Amiri Baraka and Bob Kaufman, major writers "of color," recognized for their powerful contributions to the canon. I felt that the work of John Wieners, usually more associated with the Black Mountain School (of Charles Olson, Robert Creeley, and others), needed to be presented here, as it is particularly graced with what Corso calls "soul," in the Beat sense. There were some "hard calls." Many of these writers have vigorously continued their work over the decades, and rather than be constrained by the historical, Beat time frame, I included more recent writing as well. Periodic reunions and Beat conferences around the country and abroad continually keep the lines of literary communication open. Beat writers have also influenced and encouraged subsequent generations of writers by prodigious example, their linguistic and psychological breakthroughs cutting a path for the ongoing literary avant garde.

The authors included here are each unique, in both their literary styles and their life styles, but they all shared an auspicious "moment" in the vast landscape of American belletristic time; a blink of an eye, perhaps, that had extraordinarily far-ranging ramifications for the culture at large. What continues to survive in the writing is the sensitive and smart impulse to catch the world magically through language as it flies. Open this book at any page and taste the tough and tender words of these cherished legendary scribes.

ANNE WALDMAN
The Jack Kerouac School
of Disembodied Poetics

GREGORY CORSO

GREGORY CORSO was born in 1930 in Greenwich Village, New York City, to teenage immigrant parents. His mother returned to Italy the next year, and Corso spent his youth in a number of foster homes and youth centers, with periodic stints with his father, but invariably running away. At age seventeen he went to prison for three years, where he became an avid reader: "An old man handed me *Karamazov, Les Misérables, Red and Black,* and thus I learned, and was free to think and feel and write." Corso was released at age twenty, "in love with Chatterton, Marlowe, and Shelley." He returned to Greenwich Village where "one night 1950 in a dark empty bar sitting with my prison poems I was graced with a deep-eyed apparition: Allen Ginsberg." A friendship with Ginsberg and Kerouac ensued. (Kerouac described Corso as "a tough young kid from the Lower East Side who rose like an angel over the rooftops.") In 1954, he attended Harvard, where a group of fellow students funded the publication of his first book, *The Vestal Lady of Brattle Street.* Then, in 1956, Corso migrated to San Francisco to join poet-friends. Lawrence Ferlinghetti asked for his manuscript *Gasoline* and published it in the City Lights Pocket Poets series. Ginsberg describes Corso's poetry as "pure velvet, close to John Keats for our time." Over the years, he divided his time between San Francisco and New York and was also a regular visiting faculty member at the Jack Kerouac School of Naropa University (where he can be seen in the film

What Happened to Kerouac). He died on January 17, 2001. *An Accidental Autobiography: The Selected Letters,* with an introduction by Patti Smith, was published in 2003.

―――――――

Sea Chanty

My mother hates the sea
my sea especially
I warned her not to
it was all I could do
Two years later
the sea ate her
Upon the shore I found a strange
yet beautiful food
I asked the sea if I could eat it
and the sea said that I could
—Oh, sea, what fish is this
so tender and so sweet?
—Thy mother's feet

The Last Gangster

Waiting by the window
my feet enwrapped with the dead bootleggers of Chicago
I am the last gangster, safe, at last,
waiting by a bullet-proof window.

I look down the street and know
the two torpedoes from St. Louis.
I've watched them grow old
. . . guns rusting in their arthritic hands.

Amnesia in Memphis

Who am I, flat beneath the shades of Isis,
This clay-skinned body, made study
By the physicians of Memphis?
Was it always my leaving the North
Snug on the back of the crocodile?
Do I remember this whorl of mummy cloth
As I stood fuming by the Nile?
O life abandoned! half-embalmed, I beat the soil!
For what I am; who I am, I cannot regain,
Nor sponge my life back with the charm of Ibis oil—
Still-omen of the dribbling Scarab!
Fate that leads me into the chamber of blue perfumes!
Is there no other worthy of prophecy
Than that Decker who decks my spine with ostrich plumes?

No more will the scurvy Sphinx
With beggy prophets their prophecies relate—

For Homer

There's rust on the old truths
—Ironclad clichés erode
New lies don't smell as nice
as new shoes
I've years of poems to type up
40 years of smoking to stop
I've no steady income
No home
And because my hands are autochthonic
I can never wash them enough
I feel dumb
I feel like an old mangy bull
crashing through the red rag

of an alcoholic day
Yet it's all so beautiful
isn't it?
How perfect the entire system of things
The human body
all in proportion to its form
Nothing useless
Truly as though a god had indeed warranted it so
And the sun for day the moon for night
And the grass the cow the milk
That we all in time die
You'd think there would be chaos
the futility of it all
But children are born
oft times spitting images of us
And the inequities
millions doled one
nilch for another
both in the same leaky lifeboat
I've no religion
and I'd as soon worship Hermes
And there is no tomorrow
there's only right here and now
you and whomever you're with
alive as always
and ever ignorant of that death you'll never know
And all's well that is done
A Hellene happiness pervades the peace
and the gift keeps on coming . . .
a work begun splendidly done
To see people aware & kind
at ease and contain'd of wonder
like the dreams of the blind
The heavens speak through our lips
All's caught what could not be found
All's brought what was left behind

The Mad Yak

I am watching them churn the last milk
    they'll ever get from me.
They are waiting for me to die;
They want to make buttons out of my bones.
Where are my sisters and brothers?
That tall monk there, loading my uncle,
    he has a new cap.
And that idiot student of his—
    I never saw that muffler before.
Poor uncle, he lets them load him.
How sad he is, how tired!
I wonder what they'll do with his bones?
And that beautiful tail!
How many shoelaces will they make of that!

Zizi's Lament

I am in love with the laughing sickness
it would do me a lot of good if I had it—
I have worn the splendid gowns of Sudan,
carried the magnificent halivas of Boudodin Bros.,
kissed the singing Fatimas of the pimp of Aden,
wrote glorious psalms in Hakhaliba's cafe,
but I've never had the laughing sickness,
so what good am I?

The fat merchant offers me opium, kief, hashish,
    even camel juice,
all is unsatisfactory—
O bitter damned night! you again! must I yet
pluck out my unreal teeth
undress my unlaughable self

put to sleep this melancholy head?
I am nothing without the laughing sickness.

My father's got it, my grandfather had it;
surely my Uncle Fez will get it, but me, me
who it would do the most good,
will I ever get it?

I Held a Shelley Manuscript

(written in Houghton Library, Harvard)

My hands did numb to beauty
as they reached into Death and tightened!

O sovereign was my touch
upon the tan-ink's fragile page!

Quickly, my eyes moved quickly,
sought for smell for dust for lace
              for dry hair!

I would have taken the page
breathing in the crime!
For no evidence have I wrung from dreams—
yet what triumph is there in private credence?

Often, in some steep ancestral book,
when I find myself entangled with leopard-apples
              and torched-mushrooms,
my cypressean skein outreaches the recorded age
and I, as though tipping a pitcher of milk,
pour secrecy upon the dying page.

Poets Hitchhiking on the Highway

Of course I tried to tell him
but he cranked his head
    without an excuse.
I told him the sky chases
    the sun
And he smiled and said:
    'What's the use.'
I was feeling like a demon
    again
So I said: 'But the ocean chases
    the fish.'
This time he laughed
    and said: 'Suppose the
        strawberry were
            pushed into a mountain.'
After that I knew the
    war was on—
So we fought:
He said: 'The apple-cart like a
            broomstick-angel
      snaps & splinters
            old dutch shoes.'
I said: 'Lightning will strike the old oak
        and free the fumes!'
He said: 'Mad street with no name.'
I said: 'Bald killer! Bald killer! Bald killer!'
He said, getting real mad,
    'Firestoves! Gas! Couch!'
I said, only smiling,
      'I know God would turn back his head
      if I sat quietly and thought.'
We ended by melting away,
    hating the air!

Dream of a Baseball Star

I dreamed Ted Williams
leaning at night
against the Eiffel Tower, weeping.

He was in uniform
and his bat lay at his feet
—knotted and twiggy.

'Randall Jarrell says you're a poet!' I cried.
'So do I! I say you're a poet!'

He picked up his bat with blown hands;
stood there astraddle as he would in the batter's box,
and laughed! flinging his schoolboy wrath
toward some invisible pitcher's mound
—waiting the pitch all the way from heaven.

It came; hundreds came! all afire!
He swung and swung and swung and connected not one
sinker curve hook or right-down-the-middle.
A hundred strikes!
The umpire dressed in strange attire
thundered his judgement: YOU'RE OUT!
And the phantom crowd's horrific boo
dispersed the gargoyles from Notre Dame.

And I screamed in my dream:
God! throw thy merciful pitch!
Herald the crack of bats!
Hooray the sharp liner to left!
Yea the double, the triple!
Hosannah the home run!

Spontaneous Requiem For the American Indian

Wakonda! Talako! deathonic turkey gobbling in the soft-
  footpatch night!
Blue-tipped yellow-tipped red-tipped feathers of whort dye
  fluffing in fire mad dance whaa whaa dead men red men
  feathers-in-their-head-men night!
Deerskin rage of flesh on the bone on the hot tobacco ground!
Muskhogean requiems america southeastern, O death of
  Creeks, Choctaws,
The youthful tearful Brave, in his dying hand trout, well-caught
  proud trout,
Softest of feet, fleet, o america dirge, o america norwegians
  swedes of quid and murder and boots and slaughter and
  God and rot-letters,
O pinto brays! O deatheme sled mourning the dying chief!
Berries, spruce, whortle, cranky corn, bitter wheat; o scarcity
  of men!
High-throttled squawlark, sister warrior, teepee maid, scar
  lover, crash down thy muskrat no longer thy flesh hand
  and rage and writhe and pound thy Indianic earth with
  last pang of love of love,
o america, o requiems—

Ghost-herds of uneaten left to rot animals thundering across
  the plains
Chasing the ghost of England across the plains forever ever,
  pompous Kiwago raging in the still Dakotas, o america—
America o mineral scant america o mineralize america o
  conferva of that once
great lovely Muskhogean pool, o oil-suck america despite, oil
  from forgetive days, hare to arrow, muskellunge to spear,
  fleet-footed know ye speed-well the tribes thence outraced
  the earth to eat to love to die,
o requiems, Hathor off-far bespeaks Wakonda,

heraldic henequen tubas whittled in coyote tune to mourn the
    death of the going sun the going sled of each dying, sad
    and dying, shake of man, the tremble of men, of each
    dying chief slow and red and leather fur hot—
Shake slow the rattler, the hawk-teeth, the bettle-bells, shake
    slow dirge, o dirge, shake slow the winds of winds, o
    feathers withered and blown,
Dirge the final pinto-led sled, the confused hurt sad king of
    Montanas,
Strike dumb the French fur trappers in their riverboat brool
    mockery, no chant of death in such a wealth of muskrat
    and beaver, shun them,
O slam squaw hysteria down on america, the covered wagon
    america, the arrow flamed wagons of conquest, the death
    stand of quakers and white-hooded hags and proud new
    men, young and dead,
O Geronimo! hard nickel faced Washington Boliva of a dying
    city that never was, that monster-died, that demons
    gathered to steal and did,
O Sitting Bull pruneman Jefferson Lenin Lincoln reddeadman,
    force thy spirit to wings, cloud the earth to air, o the
    condor the vulture the hawk fat days are gone, and you
    are gone, o america, o requiems,
Dry valleys, deathhead stones, high Arizonas, red sun earth, the
    sled,
The weeping bray, the ponymarenight, the slow chief of death,
    wrinkled and sad and manless, vistaless, smokeless, proud
    sad dying—
Toward the coyote reach of peak and moon, howl of heyday,
    laugh proud of men and men, Blackfoot, Mohawk,
    Algonquin, Seneca, all men, o american, peaked there then
    bow
Thy white-haired straw head and, pinto imitated, die with the
    rising moon, hotnight, lost, empty, unseen, musicless,
    mindless; no wind—
In the grim dread light of the Happy Hunting Ground
A century of chiefs argue their many scalps, whacking the

yellow strands of a child against the coaly misty harsh of
tent;

It falls apart in a scatter of strewn, away, gone, no more, back
free out of the quay, into the bladder seep of the bald dead
seeking the hairless rawhead child of whiteman's grave;

O there is more an exact sorrow in this Indianical eternity,

Sure o america woof and haw and caw and wooooo whirl
awhirl here o weep!

Indianhill woe! never was the scalp of men the prime knife in
the heart of a savagengence era, Clevelandestroyer of
manland, o requiems,

O thundercloud, thunderbird, rain-in-the-face, hark in the
gloom, death,

And blankets and corn, and peaceful footings of man in quest
of Kiwago, america, Kiwago, america, corn america,
earthly song of a sad boy's redfleshed song in the night
before the peered head intrusive head of laughing
thunderbolt Zeus, o the prank, o the death, o the night,

Requiem, america, sing a dirge that might stalk the white wheat
black in praise of Indianever again to be, gone, gone,
desolate, and gone;

Hear the plains, the great divide, hear the wind of this night
Oklahoma race to weep first in the dirge of mountains and
streams and trees and birds and day and night and the
bright yet lost apparitional sled,

The bowed head of an Indian is enough to bow the horse's
head and both in unison die and die and die and never
again die for once the night eats up the dying it eats up the
pain and there is no Indian pain no pregnant squaw no
wild-footed great-eyed boy no jolly stern fat white-furred
chief of tobacco damp and sweet, o america america—

Each year Kiwago must watch its calves thin out; must watch
with all its natural killers dead, the new marksmen of
machines and bullets and trained studied eyes aim and fire
and kill the oldest bull, the king, the Kiwago of the
reminiscent plain—

Each year Wakonda must watch the motionless desert, the dry

tearless childless desert, the smokeless desert, the
    Indianlessadly desert—
Each year Talako must watch the bird go arrowless in his peace
    of sky in his freedom of the mouth of old america, raw
    wild calm america,
O america, o requiem, o tumbleweed, o Western Sky, each year
    is another year the soft football doesn't fall, the thin strong
    arm of spear never raised, the wise council of gathered
    kings no longer warm with life and fur and damp and heat
    and hotcorn and dry jerky meat, each year no squaw titters
    her moony lover of hard love and necessary need of man
    and wife and child child, each year no child, no mien of
    life, good life, no, no, america, but the dead stones, the dry
    trees, the dusty going winded earth—requiem.
Pilgrim blunderbuss, buckles, high hat, Dutch, English, patent
leather shoes, Bible, pray, snow, careful, careful, o but feast,
turkey, corn, pumpkin, sweet confused happy hosty guests,
Iroquois, Mohawk, Oneida, Onondaga, Thanksgiving!
O joy! o angels! o peace! o land! land land land, o death,
O fire and arrow and buckshot and whisky and rum and death
    and land,
O witches and taverns and quakers and Salem and New
    Amsterdam and corn,
And night, softfeet, death, massacre, massacre, o america, o
    requiem—
Log-cabins, forts, outposts, trading-posts, in the distance,
    clouds,
Dust, hordes, tribes, death, death, blonde girls to die, gowns of
    ladies to burn, men of redcoats and bluecoats to die, boys
    to drum and fife and curse and cry and die, horses . . . to
    die, babies . . . to die;
Yeeeeeeeeeeeeeeeooooooooooooo!Harrrrrrrrrrrrrrraaaaaaaaa!
EEEEEEEEeeeeeeeeEEEEEEaaaaaaaaaaaaaaaah!
To die to die to die to die to die to die . . . america, requiem.
Corn, jerky, whortly, the Seneca in a deacon's suit, gawky,
    awkward, drunk,
Tired, slouched—the gowns and bright boots pass, the quick
take-your-partner-swing-to-the-left-swing-to-the-right hums

all is over, done, the Seneca sleeps, no sled, no pinto, no end,
but sleep, and a new era, a new day, a new light and the corn
grows plenty, and the night is forever, and the day;
The jetliner streams down upon Texas,
                    Requiem.

Motorcyclist Blackfoot his studded belt at night wilder than
bright hawk-eyes sits on his fat bike black smelly brusqued assy
about to goggleeye himself down golden ventures whizzing
faster than his ancestral steed past smokestacks bannershacks
O the timid shade of Kiwago now! the mad roar exhaustpipe
Indian like a fleeing oven clanking weeeeee weeeeeee no
feathers in his oily helmet O he's a fast engine of steam
zooming unlaurelled by but he's stupid he sits in Horn &
Hardart's his New York visit and he's happy with his short
girls with pink faces and bright hair talking about his big fat
bike and their big fat bike, O he's an angel there though sinister
sinister in shape of Steel Discipline smoking a cigarette in a
fishy corner in the night, waiting, america, waiting the end, the
last Indian, mad Indian of no fish or foot or proud forest haunt,
mad on his knees ponytailing & rabbitfooting his motorcycle,
his the final requiem the final america READY THE FUNERAL
STOMP goodluck charms on, tire aired, spikes greased, morose
goggles on, motor gas brakes checked! 1958 Indians, heaps of
leather—ZOOM down the wide amber speedway of Death,
Little Richard, tuba mirum, the vast black jacket brays in the
full forced fell.

The Whole Mess . . . Almost

I ran up six flights of stairs
to my small furnished room
opened the window
and began throwing out
those things most important in life

First to go, Truth, squealing like a fink:
"Don't! I'll tell awful things about you!"
"Oh yeah? Well, I've nothing to hide . . . OUT!"
Then went God, glowering & whimpering in amazement:
"It's not my fault! I'm not the cause of it all!" "OUT!"
Then Love, cooing bribes: "You'll never know impotency!
All the girls on *Vogue* covers, all yours!"
I pushed her fat ass out and screamed:
"You always end up a bummer!"
I picked up Faith Hope Charity
all three clinging together:
"Without us you'll surely die!"
"With you I'm going nuts! Goodbye!"

Then Beauty . . . ah, Beauty—
As I led her to the window
I told her: "You I loved best in life
. . . but you're a killer; Beauty kills!"
Not really meaning to drop her
I immediately ran downstairs
getting there just in time to catch her
"You saved me!" she cried
I put her down and told her: "Move on."

Went back up those six flights
went to the money
there was no money to throw out
The only thing left in the room was Death
hiding beneath the kitchen sink:
"I'm not real!" It cried
"I'm just a rumor spread by life . . ."
Laughing I threw it out, kitchen sink and all
and suddenly realized Humor
was all that was left—
All I could do with Humor was to say:
"Out the window with the window!"

Rembrandt—Self Portrait

When I draw the magnificent Dutch girl
When I unshackle the peachwolf from browngold air
When I have the shepherd foxglove the chin of an angel
It'll make no difference whether I believe in God or not—

How do I paint the sorrow of men
—a group of singers lamenting the death of a friend?
Who stands so detached from life
and study if there be sadness in men?
Get me the saddest man!
Each brush stroke to break all systems
           the feeding circumference
       the spectric void—Devourer!
Paint! to compel hypocrisy
the face of the human
           become the face of the inhuman
get me gold linen! cold jewels!
           let me lightdrench the saddest of men—

JACK KEROUAC

||||||||||||||||||||||||||||||||||||||||||||||||||||||||||||||||||||||||||||||||||||||||||||||||||||||||||||||||||||||||||||

JACK KEROUAC was born in 1922 in Lowell, Massachusetts. He met Ginsberg and Burroughs in New York City while on a Columbia University football scholarship. He also befriended Neal Cassady, who became the focus for Kerouac's innovative epic, *Visions of Cody,* and *On the Road,* which brought both men instant notoriety on publication in 1957. Kerouac was the author of a dozen novels—"The Duluoz Legend," he called them collectively—envisioning each as an episode in an ongoing American saga. He also wrote books of poetry, the best-known being *Mexico City Blues,* which Kerouac wrote while imagining himself as a blues saxophonist. Later, he performed his writings to jazz accompaniment, inspiring wide interest in the poetry-jazz collaborations begun by Kenneth Patchen, Kenneth Rexroth, and Lawrence Ferlinghetti. While on the West Coast he befriended Gary Snyder, who introduced him to Buddhism. Kerouac's book *The Dharma Bums* adopts a loosely veiled Snyder as its central figure and is said to have set off the "rucksack revolution"—young people living on the cheap, at home in city and wilderness alike, with a resolute spirituality more at ease with Buddhist and Taoist thought than with any Western philosophical system. Kerouac died in 1969 of complications from alcoholism. The mythology that arose around his life and work have created a fierce commercialism, spawning movies (director Francis Ford Coppola owns the movie rights to *On the Road*), clothing, books, even the possibility of a U.S. postage stamp. Books culled from Kerouac's notebooks continue to be published to this day, including *Some of the Dharma* (1999) and *Book of Sketches* (2006).

---

from The Origins of the Beat Generation

It goes back to the inky ditties of old cartoons (Krazy Kat with the irrational brick)—to Laurel and Hardy in the Foreign Legion—to Count Dracula and his *smile* to Count Dracula shivering and hissing back before the Cross—to the Golem horrifying the persecutors of the Ghetto—to the quiet sage in a movie about India, unconcerned about the plot—to the giggling old Tao Chinaman trotting down the sidewalk of old Clark Gable Shanghai—to the holy old Arab warning the hotbloods that Ramadan is near. To the Werewolf of London a distinguished doctor in his velour smoking jacket smoking his pipe over a lamplit tome on botany and suddenly hairs grown on his hands, his cat hisses, and he slips out into the night with a cape and a slanty cap like the caps of people in breadlines—to Lamont Cranston so cool and sure suddenly becoming the frantic Shadow going mwee hee hee ha ha in the alleys of New York imagination. To Popeye the sailor and the Sea Hag and the meaty gunwales of boats, to Cap'n Easy and Wash Tubbs screaming with ecstasy over canned peaches on a cannibal isle, to Wimpy looking X-eyed for a juicy hamburger such as they make no more. To Jiggs ducking before a household of furniture flying through the air, to Jiggs and the boys at the bar and the corned beef and cabbage of old wood-fence noons—to King Kong his eyes looking into the hotel window with tender huge love for Fay Wray—nay, to Bruce Cabot in mate's cap leaning over the rail of a fogbound ship saying "Come aboard." It goes back to when grapefruits were thrown at crooners and harvestworkers at bar-rails slapped burlesque queens on the rump. To when fathers took their sons to the Twi League game. To the days of Babe Callahan on the waterfront, Dick Barthelmess camping under a London street-lamp. To dear old Basil Rathbone looking for the Hound of the Baskervilles (a dog big as the Gray Wolf who will destroy Odin)—to dear old bleary Doctor Watson with a brandy in his hand. To Joan Crawford her raw shanks in the fog, in striped blouse smoking a cigarette at sticky lips in the door of the waterfront dive. To train whistles of steam engines out above the moony pines. To Maw and Paw in the Model A clanking on to get a job in California selling used cars making a whole lotta money. To the glee of America, the honesty of America, the honesty of oldtime grafters in straw hats as well as the honesty of oldtime waiters in line at the Brooklyn Bridge in *Winterset,* the funny spitelessness of old bigfisted America like Big Boy Williams saying "Hoo? Hee? Huh?" in a movie about Mack Trucks and slidingdoor lunchcarts. To Clark Gable, his certain smile, his confident leer. Like my grandfather this America was invested with wild selfbelieving individuality and this had begun to disappear around the end of World War II with so many great guys dead (I can think of half a dozen from my own boyhood groups) when suddenly it began to emerge again, the hipsters began to appear gliding around saying "Crazy, man."

Buddha

I used to sit under trees and meditate
on the diamond bright silence of darkness
and the bright look of diamonds in space
and space that was stiff with lights
and diamonds shot through, and silence

And when a dog barked I took it for soundwaves
and cars passing too, and once I heard
a jet-plane which I thought was a mosquito
in my heart, and once I saw salmon walls
of pine and roses, moving and ululating
with the drapish

Once I forgave dogs, and pitied men, sat
in the rain countin Juju beads, raindrops
are ecstasy, ecstasy is raindrops—birds
sleep when the trees are giving out light
in the night, rabbits sleep too, and dogs

I had a path that I followed thru piney woods
and a phosphorescent white hound-dog named Bob
who led me the way when the clouds covered
the stars, and then communicated to me
the sleepings of a loving dog enamoured
of God

On Saturday mornings I was there, in the sun,
contemplating the blue-bright air, as eyes
of Lone Rangers penetrated the dust
of my canyon thoughts, and Indians
and children, and movie shows

Or Saturday Morning in China when all is so fair
crystal imaginings of pristine lakes, talk
with rocks, walks with a Chi-pack across
Mongolias and silent temple rocks in valleys
of boulder and tarn-washed clay,—shh—
sit and otay

And if men were dyin or sleepin in rooftops
beyond, or frogs croaked once or thrice
to indicate supreme mystical majesty, what's
the diff? and I saw blue sky no different
from dead cat—and love and marriage

No different than mud—that's blood—
and lighted clay too—illuminated intelligent
faces of angels everywhere, with Dostoevsky's
unease praying in their X-brow faces,
twisted and great,

And many a time the Buddha played a leaf
on me at midnight thinkin-time, to
remind me 'This Thinking Has Stopped,'
which it had, because no thinking was there
but wasnt liquidly mysteriously brainly there

And finally I turned into a diamond stone
and sat rigid and golden, gold too—didnt dare
breathe, to break up the diamond that cant
even cut into butter anyway, how brittle
the diamond, how quick returned thought,—
Impossible to exist
      Buddha say:
      'All's possible'

from On the Road

6

Immediately outside Gregoria the road began to drop, great trees arose on each side, and in the trees as it grew dark we heard the great roar of billions of insects that sounded like one continuous high-screeching cry. "Whoo!" said Dean, and he turned on his headlights and they weren't working. "What! what! damn now what?" And he punched and fumed at his dashboard. "Oh, my, we'll have to drive through the jungle without lights, think of the horror of that, the only time I'll see is when another car comes by and there just *aren't* any cars! And of course no lights? Oh, what'll we do, dammit?"

"Let's just drive. Maybe we ought to go back, though?"

"No, never-never! Let's go on. I can barely see the road. We'll make it." And now we shot in inky darkness through the scream of insects, and the great, rank, almost rotten smell descended, and we remembered and realized that the map indicated just after Gregoria the beginning of the Tropic of Cancer, "We're in a new tropic! No wonder the smell! Smell it!" I stuck my head out the window; bugs smashed at my face; a great screech rose the moment I cocked my ear to the wind. Suddenly our lights were working again and they poked ahead, illuminating the lonely road that ran between solid walls of drooping, snaky trees as high as a hundred feet.

"Son-of-a-*bitch!*" yelled Stan in the back. "Hot *damn!*" He was still so high. We suddenly realized he was still high and the jungle and troubles made no difference to his happy soul. We began laughing, all of us.

"To hell with it! We'll just throw ourselves on the gawddamn jungle, we'll sleep in it tonight, let's go!" yelled Dean. "Ole Stan is right. Ole Stan don't care! He's so high on those women and that tea and that crazy out-of-this-world impossible-to-absorb mambo blasting so loud that my eardrums still beat to it—whee! he's so high he knows what he's doing!" We took off our T-shirts and roared through the jungle, barechested. No towns, nothing, lost jungle, miles and miles, and down-going, getting hotter, the insects screaming louder, the vegetation growing higher, the smell ranker and hotter until we began to get used to it and like it. "I'd just like to get naked and roll and roll in that jungle," said Dean. "No, hell, man, that's what I'm going to do soon's I find a good spot." And suddenly Limón appeared before us, a jungle town, a few brown lights, dark shadows, enormous skies overhead, and a cluster of men in front of a jumble of woodshacks—a tropical crossroads.

We stopped in the unimaginable softness. It was as hot as the inside of a baker's oven on a June night in New Orleans. All up and down the street whole families were sitting around in the dark, chatting; occasional girls came by, but extremely young and only curious to see what we looked like. They were barefoot and dirty. We leaned on the wooden porch of a broken-down general store with sacks of flour and fresh pineapple rotting with flies on the counter. There was one oil lamp in here, and outside a few more brown lights, and the rest all black, black, black. Now of course we were so tired we had to sleep at once and moved the car a few yards down a dirt road to the backside of town. It was so incredibly hot it was impossible to sleep. So Dean took a blanket and laid it out on the soft, hot sand in the road and flopped out. Stan was stretched on the front seat of the Ford with both doors open for a draft, but there wasn't even the faintest puff of a wind. I, in the back seat, suffered in a pool of sweat. I got out of the car and stood swaying in the blackness. The whole town had instantly gone to bed; the only noise now was barking dogs. How could I ever sleep? Thousands of mosquitoes had already bitten all of us on chest and arms and ankles. Then a bright idea came to me: I jumped up on the steel roof of the car and stretched out flat on my back. Still there was no breeze, but the steel had an element of coolness in it and dried my back of sweat, clotting up thousands of dead bugs into cakes on my skin, and I realized the jungle takes you over and you become it. Lying on the top of the car with my face to the black sky was like lying in a closed trunk on a summer night. For the first time in my life the weather was not something that touched me, that caressed me, froze or sweated me, but became me. The atmosphere and I became the same. Soft infinitesimal showers of microscopic bugs fanned down on my face as I slept, and they were extremely pleasant and soothing. The sky was starless, utterly unseen and heavy. I could lie there all night long with my face exposed to the heavens, and it would do me no more harm than a velvet drape drawn over me. The dead bugs mingled with my blood; the live mosquitoes exchanged further portions; I began to tingle all over and to smell of the rank, hot, and rotten jungle, all over from hair and face to feet and toes. Of course I was barefoot. To minimize the sweat I put on my bug-smeared T-shirt and lay back again. A huddle of darkness on the blacker road showed where Dean was sleeping. I could hear him snoring. Stan was snoring too.

Occasionally a dim light flashed in town, and this was the sheriff making his rounds with a weak flashlight and mumbling to himself in the jungle night. Then I saw his light jiggling toward us and heard his footfalls coming soft on the mats of sand and vegetation. He stopped and flashed the car. I sat up and looked at him. In a quivering, almost querulous, and extremely tender voice he said, "*Dormiendo?*" indicating Dean in the road. I knew this meant "sleep."

"Si, dormiendo."

"Bueno, bueno," he said to himself and with reluctance and sadness turned away and went back to his lonely rounds. Such lovely policemen God hath never wrought in America. No suspicions, no fuss, no bother: he was the guardian of the sleeping town, period.

I went back to my bed of steel and stretched out with my arms spread. I didn't even know if branches or open sky were directly above me, and it made no difference. I opened my mouth to it and drew deep breaths of jungle atmosphere. It was not air, never air, but the palpable and living emanation of trees and swamp. I stayed awake. Roosters began to crow the dawn across the brakes somewhere. Still no air, no breeze, no dew, but the same Tropic of Cancer heaviness held us all pinned to earth, where we belonged and tingled. There was no sign of dawn in the skies. Suddenly I heard the dogs barking furiously across the dark, and then I heard the faint clip-clop of a horse's hooves. It came closer and closer. What kind of mad rider in the night would this be? Then I saw an apparition: a wild horse, white as a ghost, came trotting down the road directly toward Dean. Behind him the dogs yammered and contended. I couldn't see them, they were dirty old jungle dogs, but the horse was white as snow and immense and almost phosphorescent and easy to see. I felt no panic for Dean. The horse saw him and trotted right by his head, passed the car like a ship, whinnied softly, and continued on through town, bedeviled by the dogs, and clip-clopped back to the jungle on the other side, and all I heard was the faint hoofbeat fading away in the woods. The dogs subsided and sat to lick themselves. What was this horse? What myth and ghost, what spirit? I told Dean about it when he woke up. He thought I'd been dreaming. Then he recalled faintly dreaming of a white horse, and I told him it had been no dream. Stan Shephard slowly woke up. The faintest movements, and we were sweating profusely again. It was still pitch dark. "Let's start the car and blow some air!" I cried. "I'm dying of heat."

"Right!" We roared out of town and continued along the mad highway with our hair flying. Dawn came rapidly in a gray haze, revealing dense swamps sunk on both sides, with tall, forlorn, viny trees leaning and bowing over tangled bottoms. We bowled right along the railroad tracks for a while. The strange radio-station antenna of Ciudad Mante appeared ahead, as if we were in Nebraska. We found a gas station and loaded the tank just as the last of the jungle-night bugs hurled themselves in a black mass against the bulbs and fell fluttering at our feet in huge wriggly groups, some of them with wings a good four inches long, others frightful dragonflies big enough to eat a bird, and thousands of immense yangling mosquitoes and unnamable spidery insects of all sorts. I hopped up and down on the pavement for fear of them; I finally ended up in the car with my feet in my hands, looking fearfully at the ground where they swarmed around our wheels. "Lessgo!" I yelled. Dean and Stan weren't perturbed at all by the bugs; they calmly drank a couple of bottles of Mission Orange and kicked them away from the water cooler. Their shirts and pants, like mine, were soaked in the blood and black of thousands of dead bugs. We smelled our clothes deeply.

"You know, I'm beginning to like this smell," said Stan. "I can't smell myself any more."

"It's a strange, good smell," said Dean. "I'm not going to change my shirt till Mexico City, I want to take it all in and remember it." So off we roared again, creating air for our hot caked faces.

Then the mountains loomed ahead, all green. After this climb we would be on the great central plateau again and ready to roll ahead to Mexico City. In no time at all we soared to an elevation of five thousand feet among misty passes that overlooked steaming yellow rivers a mile below. It was the great River Moctezuma. The Indians along the road began to be extremely weird. They were a nation in themselves, mountain Indians, shut off from everything else but the Pan-American Highway. They were short and squat and dark, with bad teeth; they carried immense loads on their backs. Across enormous vegetated ravines we saw patchworks of agriculture on steep slopes. They walked up and down those slopes and worked the crops. Dean drove the car five miles an hour to see. "Whooee, this I never thought existed!" High on the highest peak, as great as any Rocky Mountain peak, we saw bananas growing. Dean got out of the car to point, to stand around rubbing his belly. We were on a ledge where a little thatched hut suspended itself over the precipice of the world. The sun created golden hazes that obscured the Moctezuma, now more than a mile below.

In the yard in front of the hut a little three-year-old Indian girl stood with her finger in her mouth, watching us with big brown eyes. "She's probably never seen anybody parked here before in her entire life!" breathed Dean. "Hel-lo, little girl. How are you? Do you like us?" The little girl looked away bashfully and pouted. We began to talk and she again examined us with finger in mouth. "Gee, I wish there was something I could give her! *Think of it,* being born and living on this ledge—this ledge representing all you know of life. Her father is probably groping down the ravine with a rope and getting his pineapples out of a cave and hacking wood at an eighty-degree angle with all the bottom below. She'll never, never leave here and know anything about the outside world. It's a nation. Think of the wild chief they must have! They probably, off the road, over that bluff, miles back, must be even wilder and stranger, yeah, because the Pan-American Highway partially civilizes this nation on this road. Notice the beads of sweat on her brow," Dean pointed out with a grimace of pain. "It's not the kind of sweat we have, it's oily and it's *always there* because it's *always* hot the year round and she knows nothing of non-sweat, she was born with sweat and dies with sweat." The sweat on her little brow was heavy, sluggish; it didn't run; it just stood there and gleamed like a fine olive oil. "What that must do to their souls! How different they must be in their private concerns and evaluations and wishes!" Dean drove on with his mouth hanging in awe, ten miles an hour, desirous to see every possible human being on the road. We climbed and climbed.

As we climbed, the air grew cooler and the Indian girls on the road wore shawls over their heads and shoulders. They hailed us desperately; we stopped to see. They wanted to sell us little pieces of rock crystal. Their great brown, innocent eyes looked into ours with such soulful intensity that not one of us had the slightest sexual thought about them; moreover they were very young, some of them eleven and looking almost thirty. "Look at those eyes!" breathed Dean. They were like the eyes of the Virgin Mother when she was a child. We saw in them the tender and forgiving gaze of Jesus. And they stared unflinching into ours. We rubbed our nervous blue eyes and looked again. Still they penetrated us with sorrowful and hypnotic gleam. When they talked they suddenly became frantic and almost silly. In their silence they were themselves. "They've only *recently* learned to sell these crystals, since the highway was built about ten years back—up until that time this entire nation must have been *silent!*"

The girls yammered around the car. One particularly soulful child gripped at Dean's sweaty arm. She yammered in Indian. "Ah yes, ah yes, dear one," said Dean tenderly and almost sadly. He got out of the car and went fishing around in the battered trunk in the back—the same old tortured American trunk—and pulled out a wristwatch. He showed it to the child. She whimpered with glee. The others crowded around with amazement. Then Dean poked in the little girl's hand for "the sweetest and purest and smallest crystal she has personally picked from the mountain for me." He found one no bigger than a berry. And he handed her the wristwatch dangling. Their mouths rounded like the mouths of chorister children. The lucky little girl squeezed it to her ragged breastrobes. They stroked Dean and thanked him. He stood among them with his ragged face to the sky, looking for the next and highest and final pass, and seemed like the Prophet that had come to them. He got back in the car. They hated to see us go. For the longest time, as we mounted a straight pass, they waved and ran after us. We made a turn and never saw them again, and they were still running after us. "Ah, this breaks my heart!" cried Dean, punching his chest. "How far do they carry out these loyalties and wonders! What's going to happen to them? Would they try to follow the car all the way to Mexico City if we drove slow enough?"

"Yes," I said, for I knew.

We came into the dizzying heights of the Sierra Madre Oriental. The banana trees gleamed golden in the haze. Great fogs yawned beyond stone walls along the precipice. Below, the Moctezuma was a thin golden thread in a green jungle mat. Strange crossroad towns on top of the world rolled by, with shawled Indians watching us from under hatbrims and *rebozos*. Life was dense, dark, ancient. They watched Dean, serious and insane at his raving wheel, with eyes of hawks. All had their hands outstretched. They had come down from the back mountains and higher places to hold forth their hands for something they thought civilization could offer, and they never dreamed the sadness and the poor broken delusion of it. They didn't know that a bomb had come that could crack all our bridges and roads and reduce them to jumbles, and we would be as poor as they someday, and stretching out our hands in the same, same way. Our broken Ford, old thirties upgoing America Ford, rattled through them and vanished in dust.

We had reached the approaches of the last plateau. Now the sun was golden, the air keen blue, and the desert with its occasional rivers a riot of sandy, hot space and sudden Biblical tree shade. Now Dean was sleeping and Stan driving. The shepherds appeared, dressed as in first times, in long flowing robes, the women carrying golden bundles of flax, the men staves. Under great trees on the shimmering desert the shepherds sat and convened, and the sheep moiled in the sun and raised dust beyond. "Man, man," I yelled to Dean, "wake up and see the shepherds, wake up and see the golden world that Jesus came from, with your own eyes you can tell!"

He shot his head up from the seat, saw one glimpse of it all in the fading red sun, and dropped back to sleep. When he woke up he described it to me in detail and said, "Yes, man, I'm glad you told me to look. Oh, Lord, what shall I do? Where will I go?" He rubbed his belly, he looked to heaven with red eyes, he almost wept.

The end of our journey impended. Great fields stretched on both sides of us; a noble wind blew across the occasional immense tree groves and over old missions turning salmon pink in the late sun. The clouds were close and huge and rose. "Mexico City by dusk!" We'd made it, a total of nineteen hundred miles from the afternoon yards of Denver to these vast and Biblical areas of the world, and now we were about to reach the end of the road.

"Shall we change our insect T-shirts?"

"Naw, let's wear them into town, hell's bells." And we drove into Mexico City.

A brief mountain pass took us suddenly to a height from which we saw all of Mexico City stretched out in its volcanic crater below and spewing city smokes and early dusklights. Down to it we zoomed, down Insurgentes Boulevard, straight toward the heart of town at Reforma. Kids played soccer in enormous sad fields and threw up dust. Taxi-drivers overtook us and wanted to know if we wanted girls. No, we didn't want girls now. Long, ragged adobe slums stretched out on the plain; we saw lonely figures in the dimming alleys. Soon night would come. Then the city roared in and suddenly we were passing crowded cafés and theaters and many lights. Newsboys yelled at us. Mechanics slouched by, barefoot, with wrenches and rags. Mad barefoot Indian drivers cut across us and surrounded us and tooted and made frantic traffic. The noise was incredible. No mufflers are used on Mexican cars. Horns are batted with glee continual. "Whee!" yelled Dean. "Look out!" He staggered the car through the traffic and played with everybody. He drove like an Indian. He got on a circular glorietta drive on Reforma Boulevard and rolled around it with its eight spokes shooting cars at us from all directions, left, right, *izquierda,* dead ahead, and yelled and jumped with joy. "This is traffic I've always dreamed of! Everybody *goes!*" An ambulance came balling through. American ambulances dart and weave through traffic with siren blowing; the great world-wide Fellahin Indian ambulances merely come through at eighty miles an hour in the city streets, and everybody just has to get out of the way and they don't pause for anybody or any circumstances and fly straight through. We saw it reeling out of sight on skittering wheels in the breaking-up moil of dense downtown traffic. The drivers were Indians. People, even old ladies, ran for buses that never stopped. Young Mexico City

businessmen made bets and ran by squads for buses and athleti-
cally jumped them. The bus-drivers were barefoot, sneering
and insane, and sat low and squat in T-shirts at the low, enor-
mous wheels. Ikons burned over them. The lights in the buses
were brown and greenish, and dark faces were lined on wooden
benches.

In downtown Mexico City thousands of hipsters in floppy
straw hats and long-lapeled jackets over bare chests padded
along the main drag, some of them selling crucifixes and weed
in the alleys, some of them kneeling in beat chapels next to
Mexican burlesque shows in sheds. Some alleys were rubble,
with open sewers, and little doors led to closet-size bars stuck
in adobe walls. You had to jump over a ditch to get your drink,
and in the bottom of the ditch was the ancient lake of the Aztec.
You came out of the bar with your back to the wall and edged
back to the street. They served coffee mixed with rum and nut-
meg. Mambo blared from everywhere. Hundreds of whores
lined themselves along the dark and narrow streets and their
sorrowful eyes gleamed at us in the night. We wandered in a
frenzy and a dream. We ate beautful steaks for forty-eight cents
in a strange tiled Mexican cafeteria with generations of ma-
rimba musicians standing at one immense marimba—also wan-
dering singing guitarists, and old men on corners blowing
trumpets. You went by the sour stink of pulque saloons; they
gave you a water glass of cactus juice in there, two cents. Noth-
ing stopped; the streets were alive all night. Beggars slept
wrapped in advertising posters torn off fences. Whole families
of them sat on the sidewalk, playing little flutes and chuckling
in the night. Their bare feet stuck out, their dim candles
burned, all Mexico was one vast Bohemian camp. On corners
old women cut up the boiled heads of cows and wrapped mor-
sels in tortillas and served them with hot sauce on newspaper
napkins. This was the great and final wild uninhibited Fellahin-
childlike city that we knew we would find at the end of the
road. Dean walked through with his arms hanging zombie-like
at his sides, his mouth open, his eyes gleaming, and conducted
a ragged and holy tour that lasted till dawn in a field with a boy

in a straw hat who laughed and chatted with us and wanted to play catch, for nothing ever ended.

Then I got fever and became delirious and unconscious. Dysentery. I looked up out of the dark swirl of my mind and I knew I was on a bed eight thousand feet above sea level, on a roof of the world, and I knew that I had lived a whole life and many others in the poor atomistic husk of my flesh, and I had all the dreams. And I saw Dean bending over the kitchen table. It was several nights later and he was leaving Mexico City already. "What you doin, man?" I moaned.

"Poor Sal, poor Sal, got sick. Stan'll take care of you. Now listen to hear if you can in your sickness: I got my divorce from Camille down here and I'm driving back to Inez in New York tonight if the car holds out."

"All that again?" I cried.

"All that again, good buddy. Gotta get back to my life. Wish I could stay with you. Pray I can come back." I grabbed the cramps in my belly and groaned. When I looked up again bold noble Dean was standing with his old broken trunk and looking down at me. I didn't know who he was any more, and he knew this, and sympathized, and pulled the blanket over my shoulders. "Yes, yes, yes, I've got to go now. Old fever Sal, good-by." And he was gone. Twelve hours later in my sorrowful fever I finally came to understand that he was gone. By that time he was driving back alone through those banana mountains, this time at night.

When I got better I realized what a rat he was, but then I had to understand the impossible complexity of his life, how he had to leave me there, sick, to get on with his wives and woes. "Okay, old Dean, I'll say nothing."

from Maggie Cassidy

15

From Pawtucketville to South Lowell the route by bus encompassed the city—down Moody, to Kearney Square below the high school, the fleet of buses, the people huddled waiting against doorfronts of soda parlors, 5 & 10s, drugstores— The sad traffic crunching in from winter, out to winter— The bleak blue raw feel of the wind from the woods citifying by the few sad lights— There I changed to the South Lowell bus— It would show up always catching at my throat—the mere name of it as the busdriver'd rolled it in the window enough to make my heart beat—I'd look at other people's faces to see if they saw the magic— The ride itself grew grimmer— From the Square out up Central, to Back Central, to the outlying dark long streets of the town where dim frost sits the night by howling-wind garbage pails in cold moonlight— Out along the Concord where factories enlisted its famous flow—out beyond even them—to a dark highway where Massachusetts Street under a brown dumb streetlamp spoked in, small, mean, old, full of my love and the name of it— There I'd get off the bus, among trees, by the river, and dodge the mudholes, seven cottages down on the right to her rambling old unfenced brown-windowed house overtopped by clacking skeletal trees of the sudden from-Boston sea winds blown over wilderness, railyards and hoar— Each house meant my heart beat faster as it passed my rapid step. Her actual house, the actual light that actually upon her was bestowing and around her bathing, mote by mote made rare gold, dear magic, was the commotion hysterical light of wonder— Shadows on her porch? Voices in the street, in the yard? Not a sound, but the dull Victorian wind moaning New England by the river in the winter night—I'd stop in the street outside her house. One figure within—her mother—gloomy pawing in the kitchen, turning sadly in life, putting away her sweet dishes that some day they'd pack away with guilt and sorrow and say "I never knew, I never knew!"— The dumb, the spittling mankind crawing in his groin to make nothing.

Where is Maggie? O wind, songs have ye in her name? Plucked her did ye from midnight blasted millyard winds and made her renown ring in stone and brick and ice? Hard implacable bridges of iron cross her milk of brows? God bent from his steel arc welded her a hammer of honey and of balm?

The rutted mud of hardrock Time . . . was it wetted, springi-

fied, greened, blossomied for me to grow in nameless bloodied
lutey naming of her? Wood on cold trees would her coffin bare?
Keys of stone rippled by icy streaks would ope my needy warm
interiors and make her eat the soft sin of me? No iron bend or
melt to make my rocky travail ease—I was all alone, my fate
was banged behind an iron door, I'd come like butter looking
for Hot Metals to love, I'd raise my feeble orgone bones and
let them be rove and split the half and goop the big sad eyes to
see it and say nothing. The laurel wreath is made of iron, and
thorns of nails; acid spit, impossible mountains, and incompre-
hensible satires of blank humanity—congeal, cark, sink and
seal my blood—

"*There* you are. What are you standing out in the road for?
What'd ya come for?"

"Didnt we decide on the phone?"

"Oh . . . maybe you did."

This made me mad and I didnt say anything; now she was in
her element.

"What are you so quiet about, Jacky Boy?"

"You oughta know. Dont call me Jacky Boy. Why were you
on the porch. I didnt see you!"

"I saw you comin down the street. All the way from the
bus."

"It's cold out."

"I'm wrapped in my coat snug. Come on in with me."

"In your coat."

Laugh. "Silly. In the house. Nobody home. My mother's goin
to Mrs. O'Garra tonight to hear the Firestone Hour, some
singer."

"I though you didnt want me to come. Now you're glad."

"How do y'know?"

"When you squeeze my hand like that."

"Sometimes you get me. Sometimes I cant stand how I love
you."

"Hah?"

"Jacky!" And she was on me, all of her, thrown socko into
me all huddled to my frame, clung, kissing me wild and deep
and hot—desperate—it would never have happened on a regu-

lar Wednesday or Saturday night planned date—I closed my eyes, felt faint, lost, heartbroken, salt-sunk drowned.

In my ear, warm, hot lips, whisperings, "I love you Jacky. Why do you make me so mad! Oh you make me so mad! Oh I love you so! Oh I wanta kiss you! Oh you damn fool I want you to take me. I'm yours dont you know?—all, all yours—you're a fool Jacky—Oh poor Jacky—Oh kiss me—*hard*—save me!—I need you!" Not even inside the house yet. In there, by the hissing radiator, on the couch, we practically did everything there is to do but I never touched her in the prime focal points, previous trembling places, breasts, the moist star of her thighs, even her legs—I avoided it to please her— Her body was like fire, packed soft and round in a soft dress, young—firm-soft, rich—a big mistake—her lips burned all over my face. We didnt know where we were, what to do. And dark moved the Concord in the winter night.

"I'm glad I came!" I told myself jubilantly. "If Pa could see this or feel this he'd *know* now, he wouldnt be disappointed—Lousy too!—Ma!—I'm gonna marry Maggie, I'm gonna tell Ma!"—I pulled her yielding yearning waist, it popped her pelvis bone right into mine, I gritted my teeth in the memory of the future—

"I'm goin to the Rex Saturday night," she said, pouting in the dark as I licked her lower lip with my fingertip then threw my hand on the floor off the couch and she was suddenly stroking my profile. ("You look like you're cut out of rock.")

"I'll meet you there."

"I wish you were older."

"Why?"

"You'd know more what to do with me—"

"If—"

"No! You dont know how. I love you too much. What's the use? Oh hell—I love you so! But I hate you! Oh go home!! Kiss me! Lie on top of me, crush me—" Kisses—"Jacky I wrote you a big note today and tore it up—too much in it—"

"I read the one—"

"I finally sent that one—I wanted you to marry me in my first note— I know you're too young, I'm robbing the high school cradle."

"Ah—"

"You have no trade—You have a career ahead of you—"

"No no—"

"—be a brakeman on the railroad, we'll live in a little house by the tracks, play the 920 Club, have babies— I'll paint my kitchen chairs red—I'll paint the walls of our bedroom deep dark green or sumpin—I'll kiss you to wake up in the morning—"

"Oh Maggie that's what I want!" (Maggie Cassidy? I thought wildly. Maggie Cassidy! Maggie Cassidy!)

"No!" Slapping me on the face—pushing it—angry, pouting, rolling away, sitting up to roundabout her dress again straight. "Hear me? No!"

I'd wrestle her to the bottom of the dark couch retwisting her dresses slips belts and girdly toot pots both of us panting, sweating, burning— Hours passed, it was midnight, my day was not done— Reverently my hair was falling in her eyes.

"Oh Jack it's too late."

"I dont wanta go."

"You gotta go."

"Ah okay."

"I dont want you to go—I love you to kiss me— Dont let that Pauline Cole steal you away from me. Dont make faces like that I'll get up and walk away—Jacky—I love you I love I love you—" She kept saying it into my mouth—through my teeth, bit my lip—There were tears of joy in her eyes, on her cheeks; her warm body smelled ambrosial brew in the profound struggle we waged sinking in pillows, bliss, madness, night—hours on end—

"You better go home, dear— You gotta go to school tomorrer— You'll never get up."

"Okay Maggie."

"Say you love me when you wake up in the morning, to yourself—"

"How could I . . . otherwise . . . do . . ."

"Call me tomorrer night—come Friday—"

"W—"

"I mean Wednesday! Kiss me! Hold me! I love you I always will and no one else ever ever—I never was so much in love— never again—you damn Canook you—"

"I cant leave."

"Leave. Dont let anybody tell you nothin about me."

"Nobody *does!*"

"If they do . . .

"If they did I wouldnt listen—Maggie that house by the railroad tracks, the red chairs . . . I . . . I . . . cant—dont want to do anything else with anybody else—ever— I'll tell—I'll— we'll— Ah Maggie."

She'd cradle my broken head in her all-healing lap that beat like a heart; my eyes hot would feel the soothe fingertips of cool, the joy, the stroke and barely-touch, the feminine sweet lost bemused inward-biting far-thinking deep earth river-mad April caress—the brooding river in her unfathomable springtime thoughts— The dark flowing enriched silty heart— Irish as peat, dark as Kilkenny night, sorcerous as elf, red-lipped as red-rubied morn on the Irish Sea on the east coast as I have seen it, promising as the thatched roofs and green swards there bringing tears to my eyes to be an Irishman too and lost and sunk inside her forever—her brother, husband, lover, raper, owner, friend, father, son, grabber, kisser, keener, swain, sneaker-upper, sleeper-with, feeler, railroad brakeman in red house of red babycribs and the joyous wash Saturday morning in the glad ragged yard—

I walked home in the dead of Lowell night—three miles, no buses—the dark ground, roads, cemeteries, streets, construction ditches, millyards— The billion winter stars hugeing overhead like frozen beads frozen suns all packed and inter-allied in one rich united universe of showery light, beating, beating, like great hearts in the non-understandable bowl void black.

To which nevertheless I offered up all my songs and longwalk sighs and sayings, as if they could hear me, know, care.

from Old Angel Midnight

1

Friday afternoon in the universe, in all directions in & out
you got your men women dogs children horses pones tics perts
parts pans pools palls pails parturiences and petty Thieveries
that turn into heavenly Buddha—I know boy what's I talkin
about case I made the world & when I made it I no lie & had
Old Angel Midnight for my name and concocted up a world so
nothing you had forever thereafter make believe it's real—but
that's alright because now everything'll be alright & we'll
soothe the forever boys & girls & before we're thru we'll find
a name for his Goddam Golden Eternity & tell a story too—
and but d y aver read a story as vast as this that begins Friday
Afternoon with workinmen on scaffolds painting white
paint & ants merlying in lil black dens & microbes warring in
yr kidney & mesaroolies microbing in the innards of mer-
cery & microbe microbes dreaming of the ultimate microbe-
hood which then ultimates outward to the endless vast empty
atom which is this imaginary universe, ending nowhere & ne'er
e'en born as Bankei well poled when he ferried his mother over
the rocks to Twat You Tee and people visit his hut to enquire
"What other planet features this?" & he answers "What other
planet?" tho the sounds of the entire world are now swimming
thru this window from Mrs McCartiola's twandow & Ole
Poke's home dronk again & acourse you hear the cats wailing
in the wailbar wildbar wartfence moonlight midnight Angel
Dolophine immensity Visions of the Tathagata's Seat of Pu-
rity & Womb so that here is all this infinite immaterial mead-
owlike golden ash swimswarming in our enlighten brains & the
silence Shh shefallying in our endless ear & still we refuse
naked & blank to hear What the Who? the Who? Too What
You? will say the diamond boat & Persepine, Recipine, Mill
town, Heroine, & Fack matches the silver ages everlasting
swarmswallying in a simple broom—and at night ya raise the
square white light from your ghost beneath a rootdrinkin

tree & Coyote wont hear ya but you'll ward off the inexistency
devils just to pass the time away & meanwhile it's timeless to
the ends of the last lightyear it might as well be gettin late Fri-
day afternoon where we start so's old Sound can come home
when worksa done & drink his beer & tweak his children's
eyes—

2

and what talents it takes to bail boats out you'd never flank
till flail pipe throwed howdy who was it out the bar of the seven
seas and all the Italians of 7th Street in Sausaleety slit sleet with
paring knives that were used in the ream kitchens to cut the
innards of gizzards out on a board, wa, twa, wow, why, shit,
Ow, man, I'm tellin you—Wait—We bait the rat and forget
to mark the place and soon Cita comes and eat it and puke
out grit—fa yen pas d cas, fa yen pas d case, chanson d idiot,
imbecile, vas malade—la sonora de madrigal—but as soon as
someone wants to start then the world takes on these new
propensities:
1. Bardoush
   (the way the craydon bi fa shta ma j en vack)
2. Flaki—arrete—interrupted chain saw sting eucalyptus
words inside the outside void that good God we cant believe is
anything so arsaphallawy any the pranaraja of madore with his
bloody arse kegs, shit—go to three.

3

Finally just about the time they put wood to the poets of
France & fires broke out recapitulating the capitulation of the
continent of Mu located just south of Patch, Part, with his hair
askew and wearing goldring ears & Vaseline Hair Oil in his
arse ass hole flaunted all the old queers and lecherous cardinals
who wrote (write) pious manuals & announced that henceforth
he was to be the sole provender provider this side of Kissthat.
Insteada which hey marabuda you son of a betch you cuck-
sucker you hey hang dat board down here I'll go cot you on
the Yewneon ya bum ya—lick, lock, lick, lock, mix it for pa-tit

a a lamana lacasta reda va da Poo moo koo—la—swinging Friday afternoon in eternity here comes Kee pardawac with long golden robe flowing through the Greek Islands with a Bardic (forgot) with a lard (?) with a marde manual onder his Portugee Tot Sherry Rotgut, singing "Kee ya."

Tried to warn all of you, essence of stuff wont do—God why did you make the world?

Answer:—Because I gwt pokla renamash ta va in ming the atss are you forever with it?

I like the bliss of mind.

Awright I'll call up all the fuckin Gods, right now! Parya! Arrive! Ya damn hogfuckin lick lip twillerin fishmonger! Kiss my purple royal ass baboon! Poota! Whore! You and yr retinues of chariots & fucks! Devadatta! Angel of Mercy! Prick! Lover! Mush! Run on ya dog eared kiss willying nilly Dexter Michigan ass-warlerin ratpole! The rat in my cellar's an old canuck who wasnt fooled by rebirth but b God gotta admit I was born for the same reason I bring this glass to my lip—?

Rut! Old God whore, the key to ecstasy is forevermore furthermore blind! Potanyaka! God of Mercy! Boron O Mon Boron! All of ye! Rush! Ghosts & evil spirits, if you appear I'm saved. How can you fool an old man with a stove & wine drippin down his chin? The flowers are my little sisters and I love them with a dear heart. Ashcans turn to snow and milk when I look. I know sinister alleys. I had a vision of Han Shan a darkened by sun bum in odd rags standing short in the gloom scarey to see. Poetry, all these vicious writers and bores & Scriptural Apocraphylizers fucking their own dear mothers because they want ears to sell—

And the axe haiku.

All the little fine angels amercyin and this weary prose hand handling dumb pencils like in school long ago the first redsun special. Henry Millers everywhere Fridaying the world— Rexroths. Rexroths not a bad egg. Creeley. Creeley. Real magination realizing rock roll rip snortipatin oyster stew of Onatona Scotiat Shores where six birds week the nest and part wasted his twill till I.

Mush. Wish. Wish I could sing ya songs of a perty nova

spotia patonapeein pack wallower wop snot polly—but caint—
cause I'll get sick & die anyway & you too, born to die, little
flowers. Fiorella. Look around. The burlap's buried in the
wood on an angle, axe haiku. La religion c'est d la marde! Pa!
d la marde! J m en dor.—

God's asleep dreaming, we've got to wake him up! Then all
of a sudden when we're asleep dreaming, he comes and wakes
us up—how gentle! How are you Mrs Jones? Fine Mrs Smith!
Tit within Tat—Eye within Tooth—Bone within Light, like—
Drop some little beads of sweetness in that stew (O Phoney
Poetry!)—the heart of the onion—That stew's too good for me
to eat, you!—

People, shmeople

4

Boy, says Old Angel, this amazing nonsensical rave of yours
wherein I spose you'd think you'd in some lighter time find
hand be-almin ya for the likes of what ya davote yaself to,
pah—bum with a tail only means one thing,—They know that
in sauerkraut bars, god the chew chew & the wall lips—And
not only that but all them in describable paradises—aye ah—
Old Angel m boy—Jack, the born with a tail bit is a deal that
you never dream'd to redeem—verify—try to see as straight—
you wont believe even in God but tbe devil worries you—
you & Mrs Tourian—great gaz-zuz & I'd as lief be scoured
with a leaf rust as hear this poetizin horseshit everyhere I want
to hear the sounds thru the window you promised me when the
Midnight bell on 7th St did toll bing bong & Burroughs and
Ginsberg were asleep & you lay on the couch in that timeless
moment in the little red bulblight bus & saw drapes of eternity
parting for your hand to begin & so's you could affect—&
*ee*ffect—the total turningabout & deep revival of world robe-
flowing literature till it shd be something a man'd put his eyes
on & continually read for the sake of reading & for the sake
of the Tongue & not just these insipid stories writ in insipid
aridities & paranoias bloomin & why yet the image—let's hear
the Sound of the Universe, son, & no more part twaddle—And

dont expect nothing from me, my middle name is Opprobrium, Old Angel Midnight Opprobrium, boy, O.A.M.O.—

Pirilee pirilee, tzwé tzwi tzwa,—tack tick—birds & firewood. The dream is already ended and we're already awake in the golden eternity.

5

Then when rat tooth come ravin and fradilaboodala backala backed up, trip tripped himself and fell falling on top of Old Smokey because *his pipe* was not right, had no molasses in it, tho it looked like a morasses brarrel, but then the cunts came. She had a long cunt that sitick out of her craw a mile long like Mexican Drawings showing hungry drinkers reaching Surrealistic Thirsts with lips like Aztec—Akron Lehman the Hart Crane Hero of Drunken Records came full in her cunt spoffing & overflowing white enlightened seminal savior juice out of his canal-hole into her hungry river bed and that made the old nannies gab and kiss that.

6

O he was quite racy—real estate queen—Europe & Niles— for pleasure—stom stomp absulute raze making noise—I can write them but I cant puctuate them—then he said comma comma comma—That skinny guy with black hair—Atlean Rage—in India in the last year he's getting even ignoring all common publications & getting Urdu Nothing Sanskrit by Sir Yak Yak Yak forty page thing Norfolk—let's all get drunk I wanta take pictures—dont miss with Mrs. lately in trust picture pitcher pithy lisp—that's an artistic kit for sex—Trying to think of a rule in Sankrit Mamma Sanskrit Sounding obviously twins coming in here Milltown Equinell Miopa Parte Watacha Peemana Kowava you get sticky ring weekends & wash the tub, Bub—I'll be gentle like a Iamb in the Bible—Beautiful color yr lipstick thanx honey—Got a match Max?—Taxi crabs & murdercycles—Let's go to Trilling & ask him—I gotta wash my conduct—Dont worry about nothin—I love Allen Ginsberg—Let that be recorded in heaven's unchangeable heart—

Either bway—Rapples—Call up Allen Price Jones—Who is
that?—They re having fun on the bed there—Soo de ya bee
la—And there came the picture of Ang Bong de Beela—Fuck it
or get it in or wait something for the bee slime—Then the
ants'll crawl over bee land—Ants in bands wailing neath my
bloody ow pants, owler pants—Ta da ba dee—He thinlis I'm
competive in a long pleasant souse of Wishing all of ye bleed
stay meditation everybody martini destroy my black—Allen ye
better voice the stare, this beer these room sandwiches—Where
did you get these? Big greasy socialists—Are you gonna konk,
Allen? Mighty tall in the saddle—Anybody got a ceegiboo?—
The moon is a piece of tea—(Under the empty blue sky, verte-
brate zoology.)

How to Meditate

                    —lights out—
fall, hands a-clasped, into instantaneous
ecstasy like a shot of heroin or morphine,
the gland inside of my brain discharging
the good glad fluid (Holy Fluid) as
I hap-down and hold all my body parts
down to a deadstop trance—Healing
all my sicknesses—erasing all—not
even the shred of a "I-hope-you" or a
Loony Balloon left in it, but the mind
blank, serene, thoughtless. When a thought
comes a-springing from afar with its held-
forth figure of image, you spoof it out,
you spuff it off, you fake it, and
it fades, and thought never comes—and
with joy you realize for the first time
"Thinking's just like not thinking—
So I dont have to think
    any
    more"

from Doctor Sax

1

The other night I had a dream that I was sitting on the sidewalk on Moody Street, Pawtucketville, Lowell, Mass., with a pencil and paper in my hand saying to myself "Describe the wrinkly tar of this sidewalk, also the iron pickets of Textile Institute, or the doorway where Lousy and you and G.J.'s always sittin and dont stop to think of words when you do stop, just stop to think of the picture better—and let your mind off yourself in this work."

Just before that I was coming down the hill between Gershom Avenue and that spectral street where Billy Artaud used to live, towards Blezan's corner store, where on Sundays the fellows stand in bestsuits after church smoking, spitting, Leo Martin saying to Sonny Alberge or Joe Plouffe, *"Eh, batêge, ya faite un grand sarman s'foi icite"*—("Holy Batchism, he made a long sermon this time") and Joe Plouffe, prognathic, short, glidingly powerful, spits into the large pebblestones of Gershom paved and walks on home for breakfast with no comment (he lived with his sisters and brothers and mother because the old man had thrown em all out—"Let my bones melt in this rain!"—to live a hermit existence in the darkness of his night—rheumy red-eyed old sickmonster scrooge of the block)—

Doctor Sax I first saw in his earlier lineaments in the early Catholic childhood of Centralville—deaths, funerals, the shroud of that, the dark figure in the corner when you look at the dead man coffin in the dolorous parlor of the open house with a horrible purple wreath on the door. Figures of coffin-bearers emerging from a house on a rainy night bearing a box with dead old Mr. Yipe inside. The statue of Ste. Thérèse turning her head in an antique Catholic twenties film with Ste. Thérèse dashing across town in a car with W. C. Fieldsian close shaves by the young religious hero while the doll (not Ste. Thérèse herself but the lady hero symbolic thereof) heads for her saintliness with wide eyes of disbelief. We had a statue of Ste. Thérèse in my house—on West Street I saw it turn its head at me—in the dark. Earlier, too, horrors of the Jesus Christ of passion plays in his shrouds and vestments of saddest doom mankind in the Cross Weep for Thieves and Poverty—he was at the foot of my bed pushing it one dark Saturday night (on Hildreth & Lilley secondfloor flat full of Eternity outside)— either He or the Virgin Mary stooped with phosphorescent profile and horror pushing my bed. That same night an elfin, more cheery ghost of some Santa Claus kind rushed up and slammed my door; there was no wind; my sister was taking a bath in the rosy bathroom of Saturday night home, and my mother scrubbing her back or tuning Wayne King on the old mahogany radio or glancing at the top Maggie and Jiggs funnies just come in from wagon boys outside (same who rushed among the downtown redbricks of my Chinese mystery) so I called out "Who slammed my door *(Qui a farmez ma porte?)*" and they said nobody *("Parsonne voyons donc")*—and I knew I was haunted but said nothing; not long after that I dreamed the horrible dream of the rattling red livingroom, newly painted a strange 1929 varnish red and I saw it in the dream all dancing and rattling like skeletons because my brother Gerard haunted them and dreamed I woke up screaming by the phonograph machine in the adjoining room with its Masters Voice curves in the brown wood— Memory and dream are intermixed in this mad universe.

2

In the dream of the wrinkly tar corner I saw it, hauntingly, Riverside Street as it ran across Moody and into the fabulously rich darknesses of Sarah Avenue and Rosemont the Mysterious . . . Rosemont:—community built in the floodable river flats and also on gentle slopes uprising that to the foot of the sand-bank, the cemetery meadows and haunted ghostfields of Luxy Smith hermits and Mill Pond so mad—in the dream I only fancied the first steps from that "wrinkly tar," right around the corner, views of Moody Street Lowell—arrowing to the City

Hall Clock (with time) and downtown red antennas and Chinese restaurant Kearney Square neons in the Massachusetts Night; then a glance to the right at Riverside Street running off to hide itself in the rich respectaburban wildhouses of Fraternity presidents of Textile (O!—) and oldlady Whitehairs landladies, the street suddenly emerging from this Americana of lawns and screens and Emily Dickinson hidden schoolteachers behind lace blinds into the raw drama of the river where the land, the New England rockyland of high-bluffs dipped to kiss the lip of Merrimac in his rushing roars over tumult and rock to the sea, fantastic and mysterious from the snow North, goodbye;—walked to the left, passed the holy doorway where G.J. and Lousy and I hung sitting in the mystery which I now see hugens, huger, into something beyond my Grook, beyond my Art & Pale, into the secret of what God has done with my Time;—tenement standing on the wrinkly tar corner, four stories high, with a court, washlines, clothespins, flies drumming in the sun (I dreamed I lived in that tenement, cheap rent, good view, rich furniture, my mother glad, my father "off playing cards" or maybe just dumbly sitting in a chair agreeing with us, the dream)— And the last time I was in Massachusetts I stood in the cold winter night watching the Social Club and actually seeing Leo Martin breathing winter fogs cut in for aftersupper game of pool like when I was small, and also noticing the corner tenement because the poor Canucks my people of my God-gave-me-life were burning dull electric lights in a brown doom gloom of kitchen with Catholic calendar in the toilet door (Ah Me), a sight full of sorrow and labor—the scenes of my childhood— In the doorway G.J., Gus J. Rigopoulos, and I, Jackie Duluoz, local sandlot sensation and big punk; and Lousy, Albert Lauzon, the Human Cave-In (he had a Cave-In chest), the Kid Lousy, World's Champion Silent Spitter and also sometimes Paul Boldieu our pitcher and grim driver of later jaloppy limousines of adolescent whim—

"Take note, take note, well of them take note," I'm saying to myself in the dream, "when you pass the doorway look very close at Gus Rigopoulos, Jackie Duluoz and Lousy."

I see them now on Riverside Street in the waving high dark.

3

There are hundreds of people strolling in the street, in the
dream . . . it's Sanurday Sun Night, they're all roshing to the
Clo-Sol— Downtown, in real restaurants of reality, my mother
and father, like shadows on a menu card sitting by a shadow-
grill window with 1920's drapes hanging heavy behind them,
all an ad, saying "Thank you, call again to dine and dance at
Ron Foo's 467 Market Street Rochester,"—they're eating at
Chin Lee's, he's an old friend of the family's, he knew me, gave
us lichee nut for Christmas, one time a great Ming pot (placed
on dark piano of parlor glooms and angels in dust veils with
doves, the Catholicity of the swarming dust, and my thoughts);
it's Lowell, outside the decorated chink windows is Kearney
Square teeming with life. "By Gosh," says my father patting his
belly, "that was a good meal."

Step softly, ghost.

4

Follow the great rivers on the maps of South America (origin
of Doctor Sax), trace your Putumayos to a Napofurther Ama-
zonian junction, map the incredible uncrossable jungles, the
southern Parañas of amaze, stare at the huge grook of a conti-
nent bulging with an Arctic-Antarctic—to me the Merrimac
River was a mighty Napo of continental importance . . . the
continent of New England. She fed from some snakelike source
with maws approach and wide, welled from the hidden dank,
came, named Merrimac, into the winding Weirs and Franklin
Falls, the Winnepesaukies (of Nordic pine) (and Albatrossian
grandeur), the Manchesters, Concords, Plum Islands of Time.

The thunderous husher of our sleep at night—

I could hear it rise from the rocks in a groaning wush ululat-
ing with the water, sprawlsh, sprawlsh, oom, oom, zoooo, all
night long the river says zooo, zooo, the stars are fixed in roof-
tops like ink. Merrimac, dark name, sported dark valleys: my
Lowell had the great trees of antiquity in the rocky north wav-
ing over lost arrowheads and Indian scalps, the pebbles on the
slatecliff beach are full of hidden beads and were stepped on

barefoot by Indians. Merrimac comes swooping from a north
of eternities, falls pissing over locks, cracks and froths on rocks,
bloth, and rolls frawing to the kale, calmed in dewpile stone
holes slaty sharp (we dove off, cut our feet, summer afternoon
stinky hookies), rocks full of ugly old suckers not fit to eat, and
crap from sewage, and dyes, and you swallowed mouthfuls of
the chokeful water— By moonlight night I see the Mighty Mer-
rimac foaming in a thousand white horses upon the tragic
plains below. Dream:—wooden sidewalk planks of Moody
Street Bridge fall out, I hover on beams over rages of white
horses in the roaring low,—moaning onward, armies and cav-
alries of charging Euplantus Eudronicus King Grays loop'd &
curly like artists' work, and with clay souls' snow curlicue
rooster togas in the fore front.

I had a terror of those waves, those rocks—

5

Doctor Sax lived in the woods, he was no city shroud. I see
him stalking with the incredible Jean Fourchette, woodsman
of the dump, idiot, giggler, toothless-broken-brown, scarched,
sniggerer at fires, loyal beloved companion of long childhood
walks— The tragedy of Lowell and the Sax Snake is in the
woods, the world around—

In the fall there were great sere brown sidefields sloping
down to the Merrimac all rich with broken pines and browns,
fall, the whistle was just shrilled to end the third quarter in the
wintry November field where crowds and me and father stood
watching scuffling uproars of semipro afternoons like in the
days of old Indian Jim Thorpe, boom, touchdown. There were
deer in the Billerica woods, maybe one or two in Dracut, three
or four in Tyngsboro, and a hunter's corner in the *Lowell Sun*
sports page. Great serried cold pines of October morning when
school's re-started and the apples are in, stood naked in the
northern gloom waiting for denudement. In the winter the
Merrimac River flooded in its ice; except for a narrow strip in
the middle where ice was fragile with crystals of current the
whole swingaround basin of Rosemont and the Aiken Street

Bridge was laid flat for winter skating parties that could be observed from the bridge with a snow telescope in the gales and along the Lakeview side dump minor figures of Netherlander snowscapes are marooning in the whorly world of pale white snow. A blue saw cracks down across the ice. Hockey games devour the fire where the girls are huddled, Billy Artaud with clenched teeth is smashing the opponent's hockey stick with a kick of spiked shoes in the fiendish glare of winter fighting days, I'm going backwards in a circle at forty miles an hour trailing the puck till I lose it on a bounce and the other Artaud brothers are rushing up pellmell in a clatter of Dit Clappers to roar into the fray—

This the same raw river, poor river, March melts, brings Doctor Sax and the rainy nights of the Castle.

6

There were blue holiday eves, Christmas time, be-sparkled all over town almost the length and breadth of which I could see from the back Textile field after a Sunday afternoon show, dinnertime, the roast beef waiting, or *ragout d'boullette,* the whole sky unforgettable, heightened by the dry ice of weather's winter glare, air rarefied pure blue, sad, just as it appears at such hours over the redbrick alleys and Lowell Auditorium marble forums, with snowbanks in the red streets for sadness, and flights of lost Lowell Sunday suppertime birds flying to a Polish fence for breadcrumbs—no notion there of the Lowell that came later, the Lowell of mad midnights under gaunt pines by the lickety ticky moon, blowing with a shroud, a lantern, a burying of dirt, a digging up of dirt, gnomes, axles full of grease lying in the river water and the moon glinting in a rat's eye— the Lowell, the World, you find.

Doctor Sax hides around the corner of my mind.

SCENE: A masked by night shadow flitting over the edge of the sandbank.

SOUND: A dog barking half a mile away; and river.

SMELL: Sweet sand dew.

TEMPERATURE: Summer mid night frost.

MONTH: Late August, ballgame's over, no more homeruns over the center of the arcanum of sand our Circus, our diamond in the sand, where ballgames took place in the reddy dusk,—now it's going to be the flight of the caw-caw bird of autumn, honking to his skinny grave in the Alabama pines.

SUPPOSITION: Doctor Sax has just disappeared over the sandbank and's gone home to bed.

from Visions of Cody

Suddenly out on East Colfax Boulevard bound for Fort Collins Cody saw a football game going on among kids in a field, stopped the car, said "Watch" ran out leaping madly among kids (with noble seriousness there wearing those tragic lumps like the muscles of improvised strongmen in comedies), got the ball, told one blondhaired boy with helmet tucked underarm to run like hell, clear to the goalpost, which the kid did but Cody said "Further, further," and the kid halfway doubting to get the ball that far edged on back and now he was seventy yards and Cody unleashed a tremendous soaring wobbling pass that dropped beyond the kid's most radical estimate, the pass being so high and powerful the boy completely lost it in eyrieal spaces of heaven and dusk and circled foolishly but screaming with glee—when this happened everyone was amazed except Johnson, who rushed out of the car in his sharp blue suit, leaped around frantically in a mixup of kids, got the ball (at one point fell flat because of his new shiny-bottom shoes that had only a half hour's poolroom dust on 'em) and commanded the same uncomplaining noble boy to run across the field and enragedly unfurled a long pass but Cody appeared out of nowhere in the mad lowering dusk and intercepted it with sudden frantic action of a wildfaced maniac jumping into a roomful of old ladies; spun, heaving a prodigious sky pass back over Johnson's head that Johnson sneered at as he raced back, he'd never been outdone by anybody ("Hey whee!" they yelled in the car); such a tremendous pass it was bound to be carried by the wind, fall in the road out on East Colfax, yet Johnson ran out there dodging traffic as mad red clouds fired the horizon of the mountains, to the west, and somewhere across the field littler tiny children were burning meaningless fires and screaming and playing football with socks, some just meaninglessly tackling one another all over in a great riot of October joy. Circling in the road, almost being murdered by a car driven eighty miles per by Denver's hotshot (Biff Buferd, who tooted), Johnson made a sensational fingertip sprawling-on-knees catch instantly and breathtakingly overshadowed by the fact that dramatic fantastic Cody had actually gone chasing his own pass and was now in the road yurking with outstretched hands from the agony that he was barely going to miss, himself sprawling as terrorstricken motorists swerved and screeched on all sides. This insane scene was being beheld not only by Biff Buferd laughing like hell as it receded eighty miles an hour out of his rearview window, but across the wild field with its spastic fires and purple skies (actually an empty lot sitting between the zoom-swish of Colfax traffic and some old homes, the goalposts just sticks the kids "put up with believing crudeness of primitive Christians") was propped all by itself there an old haunted house, dry gardens of Autumn planted round it by nineteenth-century lady ghouls long dead, from the weatherbeaten green latticed steps of which now descended Mr. behatted beheaded Justin G. Mannerly the mad schoolteacher with the little Hitler mustache, within months fated to be teaching Cody how to wash his ears, how to be impressive with highschool principals—Mannerly now stopped, utterly amazed, halfway down, the sight of Cody and Earl Johnson furying in the road (almost getting killed too), saying out loud "My goodness gracious what is *this?*"; same who in fact that afternoon, at the exact moment Cody was approaching Watson, sat in a grave of his own in his overcoat in an empty unheated Saturday classroom of West Denver High not a mile across town, his brow in his hand as blackboard dust swam across October fires in the corner where the window-opening pole was leaned, where it was still written in chalk from yesterday's class (in American Lit.) *When lilacs last in the dooryard bloom'd,* sat

there in a pretense of thinking for the benefit of any teachers
and even kids passing in the hall with some of whom just before
he'd in fact been joking (threw a feeble lopsided pass across the
afternoon lawn as he hustled from Studebaker to business), sat
now moveless in a pretense of remembering, with severe preci-
sion, the exact date of something that was bottlenecking his
entire day, left wrist raised for a quick look at how much time
was left, frown of accompaniment already formed, drawer
pulled with letterheaded memo paper ready to fly the instant
he smacked the desk deciding, but actually choking over loss,
choking over loss, thinking of the love, the love, the love he
missed when his face was thin and fresh, hopes were pure. O
growing old! O haggard ugly ghoul is life's decay! Started life a
sweet child believing everything beneath his father's roof; went
from that, immersed and fooled, to that mask of disgusted flesh
called a face but not the face that love had hoped for and to
that soul of a gruesome grieving ghost that now goes shudder-
ing through nightmare life cluttering up the earth as it dies. Ah
but well, Earl Johnson wanted to throw a pass to Cody and
Cody challenged him and said "Run with the ball and let's see
if I tackle you before you reach that Studebaker where the
man's standing"; and Johnson laughed because he had been
(absolutely) the outstanding runner everywhere (schools,
camps, picnics), at fifteen could do the hundred in 10:9, track
star speed; so took off not quite realizing what he'd done here
giving Cody these psychological opportunities and looking
back at him with taunts "Well come on, come on, what's the
matter?" And so that Cody furiously, as if running for his life,
not only caught up with him but even when Johnson increased
his speed in wholehearted realizing race caught up with him
easily, in his sheer excitement, with his tremendous unprece-
dented raw athletic power he could run the hundred in almost
ten flat (actually and no lie) and a sad, remote tackle took place
in the field, for a moment everybody saw Cody flyingtackling
horizontally in the dark air with his neck bulled on to prove,
his head down almost the way a dead man bows his head self-
satisfied and life-accomplished but also as if he was chuckling
up his coat sleeve at Johnson about-to-be-smeared, both arms

outstretched, in a tackling clamp that as he hung suspended in that instantaneous fix of the eye were outstretched with a particular kind of unspeakable viciousness that's always so surprising when you see it leaping out of the decent suits of men in sudden sidewalk fights, the cosmopolitan horror of it, like movie magnates fighting, this savagery explosively leaping now out of Cody's new suit with the same rage of shoulderpads and puffy arms, yet arms that also were outstretched with an unspeakable mute prophesied and profound humility like that of a head-down Christ shot out of a cannon on a cross for nothing, agonized. Crash, Johnson was tackled; Justin G. Mannerly called out "Why didn't you try that in the road I have a shovel in the car" nobody noticing, even as he drove off; and Cody, like Johnson with his knees all bruised and pants torn, had established his first great position of leadership in Tom Watson's famous gang.

Long ago in the red sun—that wow-mad Cody, whose story this is, lookout.

from Mexico City Blues

211th Chorus

The wheel of the quivering meat
       conception
Turns in the void expelling human beings,
Pigs, turtles, frogs, insects, nits,
Mice, lice, lizards, rats, roan
Racinghorses, poxy bucolic pigtics,
Horrible unnameable lice of vultures,
Murderous attacking dog-armies
Of Africa, Rhinos roaming in the
       jungle,
Vast boars and huge gigantic bull
Elephants, rams, eagles, condors,
Pones and Porcupines and Pills—

All the endless conception of living
                              beings
Gnashing everywhere in Consciousness
Throughout the ten directions of space
Occupying all the quarters in & out,
From supermicroscopic no-bug
To huge Galaxy Lightyear Bowell
Illuminating the sky of one Mind—
        Poor! I wish I was free
        of that slaving meat wheel
        and safe in heaven dead

239th Chorus

Charley Parker Looked like Buddha
Charley Parker, who recently died
Laughing at a juggler on the TV
after weeks of strain and sickness,
was called the Perfect Musician.
And his expression on his face
Was as calm, beautiful, and profound
As the image of the Buddha
Represented in the East, the lidded eyes,
The expression that says "All is Well"
—This was what Charley Parker
Said when he played, All is Well.
You had the feeling of early-in-the-morning
Like a hermit's joy, or like
                              the perfect cry
Of some wild gang at a jam session
"Wail, Wop"—Charley burst
His lungs to reach the speed
Of what the speedsters wanted
And what they wanted
Was his Eternal Slowdown.
A great musician and a great
                        creator of forms
That ultimately find expression
In mores and what have you.

from The Dharma Bums

1

Hopping a freight out of Los Angeles at high noon one day in late September 1955 I got on a gondola and lay down with my duffel bag under my head and my knees crossed and contemplated the clouds as we rolled north to Santa Barbara. It was a local and I intended to sleep on the beach at Santa Barbara that night and catch either another local to San Luis Obispo the next morning or the firstclass freight all the way to San Francisco at seven p.m. Somewhere near Camarillo where Charlie Parker'd been mad and relaxed back to normal health, a thin old little bum climbed into my gondola as we headed into a siding to give a train right of way and looked surprised to see me there. He established himself at the other end of the gondola and lay down, facing me, with his head on his own miserably small pack and said nothing. By and by they blew the highball whistle after the eastbound freight had smashed through on the main line and we pulled out as the air got colder and fog began to blow from the sea over the warm valleys of the coast. Both the little bum and I, after unsuccessful attempts to huddle on the cold steel in wraparounds, got up and paced back and forth and jumped and flapped arms at each our end of the gon. Pretty soon we headed into another siding at a small railroad town and I figured I needed a poorboy of Tokay wine to complete the cold dusk run to Santa Barbara. "Will you watch my pack while I run over there and get a bottle of wine?"

"Sure thing."

I jumped over the side and ran across Highway 101 to the store, and bought, besides wine, a little bread and candy. I ran back to my freight train which had another fifteen minutes to wait in the now warm sunny scene. But it was late afternoon and bound to get cold soon. The little bum was sitting cross-legged at his end before a pitiful repast of one can of sardines. I took pity on him and went over and said, "How about a little wine to warm you up? Maybe you'd like some bread and cheese with your sardines."

"Sure thing." He spoke from far away inside a little meek voicebox afraid or unwilling to assert himself. I'd bought the cheese three days ago in Mexico City before the long cheap bus trip across Zacatecas and Durango and Chihuahua two thousand long miles to the border at El Paso. He ate the cheese and bread and drank the wine with gusto and gratitude. I was pleased. I reminded myself of the line in the Diamond Sutra that says, "Practice charity without holding in mind any conceptions about charity, for charity after all is just a word." I was very devout in those days and was practicing my religious devotions almost to perfection. Since then I've become a little hypocritical about my lip-service and a little tired and cynical. Because now I am grown so old and neutral. . . . But then I really believed in the reality of charity and kindness and humility and zeal and neutral tranquillity and wisdom and ecstasy, and I believed that I was an oldtime bhikku in modern clothes wandering the world (usually the immense triangular arc of New York to Mexico City to San Francisco) in order to turn the wheel of the True Meaning, or Dharma, and gain merit for myself as a future Buddha (Awakener) and as a future Hero in Paradise. I had not met Japhy Ryder yet, I was about to the next week, or heard anything about "Dharma Bums" although at this time I was a perfect Dharma Bum myself and considered myself a religious wanderer. The little bum in the gondola solidified all my beliefs by warming up to the wine and talking and finally whipping out a tiny slip of paper which contained a prayer by Saint Teresa announcing that after her death she will return to the earth by showering it with roses from heaven, forever, for all living creatures.

"Where did you get this?" I asked.

"Oh, I cut it out of a reading-room magazine in Los Angeles couple of years ago. I always carry it with me."

"And you squat in boxcars and read it?"

"Most every day." He talked not much more than this, didn't amplify on the subject of Saint Teresa, and was very modest about his religion and told me little about his personal life. He is the kind of thin quiet little bum nobody pays much attention to even in Skid Row, let alone Main Street. If a cop hustled him off, he hustled, and disappeared, and if yard dicks were around in bigcity yards when a freight was pulling out, chances are they never got a sight of the little man hiding in the weeds and hopping on in the shadows. When I told him I was planning to hop the Zipper firstclass freight train the next night he said, "Ah you mean the Midnight Ghost."

"Is that what you call the Zipper?"

"You musta been a railroad man on that railroad."

"I was, I was a brakeman on the S.P."

"Well, we bums call it the Midnight Ghost cause you get on it at L.A. and nobody sees you till you get to San Francisco in the morning the thing flies so fast."

"Eighty miles an hour on the straightaways, pap."

"That's right but it gits mighty cold at night when you're flyin up that coast north of Gavioty and up around Surf."

"Surf that's right, then the mountains down south of Margarita."

"Margarity, that's right, but I've rid that Midnight Ghost more times'n I can count I guess."

"How many years been since you've been home?"

"More years than I care to count I guess. Ohio was where I was from."

But the train got started, the wind grew cold and foggy again, and we spent the following hour and a half doing everything in our power and will power not to freeze and chatter-teeth too much. I'd huddle and meditate on the warmth, the actual warmth of God, to obviate the cold; then I'd jump up and flap my arms and legs and sing. But the little bum had more patience than I had and just lay there most of the time chewing his cud in forlorn bitterlipped thought. My teeth were chattering, my lips blue. By dark we saw with relief the familiar mountains of Santa Barbara taking shape and soon we'd be stopped and warm in the warm starlit night by the tracks.

I bade farewell to the little bum of Saint Teresa at the crossing, where we jumped off, and went to sleep the night in the sand in my blankets, far down the beach at the foot of a cliff where cops wouldn't see me and drive me away. I cooked hotdogs on freshly cut and sharpened sticks over the coals of a big

wood fire, and heated a can of beans and a can of cheese maca-
roni in the redhot hollows, and drank my newly bought wine,
and exulted in one of the most pleasant nights of my life. I
waded in the water and dunked a little and stood looking up at
the splendorous night sky, Avalokitesvara's ten-wondered uni-
verse of dark and diamonds. "Well, Ray," sez I, glad, "only a
few miles to go. You've done it again." Happy. Just in my swim
shorts, barefooted, wild-haired, in the red fire dark, singing,
swigging wine, spitting, jumping, running—that's the way to
live. All alone and free in the soft sands of the beach by the sigh
of the sea out there, with the Ma-Wink fallopian virgin warm
stars reflecting on the outer channel fluid belly waters. And if
your cans are redhot and you can't hold them in your hands,
just use good old railroad gloves, that's all. I let the food cool
a little to enjoy more wine and my thoughts. I sat crosslegged
in the sand and contemplated my life. Well, there, and what
difference did it make? "What's going to happen to me up
ahead?" Then the wine got to work on my taste buds and be-
fore long I had to pitch into those hotdogs, biting them right
off the end of the stick spit, and chomp chomp, and dig down
into the two tasty cans with the old pack spoon, spooning up
rich bites of hot beans and pork, or of macaroni with sizzling
hot sauce, and maybe a little sand thrown in. "And how many
grains of sand are there on this beach?" I think. "Why, as many
grains of sand as there are stars in that sky!" (chomp chomp)
and if so "How many human beings have there been, in fact
how many living creatures have there been, since before the *less*
part of beginningless time? Why, oy, I reckon you would have
to calculate the number of grains of sand on this beach and on
every star in the sky, in every one of the ten thousand great
chilicosms, which would be a number of sand grains uncom-
putable by IBM and Burroughs too, why boy I don't rightly
know" (swig of wine) "I don't rightly know but it must be a
couple umpteen trillion sextillion infideled and busted up un-
numberable number of roses that sweet Saint Teresa and that
fine little old man are now this minute showering on your head,
with lilies."

Then, meal done, wiping my lips with my red bandana, I

washed up the dishes in the salt sea, kicked a few clods of sand, wandered around, wiped them, put them away, stuck the old spoon back in the salty pack, and lay down curled in my blanket for a night's good and just rest. Waking up in the middle of the night, "Wa? Where am I, what is the basketbally game of eternity the girls are playing here by me in the old house of my life, the house isn't on fire is it?" but it's only the banding rush of waves piling up higher closer high tide to my blanket bed. "I be as hard and old as a conch shell," and I go to sleep and dream that while sleeping I use up three slices of bread breathing. . . . Ah poor mind of man, and lonely man alone on the beach, and God watching with intent smile I'd say. . . . And I dreamed of home long ago in New England, my little kitkats trying to go a thousand miles following me on the road across America, and my mother with a pack on her back, and my father running after the ephemeral uncatchable train, and I dreamed and woke up to a gray dawn, saw it, sniffed (because I had seen all the horizon shift as if a sceneshifter had hurried to put it back in place and make me believe in its reality), and went back to sleep, turning over. "It's all the same thing," I heard my voice say in the void that's highly embraceable during sleep.

NEAL CASSADY

|||||||||||||||||||||||||||||||||||||||||||||||||||||||||||||||||||||||||||||||||||||||||||||||||||||||||||||||||||||||||||

NEAL CASSADY met Kerouac and Ginsberg in New York in 1946 after leaving a reformatory in Denver. He had grown up around Larimer Street, a skid row district, and came of age among hustlers, con men, car thieves, and drunks. Cassady was a wild and energetic conversationalist, and it spilled over into his writing. His vast, spontaneous, sexually explicit letters, full of street talk, brazen fun-seeking, and personal intimacy, helped break Kerouac free from the conventional writing found in his first book, *The Town and the City*. Ginsberg and Cassady carried on a love affair between New York and Denver; Kerouac tagged along, watching and listening, while beginning his masterpiece *Visions of Cody*, a portrait of Cassady, part of his perennial search for an American hero. That book (published only after Kerouac's death) became the basis of the other portrait of Kerouac and Cassady's comradeship, *On the Road*, which brought fame and notoriety to Cassady. Cassady's own writing consists mostly of the hundreds of letters, posted to Kerouac and others, which set so much of the tone for Beat writing. Cassady also started a book on himself—a sort of rival to Kerouac's efforts—but he only managed to write a prologue and three chapters. City Lights published this material as *The First Third*: Cassady's idea being that it would cover the first third of his life. The second "third" was to have been an account of his days with Kerouac and Ginsberg; the final part was to cover the period in the 1960s when Cassady joined Ken Kesey and the Merry Pranksters on the Magic Bus, becoming a culture hero for a whole new generation. One night, early in February of 1968, Cassady set off down the railroad tracks outside San Miguel de Allende, Mexico, to a wedding party where *pulque* (alcohol) was being served. He had taken downers to quiet amphetamine withdrawal. He died of exposure the next day.

Letter to Allen Ginsberg, May 15, 1951

Dear Allen;

I have not written anything for a month. This is not particularly bad, that is, I didn't quit in the habitual doubt and depression. There is a dissatisfaction; a basic deeply disgusting impatience and feeling of overwhelming inadequacy with words. Especially acute is the awareness of my lack of ability, an almost entire lack I fear, to delineate any character literally. Yet, as I say, this last stopping was not too frustrating since it was actuated by a rational slackening-off (altho i'm the last person recommendable to slow down, Time and my personality makes that inadvisable; in my 25 years I've written only a rambling prologue, an even weaker first 20 pages and pitifully few letters) to escape the mediocre monotone of what I'm writing by assimilating "Tender is the Night" -F. Scott Fitzgerald and a little poetry to freshen my outlook, now that my oolong is gone and to substitute for too powerful dexderine. Again, too, the RR program makes writing difficult because I'm seldom in SF more than 8 hrs. at a time. To compensate I carry a note pad and write a sentence or two as I think of it, but these caboose-lines are always, of necessity, the next ones of the book and have accumulated into a number of illegible longhand pages. Being not at home long enough to work these into a typewritten reality, I simply quit writing until such time as I can catch up. So I do have an inflexible body of swollen adjectives to attack and shall do it, tho the slowness of the labor quells my spirit. I may as well tell you why. It happens this way in my untalented case: Of course, I have in mind a rough outline which consists only of an attempt to recall my befuddled memories. To put down these happenings gives me the original impetus for each line—at best I write only from sentence to sentence and can't construct beyond this—and I begin to write. After the first statement is out, and often before, I get hopelessly involved in words to contain the increasing number of ideas. As I progress this morass becomes larger and my head more and more deeply engulfed in recurrent themes which are unfolded in sickening profusion. While on the paper, in attempting to snatch all I can before I forget, I am soon so overextended—stretched grammatically and logically to the point where any semblance of clarity is lost—that I am forced to stop. These bunched ideas cannot long be consciously retained as I write and are lost by being momentarily thrust back into the mind, each as they come except the immediate one pinpointed, and the sensitive things, once rejected for a second, shyly vanish in an unrelenting march of steady retreat into their Limbo while I'm floundering at sloppy deliberation in the choice of every new word, and thus damned up in my soul is left to rot. The limit of my foremind to tap and drain onto paper any flow from my residue of self-saturated thoughts is usually half a page at any one sitting. Naturally, the shorter the space of time between each diving-in the less satisfaction I could weave for myself and each continuing made more oppressive the friction generated by rubbing so familiarly against my blocks. When confronted with these boundaries I had once either often changed the subject upon which to think or didn't write at all, mostly the latter. Now, in my still inconsistent and inconstant fashion, I've burst thru somewhat (¿) so face bigger things. These are more of the straitjacket variety and perhaps approach your own problems of poetic thought, but that is no help and might be something else entirely. Be as it may, the way it happens is simply that a particular word one knows pops out for use. But we quickly learn not to be content with just any word and look for a second, or third, or fourth choice. (incidently, when I first began typing if I accidently hit the wrong letter to start a word I would, rather than erase, think up a word to suit the letter and as another and then another mistake came up I had soon altered completely both the meaning of what I said and the things which I was saying—with all the accompanying change in chain of thought) At last I come to the core of my writing faults, flaws in reasoning, windiness or too tight style, grammar troubles, triteness, etc, so shall put off for a minute any delving into our straitjacket problems per se, altho all is tied together I give you detailed example to show that most of my inability to get on with the book lies in my slowness in selecting words, more properly I mean my slowness in fitting into a sensible sentence the words that select themselves. My primary weakness is that I try to crowd too much in, once a word has come to me, no matter how obviously poor, I am loath to leave it out of that sentence. Seeing it won't fit I set out to manufacture another sentence for it, in doing so I create more, etc. Let us look at this a little more closely. Right away I've got a surplus of cheap old common words. In the interval it takes to make the sentence structure a few more hit me and they force the sentence into a ridiculous bulge which I must prune pronto. To load each sentence with all it can carry takes time and the longer I linger the more abstract possibilities flit across my mind. Then I'm really in for it because I start switching words about like an overzealous brakeman with poor savey. A compromise must be reached and the slow decision on one is what puts me in the hole so muchoftenfardeeply. See what I mean, those four words just popped and I had to choose. To continue this assinine level of elementary writing frustration you are to turn back to the upside down question mark on last page. I was about to modify "somewhat" by using these words—to adapt an attitude by attempting to be attuned for each topic in a subject matter—but when I began arranging the words I realized I was doing typical writing in one of my normal sentences and tho they didn't mean too much, even if poor (and they are not good words, as can be easily seen) I was about to use them because each one had just popped out in rapid order and because they had come I felt it necessary to try and put them in after "somewhat". Instead I left them out, and its most unusual for me to leave anything out just because it's stinking and that's why the ordinary level of my writing is so trite and shallow, and put in the question mark to call your attention to the space and put the words here for you instead of where they were intended to be placed when I wrote them. Enuf. Back to the straitjacket problem of control. For me to cultivate adequate management of ideas so as to keep them and to be able to put them down clearly is an everpresent difficulty to my stumbling mind. Incidently, it was along this line of trying to save something for writing until I could learn to make it all one process of just thinking and putting down that thought, that I rationalized into the decision to buy my Ekotape recorder. The experiment has proved somewhat disappointing so was abandoned in its infancy a few months ago, but when I again get 10 bucks to get it out of the repair shop (magnetized by sitting next to a radio in long disusement) I will begin a new attempt with it. Now, if I'm on the novel I write longhand and type it up with a bit of changing as I go along, if I'm writing a letter I just type word for word as I think of them, unless I get particularly involved, then I write that sentence or two in longhand before typing. In this letter, except for the majority of lines 25 to 40 on the first page and one or two other single lines, I typed right along at my average (a little better than average, I think) speed of—well, figure it up if you've the patience, I've taken exactly four (4) hours of sitting here, with a couple of times-out to piss and quiet kids, to reach this sentence, anyhow, it must surely be at least several words a minute, I guess, huh? Right now my book stands much in relationship to the above words I gave you that were supposed to follow "somewhat" on page one. That is, I have a lot of longhand junk that has each sentence in it crammed full of stupid words that make faulty reasoning and poor flow because of the jampacked verbs and adjectives. This makes for a whole stretch of pages that are not only poorer than usual, but also has no uplifting line or two to compensate. In other words, one sunday a month or so ago I wrote all of this weak part in the sunshine of the backyard (sitting on a piles-making square of concrete) and got horribly involved in my nemesis of too many poor words. So there I'm stuck because I can't throw it all away and can't satisfactorily patch it up. All I can do is finish this part and try to do better on the following pages and if I ever accumulate a great many pages I can either throw this part out or graft it on elsewhere. So its really not too bad, as I said in the beginning, it just happens to be where I am right now. Ugh, OK, I stop for the sake of intelligence and apologize that the reasoning of this whole letter would give discredit to a retarded ten-year-old. But I must say this as it seems apropos; I find, and for the first time, that when I read F. S. Fitzgerald I'm dealing with a writer that I'm about equal to. Not yet, of course, and maybe never in terms of word-use, but I know I'm in there already almost as far as he ever was. I was amazed to discover that his writing reasoning was nearly exactly paralleled by me. Not that I can approach his style, nor do I much care to, in fact, strangely enough, it seems somehow beneath me. What I perhaps mean is that I feel he and I both try with about equal intensity. If I can't come to eventually write as good as he did I fear I'll honestly be pretty much of a failure, ego? no, truth. I realize he's not much and only extolled as American (at least a dozen, including our pal Jack K. are better) and I see him as a baby compared to Proust or Celine.

[I halt these digressions so that I may begin the next page clean.]

from The First Third

Chapter 1

For a time I held a unique position. Among the hundreds of isolated creatures who haunted the streets of lower downtown Denver, there was not one so young as myself. Amid these dreary men who had committed themselves, each for his own good reason, to the task of finishing their days as pennyless drunkards, I alone as the sharer of their way of life, presented the sole replica of their own childhood to which their vision could daily turn. Being thus grafted onto them, I became the unnatural son of a few score beaten men.

It was my experience to be constantly meeting new cronies of my father's; who invariably introduced me with the proud, "This is my boy." Whereupon the pat on my head was usually followed by the quizzical look the eye reserves for uncertainty, which here conveyed the question; "Shall I give him a little drink?" Sensing the offer, backed by a half-extended bottle, my father would always say, "You'll have to ask him." I would answer, "no." Of course, this was only on those memorable occasions when an acceptable drink like wine was available. The unhappy times when there was none, or, only "canned heat" (denatured alcohol) or Bay Rum at hand, I did not have to go through my little routine.

Many times, after normal adult catering with questions to show interest in the child, (such gestures of talkative comradeship was their token parenthood, for these fathers had nothing else to give). I was usually then ignored while the talk of my father and his new friend would turn to recalling the past. These Tete-a-tetes were full of little asides which carried with them facts establishing that much of the life they had suffered was in common; mutual friends, cities visited, things done there, and so on. Their conversation had many general statements about Truth and Life, which contained the collective intelligence of all America's bums. They were drunkards whose minds, weakened by liquor and an obsequious manner of existence, seemed continually pre-occupied with bringing up short observations of obvious trash, said in such a way as to be instantly recognizable by the listener, who had heard it all before and whose own prime concern was to nod at everything said, then continue the conversation with a remark of his own, equally transparent and loaded with generalities. The simplicity of this pattern was marvelous and there was no limit to what they could agree on in this fashion and the abstract ends that could be reached. Through sheer repetitious hearing of such small-talk speculation, I came to know their minds so intimately that I could understand as they understood, and there was soon no mystery to the conversation of any of them. I as-

sumed all men thought the same and so knew *these* things, be-
cause like any child I correlated all adult action without much
actual regard for type.

All his fellow alcoholics called my father "the barber" since
he was about the only one of them who had practised that trade
and I was "the barber's boy". They all said I looked just like
him, but I didn't think this was true in the least. And they
watched me grow with comments like "Why, look there—his
head is higher than your belt already!", it wasn't such a feat,
I thought, to stand that tall, because my father had awfully
short legs.

When, in 1932, the family situation was resolved by my par-
ents' parting, I was not sorry to accompany my father in his
retreat to Larimer Street. Most especially, I was not sorry to
bid what proved to be a two-years farewell to my terrifying
bully-brother, Jimmy, and even to my less-thought-about
mother and younger sister. The prospect of adventure filled my
six-year-old head; besides, I would now be spared the sight of
violence every Sunday. With my father gone for good, my older
half-brothers Jack and Ralph would not be able to pound his
face bloody when he returned so obediently home from his Sat-
urday-night binges. Mother used to cry and beg them to stop
beating him, but, as I observed many times in the years to fol-
low, when these boys started using their fists there was only
exhaustion to stop their brain-blinding rages.

But now all this and other such terrors, as when Jimmy made
me fight other little boys, were behind me, and for the present I
took an increased interest in my new surroundings so singularly
uncommon and giving me so matchless an edification in ob-
serving the scum right from the start. Avoiding those whose
alcoholic rages made surly and dictatorial by being with
father's more brow-beaten friends, I was given certain unortho-
dox freedoms not ordinarily to be had by American boys of six.
Also, my father, being usually drunk, or trying to get that way,
was of necessity a bit lax in his discipline. Still, I didn't much
take advantage of him, since I really loved the old boy.

It was the month of my sixth birthday and a usual fierce winter was upon the city when Dad and I moved into the Metropolitan. This is a five-story building, condemned before I got there, (though still not torn down till very recently,) on the corner of 16th and Market Streets. In peril of collapse it housed about a hundred of Denver's non-transient bums and still does. On each of the upper floors there were some thirty odd cubicles whose walls failing by several feet to reach it, made the ceiling seem incongruously high. These sleeping cells mostly rented for ten or fifteen cents a night; certain superior ones cost two-bits, and we had one of these, but only paid a weekly rate of one dollar, because of the top floor location since we shared the room with a third person.

This roommate of ours slept on a sort of platform made by a plank covering a pipe elbow in the building's plumbing. Not just anyone could sleep there in comfort, for the ledge was only about three feet long, but he fit in the space snugly enough, because both his legs had been amputated at the thigh many years ago. Appropriately, he was called Shorty and this fitting of name to fact seemed very funny to me. Every morning he got up early and with his oversized arms, swung a skinny torso down those five flights of stairs. I never saw him pause to use the community washroom on the second floor and presumed the sinks were too high for him so he made toilet arrangements elsewhere. On the sidewalk he would get into a dolly-like cart and, using blocks of wood in each hand, push himself to his begging post. He usually went around the corner on Larimer Street and stationed himself before the Manhattan Restaurant. Larimer Street was Denver's main drag in the nineteenth century and the Manhattan was its best restaurant. Now, everything else has fallen to cheapness, but the fine Manhattan is still frequented by tourists and the well-to-do. Shorty's schedule was a few hours ahead of the bums with a normal length to their limbs, and he would often panhandle a dollar or more before noon because he had utilized the advantage of his handicap by displaying it in this good spot. After he had gotten the price of a bottle or two, he would return to the room and drink into a stupor.

Usually he had passed out, or was about to, by the time I got home from school, but some days were slack, and on these days he would stay out very late. It was as though he had an early afternoon deadline, and if he wasn't in the room by then he wouldn't come at all. I came to dread these times because he would then drink on the street, and it was up to me to help search the alleys and doorways until we found him. Dad would carry him home while I followed, alternately pulling up hill and coasting down on his cart with the roller-skate wheels.

Now and again, when with child-energy, I burst into the room, I would catch Shorty playing with himself. (I thought it fried eggs littering the floor.) Even though he was past forty, any preoccupation with this form of diversion was justified, I'm sure, since judging from his appearance, he must not have had a woman since his youth, if then. Encrusted with dirt, he stank of body smell and was very ugly with a no-forehead face full of a grinning rubber mouth that showed black stubbed teeth. Yet, his taste certainly did not run to boys my age, because the time or two I saw him exposed, he roared at me to get out, and these were his only incidents of anger that I recall.

My father and I lived with Shorty until June, and after these four or five months, although I looked for him out of curiosity, we never saw him again, so I never learned what became of old pal Shorty.

The first convenient Monday after we settled in the Metropolian, Dad put me back in school. My morning wash-up was dispatched with anxious hurry, tho there was the usual care to get behind my ears. A stained mirror hung suspended on the wall's cracked plaster, whose white dust crumbled into the stench of the metal sink below, and looking in it past a distorted reflection of washing men, my father gave his blurred face a final check before hustling me to a twenty-cent bolted breakfast of brains and eggs. Onto the big yellow street-car for a quick ride up Sixteenth to Welton, then left to 23rd Street. Over the block-long walk to our Glenarm Street destination, we paused for a moment to stare as Dad once again pointed out all the cluttered maze behind the window of the shoe-cobbler's next to his first Denver barber shop. Then we entered the modern building of gleaming white firebrick that is Ebert Grammar School and apprehensively approached the information desk. My old man meekly informed the girl receptionist that I was ready to go to school again. The term had started some weeks before, and he was afraid I might have to begin kindergarten all over. It was an unfounded fear, for my tardy enrollment made no difference, I was placed without question in my proper grade, the first. Filling out my card, the pretty clerk asked where I lived, and Dad was wise enough to give mother's 22nd and Stout address, only four blocks away.

This sort of lie became habitual, for all the years I was with my father I had to give the school a fictitious home address. I developed a continual worry they would find I lived outside Ebert's district; then I would be forced to attend in the district I was, and the thought of switching schools terrified me. So, in defiance of Denver's geography, I went to Ebert six straight years. And this was no mean foot-feet; I always lived at least a mile from the school and often more, even four. In fact, it was the many mornings of racing these miles, (since I seldom had carfare or would use it if I had) so as not to be late, that must have led to my becoming interested in long-distance running.

In the nighttime of Metropolitan squalor, we slept side by side, my Dad and I, in a bed without sheets. There happened to be no clock, so I relied on Daniels and Fisher's mammoth tower one to wake me for school, and it did. Or at least I think this is what woke me, because as it boomed 7:00 A.M. down to me I always opened my eyes, and from under the unwashed blanket stuck my alert head into our room's nippy air. There my father snored, and usually being too drunk to stir, was oblivious to everything. Turning from the breath's smell out of his drink-swollen face, I eased my naked self off the creaking cot with shivering quietness. I hurried into some hated remnants of brother Jimmy's clothes; too-short shoes and knickers which crept above my knees. The long wool socks I wore failed to effectively close this embarrassing gap. Most of the time Dad just snored on and on, and since Shorty's shelf was bare (he sometimes departed while it was still dark outside), I woke to no commanding voices. Slipping through our door and along a splintered floor, I passed rooms where other weakened bodies of shattered soul joined my father in giving noise to a labored sleep. Down worn stairs on silent feet and a quick step into a sunlit lavatory of activity. Ringing the enormous room were many nondescript men at their toilet. Most of them were shaving, some had the "shakes" so that it was quite a job, and, so as not to cut themselves or face the agony too often, they only shaved when they were on their way uptown to hustle a dime. Unclean trousers bagged over run-down shoes. Their heavy coats and frayed shirts hung on hooks beside them, for when washing they really splashed with janitorial unconcern. I remember sidestepping these puddles of water as I skipped to one of the room's large windows and tiptoe-peered through dirty panes to read the time by guessing at the slant of nearly illegible black hands against the dingy white glass of the Roman-numeraled clockface atop the mighty tower of Daniels and Fisher's department store, Denver's highest building—it was 7:15. After washing I tripped back upstairs to fetch my tennisball and coat and to check Dad for any signs of sobriety or interest in food, but on most school days he didn't often stir, so alone I went to my breakfast.

Again descending the stairs I went through the lobby, empty of loitering men at this hour, and on down several big steps of deeply scooped stone onto the busy 16th and Market Streets intersection. Big trucks with chain-drive and hard-rubber tires bounced over Market's slick cobblestone. Opening for the day's business were the wholesale meat dealers, poultry houses, fish markets, coffee and spice warehouses and cheese companies—I was always hungry then—and the employment agencies and restaurants and bars, and a couple of business concerns I have forgotten, that crowded into the blocks of Market between 14th and 18th. On 16th Street, arterial traffic rumbled from an overpass into North Denver—of Denver's half-dozen ones, only this viaduct had streetcar tracks—a bottleneck of oversized trams jammed with working people inching toward the Loop, Larimer, Downtown and all East Denver clanged past me as I came out of the hotel. I walked a block up 16th and turned left at the newly opened Dave Cook sporting goods store on Larimer's corner and went into the building next to it. This was the Citizen's Mission, run by a Protestant church organization and strongly backed by a good assemblyman (whose name I've forgotten although Dad in his daydreams of getting somewhere was always talking of going to see "So and so, up at the Mission" to get a steady job—now I remember, Val Higgins!). The Mission gave breakfast and supper to about two hundred men a day and in return had a well attended bi-weekly church service, a thing of which its several competitors up and down The Street could also boast, but I couldn't see why, since they handed out no food. A couple of years later Father Divine's, up Larimer on 24th in the middle of the block, began giving meals. They served only lunch, a real tasty one too, and there was a big whoopdeedo among the boys when his place opened, for the gap between breakfast and supper at the Mission had been felt by us all. But right now we had only the Mission and I was its youngest member by a good dozen years.

The facade of the Citizen's Mission was of inappropriately gay yellow stucco. The double center doors entered into an au-ditorium with massive wooden pews that could sit a hundred people. Down the aisle was a raised platform with a front-cen-ter box pulpit, also on this stage was an unmusical piano and a table with a semi-circle of chairs behind it. From the street there were single doors on each end of the building, the one on the right led upstairs to the administration offices, but I never used it and always took the door to the left instead. Getting in an orderly line of hungry men I moved slowly forward down metal stairs into a warm kitchen of smells and clatter. Being served cafeteria style, each of us picked up a tray, spoon, bowl and cup of tinny material, and we moved along the wall in a patient wait for our turn before the steam tables. The first white-aproned woman—all the food handlers were women, smiling on us and busy with a "cause"—placed two pieces of bread on the tray, the second one ladled a scoopful of oatmeal into our bowls, while the third poured hot coffee. (There was

no cream, but plenty of sugar, and one could get a second cup.)
We filed to stainless steel benches and sat before long ringing
tables of the same material which vibrated so from the impact
of our utensils that my sensitive ears filled completely. All
around men clustered and we squeezed elbow to elbow for lack
of space in the crowded basement room. Sometimes my break-
fast companions happened to talk to me, and sometimes they
didn't. Either way as I remember it was all the same. Of course
I eventually learned that almost all of them were alcoholics,
and many of them suffering a great deal from the disease, but
there were also several old-age pensioners and other indiffer-
ently bunched younger men who were just down on their luck
because of the Depression.

On the Mission's left was the Manhattan Restaurant and
seated in his cart before its building would be Shorty at work.
He sat in the bright morning sun of winter as its cold light came
to touch the sidewalk's outer edge, and turning dull eyes on
Larimer's crowd he leaned back against the base of a heavily
ornate iron drinking fountain the twin faucets of which have
long been out of service and whose infant cupids danced in
golden contrast over his head. As I passed him on my way
toward 17th Street he gave a languid nod which contrasted
with the grinning mouth he exhibited in our room's privacy
and I realized he put on a different face for the public.

My route to Ebert was an always careful Zig Zag. The game
was to find hurrying shortcuts, and to not waste a step, espe-
cially by the crime of missing a bounce of the dirty tennis ball's
constant dribble. I also avoided cracks in the concrete, as a
substitute for the impractical game of "Sidewalk's Poison"
which, on later trips to school from residential districts, I devel-
oped into a Fine Art. I went past some of Larimer's row of
bars and pawn shops, then up 17th Street to the newly-created
Federal Reserve Bank with its massive marble squares and with
elegant iron bars protecting its windows. Unlike other banks
on 17th Street its enormous bronze doors of scrolled bas-relief
featuring charioteered archers were never open and I wondered
the mystery of its vaults. Another left turn and along a block

of Arapahoe street whorehouses I later patronized. Then a right, onto busy 18th Street with its noisy sheet metal shops and motorcycle showrooms and garages. Across Curtis Street's corner of candy company, parking lot, cheap hotel and cheaper restaurant, and up to Champa Street with the mighty colonnaded structure of the Post Office. Along this block there occasionally came from the depths of musty smelling second-hand clothing stores the squeaky screech of serious adolescent violin lessons. On the Post Office corner I would pause for a quick drink at the public fountain which—unlike most of Denver's—was not shut off in winter so that conical ice attacked the spout's silvery knob, and on certain cold days it victoriously choked the bowl and froze the overflow basin outlet. The idea was to avoid torrents of backlogged water, leap on the fountain to snatch a gulp, then rush a retreat before my shoes were filled. If it had no fresh snow on which to slip, I'd next canter over a huge stone bench whose giant size made even adults use only its edge for sitting. I made paradox of the puzzling proverb carved in its granite, for it cautioned against too much rest while offering it freely, "Desire rest but desire not too much." A springing leap up the 18th Street side of broad stairway that circumvented the Post Office to walk through the warmth of its block-long lobby. On balmier days I disdained this minute of heat, and instead, scampered in a weaving run about the fluted sides of every enormous column that fronted Stout Street. There was a hundred feet of sidewalk—filled waste space between curb and Post Office. Down the 19th Street steps three in a bound and catty-corner to a narrow wall's sharp peak which challenged my equilibrium. My tightrope was the angled top of a half-foot high sidewalk border enclosing the grounds of the new Federal building. I would pause on my tilted perch to stare upward at the white majesty of the almost completed structure that now made an equalling block square twin to the Post Office's substantial bulk. Across California Street to go into the alley behind the basement Church of the Holy Ghost, where I later served a year as altar boy without missing a day, then under a vacant lot's billboard to reach the five-pointed intersection of Welton, Broadway and 20th Avenue. The triangular Crest Hotel rose in ten luxurious floors; across from it were a miscellany of drugstore, flower shop, beauty salon, restaurant and two large groceries. Above these businesses there towered, all chunked together, hotel buildings whose solid facades were broken only by the gap of a 20 foot alley entrance. From out of this canyon-like block, so rare in Denver, I raced uphill over another rarity. It was an uncommon pavement bulge with such a stretch from curb to curb that I made a game of traversing its middle. The distinct idea of this journey was to hold my breath with no sneak inhales while on the blacktop itself, and if I didn't run at top speed, or failed to begin with an extreme expansion of chest, I didn't succeed. From the beginnings of its swell near Welton Street to its upper end on Sherman, the hill of this 20th Avenue street surface was fully two blocks long and on my path, from Lincoln to Glenarm, was easily a hundred yards in width. My ambition was to do my little no breathing stunt the long way, but a measuring look at that vast space always discouraged any effort. It was as though an entire acre or more had been thoughtlessly razed just so autos could branch out in any one of three directions with unnecessary room to spare, in fact, it had a center triangle, formed by raised oval traffic buttons that contained nothing and was for no purpose but to keep cars out, since some reckless drivers might be tempted into wild and fancy curlyques over this spacious asphalt—in later years I myself made a few tentative speedway dashes around this triangle. Reaching the sidewalk of Glenarm Street with my lungs in double tempo, I would pass a business school on the corner and then the first of the homes that fringed the downtown area. They nestled between a splendid Catholic church with matching slender spires of stone and the Denver Bible Institute, whose odd belfry was in a squat clapboard affair of afterthought that hid itself beneath the trees of the Institute's yard. Now the residential section began in earnest and from 21st to 22nd Streets only a tiny candy store disturbed the rows of solidly bunched houses. I cut the corner and entered the far side of Ebert's huge graveled playground and ran its length at full tilt for the bell was usually ringing.

I faintly remember my few weeks of kindergarten blocks and beads. Equally indistinct is the first grade, except the labored efforts to write my name. Our classroom was in the middle of the building and faced the playground; underneath its windows there was a driveway that was used by coal trucks and other delivery vehicles, and beside the driveway entrance was a small slide and row of swings intended for the younger children. Around these an iron pipe guardrail was later built which created a new excitement in the swings, for, the older boys found that if they leapt from a swing at just the right point in its highest arc they could clear this barrier. I watched the feat in awe for a long time before I dared attempt it myself; with the best of jumps, I could just graze the rail's top and often, seized by buck fever, I was so unfortunate as to drop astraddle the railing. Near the center of the playground were two old trees about a hundred feet apart; twin goals marking a basketball court's gaunt occupancy rose between their trunks of withered bark, scarred and made barren by years of carved initials. At the yard's furthest corner, was a circle of overhead rings, another slide and a bigger set of swings alongside a rough baseball diamond. Below this, near Glenarm, was the five or six room house of the school custodian, totally isolated from the playground by a high wooden fence that we children were forbidden to climb. Around the entire block-square schoolyard ran a six foot woven wire fence that was made by Cyclone, as a metal tag attached every few yards testified.

Ebert itself is an "I" shaped building of two stories with the classrooms of both floors filling the elongated center bar of the "I", except that near one end of the main corridor was a large room for the Principal and her office staff. The twin ends of the "I" contained a magnificent gym and auditorium. The school cafeteria in the basement was not used by the student body since most of the children went to their nearby homes for lunch, so the Cub Scouts, student council and other groups with similar organizational activities used this benched room for their meetings. But there were even a couple dozen of us who did eat there; the city had appropriated a small fund to supply the needy children, whose parents applied for it, (Father put off doing this for weeks), a noonday snack of milk and Graham crackers.

Returning from school, the hurried pace of morning was absent and I made leisurely detours to play. My primary cern was not to lose the ever-active tennis ball with which I played solitary catch. There was many a close squeak when, after a muff, only a frantic dash and a desperate lunge could retrieve the guttered ball. There was a great struggle with the manhole cover and a gingerly movement down the repulsive iron ladder into a frightening hole to snatch the bobbing ball from the water's stench. Often the chase led upwards, at those times when I would incorrectly judge the bounce off a rooftop's slant. Unless it was a particularly isolated roof that repelled all maneuverings, no mere hard climb ever deterred me from making the unfriendly housedrain yield its prey. I took to raiding all the raincatchers about and found veritable nests of lost balls in some of the least accessible ones.

The Citizens' Mission began supper at five o'clock. The idea was to be in the first group so as to avoid being delayed by the ever-increasing accumulation of men to be served. The line moved slowly at any time and if anyone missed being in the beginning batch it might take him much of the early evening to reach his meal. If alone, I could whiz through the entire operation in less than half an hour, for then some kindly line-crawlers would push me past them. Often in thus creeping forward to my food, I would edge around a couple dozen of these indulgent men who, while committing the cheat for me, gave to their companions a sly wink and an expansive chortle of self-satisfaction. These no-dallying dinners happened only when I was so late from school that there was no time to stop at the Metropolitan for Dad, or if he was laid up drunk. Usually, of course, we did meet and I then stayed in the line with him to wait our fair turn in the rotation of shuffling.

Perhaps the most exciting part of the day was the Metropolitan nights. Around the spacious main floor lobby were indiscriminately arranged numerous roundbacked chairs that supported with old wood squeakings of protest their pounds of weary flesh. Into this drafty high vaulted parlor of affliction those dregs crowded who had nothing to do and spent dreary hours of heavy time just sitting. But none sat in a position very near the pot-bellied stove in the rough floor's metal covered center, for, in contrast with the non-heated upper floors and the extreme cold outside, unwelcome waves of too much heat radiated from cherry colored cheeks of the overstoked stove, with its fiercely roaring always-open draft.

There was an inner lobby of smaller dimensions that was altogether more comfortable and unlike the outer lobby with its huge dirt-caked windows, on which was advertised the price of beds, this room, except for a narrow door, had no break whatsoever in the filthy walls. In its confines there existed a pleasant intimacy quite missing in the foyer, because clustered about its tables were moneyless men killing time at cards. A year or two later, when the Metropolitan became even more overstuffed with society's sediments, the landlords—executors of a deceased plumber and pipefitter's large estate that had tinyly begun in shrewd realty deals—removed what furniture filled this secondary lobby and put in cots to make a dormitory for the "one-nighters." But now, there was a continual round of knock-rummy, cribbage, Con-Can, Casino, Pieute, Pinochle, Poker and other varieties of cardplaying. Here I spent much of the night learning to play most of the games fairly well, besides several slick card tricks in which I particularly delighted. I also passed many evening hours tossing my laboriously made dart; it was a sewing needle inserted in a wooden match, the top of which was split to receive its feathers of newspaper that were held in place by thread wound around after to heal the rupture. Despite my poor child-construction this contraption would work fine for a short time it went unstepped on. Of course, the unsturdy needle needed constant realigning and especially often must I re-crease the paper rotary blades so necessary for a balanced flight. Nevertheless, I loved my fragile weapon as I made it sail to the mark with throws of erratic southpaw speed. Without letup, save for the moments of adjustment, I ran back and forth between disgruntled onlookers, loosing the dart at everything stickable. All about the roomful of sitting men were these targets; a particular spot of scum in the wall plaster above their heads, a crack in the wooden floor, an empty chair, a window sill.

To the rear of the lobby, just to one side of the dark stairway opening, the dim golden color was still to be seen on grillwork of a cashier's cage. It was furnished with typical high-legged stool and black safe, reflecting from its dull finish the light of a tiny bulb aimed upon the dial combinations. In this small office domain sat the man who every night collected the pennies of incoming lodgers' rent. As they paid, each tenant scrawled his name and hometown on an ancient ledger book. When I had exhausted myself with darts and cards, it was my quiet pleasure to take this on my lap to scan its hundreds of ink-blotched pages. It became my custom to curiously examine in regular private ritual all legible signatures and pronounce them to myself, to guess by their sound which names were aliases. Beginning with dates before my birth, the book names of long-departed guests filled my mind with fascination. I became engrossed reading the long columns listing towns and states, comparing them geographically on the huge map, and particularly did I wonder at the different surnames and their origin: *all unknown to me each man's destiny and in daydreams imagining the variety of possible fates I first consciously amazed at life.*

Leaving L.A. by Train at Night, High . . .

Dark streets, hundreds of silent autos parked almost too close to the rail, mammoth buildings, many still lit, now looming in blacker outline, isolated houses, houses of dirt, of noise, cheery ones, then dark, dark ones; one wonders, the occupation of its owners. Billboards, billboards, drink this, eat that, use all manner of things, EVERYONE, the best, the cheapest, the purest and most satisfying of all their available counterparts. Red lights flicker on every horizon, airplanes beware; cars flash by, more lights. Workers repair the gas main. Signs, signs, lights, lights, streets, streets; it is the dark between that attracts one— what's happening there at this moment? What hidden thing,

glorious perhaps, is being passed and lost forever. The conges-
tion slackens, a cone of widening sparcity stretches before the
train, now one has left the center and its core is burst past as
the interlocking plants terminate grip and entrust us to the au-
tomatic block system's meticulous care. The maze of tracks
have unwreathed from cross-over webs of railroad intellectual-
ity to become simple main line dignity; these ribbons of accu-
rate gauge so ceaselessly toiled over, respected, feared. Oh, un-
ending high rail of intrigue!

Adventures in Auto-eroticism

I stole my first automobile at 14 in 1940; by '47 when swear-
ing off such soul-thrilling pleasures to celebrate advent into
manhood, I had had illegally in my possession about 500
cars—whether just for the moment and to be taken back to its
owner before he returned (I.E. on Parking lots) or whether
taken for the purpose of so altering its appearance as to keep it
for several weeks but mostly only for joyriding.

The virgin emotion one builds when first stealing an auto—
especially when one can hardly make it function properly, so
takes full minutes to get away—is naturally strenuous on the
nervous system, and I found it most exciting. I was initiated
into this particularly exhilerating pastime (tho undeniably ut-
terly stupid) by a chance meeting with the local bad-boy, whom
I had known at school. We came upon a '38 Olds sedan which
was parked before the well-light entrance of an apartment
house. It so happens this model Olds is a bastardized type—
Olds being GM's "experimental" car—and since the ignition,
lights, radio etc, are unconventionally set off the dashboard by
bull horn-like dials; and because this unfamiliarity heightened
his panicky condition, John's efforts to start the car seemed
really ludicrous from my tree-trunk vantage point. He turned
on the radio, the lights, everything but the key I guess, anyhow,
when he finally became so flustered as to honk the horn, he
bolted away, failing to even close the door. So it was with a
genuine fear, so well-based as to make me think I was pretty
brave indeed, that we sneaked back for another try. John, altho

belittling his own fright, kept assuring me how easy it was, and this (besides the many minutes of quietude that passed after we had resumed our observation point behind a big tree) finally bolstered my courage enough to run over and drive away in the car.

Neal Talking Telling Story Fall '63

Following Fall 1963 story was taken down handwrit at kitchen table 1403 Gough Street San Francisco by Allen Ginsberg while Neal Cassady was cleaning a shoebox full of grass and describing the caracters of archetypal auto race heroes he'd imagined as for a story in True Magazine—I think the two Neals imagined would have met in a race had the story been completed.

—Allen Ginsberg

Now, let's get this down in black & white. I still wanta do the race driver. Wouldn't he be symbolic of this century & the other?

It's such a great story it deserves 2 pages. I once wrote a story about a guy in Indianapolis—the whole thing is what he had time to flashback—He had a *lot* of time to realize by flashback. Most accidents happen so quickly that a guy hasn't got time to say this is it. He also set the record in his death.

Well we'd had this mythological super race driver who was not only a national hero like Moss, but in England of course—you see he represented the Amaarican Frustration, he had an unhappy love affair with Marilyn Monroe or someone. In one-man duels in matching cars he'd bested the best in the world. Two-man duels I guess it would be. Y'could hardly have a one-man duel—Essentially I want him balanced . . . a balanced character I don't want him a freakish one . . . you have have him be a father—The point is he had not only peripheral vision—extremely wide vision—but also this faculty for thinking—perceiving actually—twice as fast as anybody else—He could see motion pix that were going 1/50th of a second & he could see them as stills—On top of that, what made him a world-beater was his fanaticism . . . he was a true fanatic—

Under no circumstances would he allow *anyone* to pass him
. . . he'd broadside in front of them, almost—Often the races
could hardly be started because he couldn't bear to let the other
pole setter draw abreast of him to start even—it was just insuf-
ferable. (What I want to give here are some examples of his
ability to justify this . . . impossible.)

Like he'd wear elbow pads in the races around houses, in
town, racing around buildings—so he could pivot, so he could
stick out his elbow at crucial spots so he could ricochet around
walls—Monte Carlo & all.

In fact that was his racing style—arms akimbo—head for-
ward—body crouched—teeth grimaced in fact everything *op-
posite* of good style, of great driving style—See, the real way
to drive is back & arms as straight as you possibly can get
them—comfortable straight see, comfortably, almost reclin-
ing—the way yr body's relaxed & you can see—The point is
he's so anxious that he can't even stand to sit back & drive,
he'd sit on the hood if it would have helped, if it would have
gotten him there any faster.

Well see I could ah—no no—dammit—He had no concern
for the machine—ah—even when he knew it was about to blow
up, break down—he simply couldn't ease off, & despite this he
won many races with sick cars that somehow held together see,
a correct driver would have eased off & tried to finish but
there's nothing within *him* capable of rational race driving be-
havior.

See there are stages in driving—first year or two a guy's got
to prove himself & be a tiger, get in over his head so many
times that if he's not dead, learns what he can & can't do—
there's no other way.

The second stage has to do with—ah—ah—I don't wanta use
"old pro" or "experience," has to do with where on this scale
of oh—I don't have to *name* it—where on this scale he's con-
tent to settle—Particular curves, circuits, cars even . . . give him,
give raise to fears that he's accumulated—imperceptibly he'll
slacken at this or that point—Then he'll try to make up for it
other ways.

As for a third stage—for the few who reach it—of real old

pro experience, know-how, where the fears have been controlled—mitigated as to be imperceptible . . . practically imperceptible . . . ah—where actually it's almost the same as the Novice—not knowing—free of the form really—yet thru the experience you see brightened up, perfected—As for this stage you may as well forget about it, there are so few to begin with—This kid disproved all that from the beginning.

He drove so continually over his head that even on the straightaway his car never seemed controlled—not just the mechanics blanching—white faced as they passed the signals, the crowd literally shuddering—The officials ever ready with the red & black flags—(You black flag a guy if you see he's too dangerous, or mechanically unsafe—The red flag is Stop)—But the car owner . . . well you know nerves tortured, often vomiting—vowing never to watch again—None had any effect on our Hero—Uncontrollable as he was—When behind the wheel of course.

What shall we do outside? I want to have a poignancy, a sadness—with a diametrical thing in the sex world—sort of like Judge Roy Bean & Lilly Langtry from afar, Eulogized Lionized—They even changed the front cover of Wheaties—Stuck on something that he can't take, like a lesbian—hooked on something—continual torment—so that his only release was winning—take it out on tearing up these machines—tearing up racing.

In the beginning, the car-owners felt he should practice like everyone else. But it soon became apparent that once begun they could hardly stop him from the trial spins—risk their lives in fact trying to wave him down—& he would, if not stopped quickly, usually end up in the wall, infield, spectator bleachers, anywhere but the pits—(I wanted to say pits)—but he could spin in the pits, he often spun there as well—dash—all this purely & simply because he would just go faster & faster—couldn't help himself, I think that's pretty clear by now we oughta get into something.

Flashbacking type—Chronologically, we'd just have a lotta dry races. or we cd even talk about, again, & emphasize, that he was never an in-&-outer, never had an off day, never had anything but the extreme of speed. Indeed he never drove without a broken torn ripped (Rip Torn) bone muscle tendon hip head shoulder rib foot hand—He himself was hurt like this on account of his having no sense of relativity. He was indestructible.

You see all this time I'm telling this I'm wanting to—get the Le Mans Story on the road.

Well the Le Mans character is different. About opposite in fact—a mediocre driver overshadowed by better, by 3 better racing driving brothers, even his own father had been captain of the Alfa Romeo team back in the 20's—A position he certainly never even approached—to be Captain Of The Team you see. Yet like those persevering dull students who become college professors, he uh—singlemindedly overcame his inaptness—his initial ineptness—became almost good. Run of the mill. One of the pack.

His initiation was in the garage practice circuit, country byways, & other scenes that his family used to increase their racing ability. His older brother was killed, as I remember, his father retired & I believe the other brothers eventually did too. But he persisted so that by now nearly middle aged & more or less suddenly without any outlet in the racing scene he found himself both frustrated and at a turning point.

But he by himself continued to build his own race car, put in all his own practice & all in all was a one man team. . . .

ALLEN GINSBERG

||||||||||||||||||||||||||||||||||||||||||||||||||||||||||||||||||||||||||||||||||||||||||||||||||||||||||||||||||||||

ALLEN GINSBERG was born in 1926, in Newark, New Jersey. In 1943, he enrolled at Columbia College, where he met Kerouac, Burroughs, Huncke, and others. Lying in bed one day in 1948, Ginsberg had an auditory vision of the poet William Blake, which initiated him into a visionary poetic lineage. In 1954, Ginsberg moved to San Francisco. Prompted by Kenneth Rexroth, he broke into the long breathline form that resulted in *Howl*. *Howl* became the object of San Francisco obscenity charges, which were eventually dismissed. But the poem made Ginsberg the notorious and charismatic leader of a newly emerging counterculture, featured in news magazines and identified with activists and outlaws like Timothy Leary, the Hell's Angels, Bob Dylan, and Abbie Hoffman. A turn toward Eastern wisdom prompted a trip to India in 1962–63, during which he visited religious teachers and meditated in charnel grounds. Returning to the U.S., he met Chögyam Trungpa Rinpoche, who in 1974 invited him to found, with Anne Waldman and Diana di Prima, the Jack Kerouac School of Disembodied Poetics at Naropa University. Throughout his life, Ginsberg was one of the preeminent teachers of poetry, traveling throughout Europe, Asia and North America, spreading the "gospel noble truth" and turning students toward Buddhism. On the political front, he was continually active, serving as a sort of unacknowledged ambassador from the United States—meeting with heads of state, fighting censorship, and working on behalf of political prisoners. He served as Distinguished Professor of English at Brooklyn College. His archives reside at Stanford University. Allen Ginsberg died on April 5, 1997, in his own loft in New York City. Tibetan Buddhist teacher Gelek Rinpoche and monks practiced and chanted for many hours with the body. A funeral was held at the Shambhala Center and included the Jewish Kaddish. Books published posthumously include *Death & Fame: Last Poems 1993–1997*, *Delibrate Prose: Selected Essays 1952–1995*, and *Spontaneous Mind: Selected Interviews 1958–1996*. In 2006, Jason Shinder published *The Poem That Changed America: "Howl" Fifty Years Later*, to commemorate Ginsberg's most celebrated work. Anniversary readings and celebrations were held all across the country.

The Blue Angel

Marlene Dietrich is singing a lament
for mechanical love.
She leans against a mortarboard tree
on a plateau by the seashore.

She's a life-sized toy,
the doll of eternity;
her hair is shaped like an abstract hat
made out of white steel.

Her face is powdered, whitewashed and
immobile like a robot.
Jutting out of her temple, by an eye,
is a little white key.

She gazes through dull blue pupils
set in the whites of her eyes.
She closes them, and the key
turns by itself.

She opens her eyes, and they're blank
like a statue's in a museum.
Her machine begins to move, the key turns
again, her eyes change, she sings

—you'd think I would have thought a plan
to end the inner grind,
but not till I have found a man
to occupy my mind.

                    Dream, Paterson, mid-1950

The Green Automobile

If I had a Green Automobile
            I'd go find my old companion
            in his house on the Western ocean.
                        Ha! Ha! Ha! Ha! Ha!

I'd honk my horn at his manly gate,
            inside his wife and three
            children sprawl naked
                        on the living room floor.

He'd come running out
            to my car full of heroic beer
            and jump screaming at the wheel
                        for he is the greater driver.

We'd pilgrimage to the highest mount
            of our earlier Rocky Mountain visions
            laughing in each other's arms,
                        delight surpassing the highest Rockies,

and after old agony, drunk with new years,
            bounding toward the snowy horizon
            blasting the dashboard with original bop
                        hot rod on the mountain

we'd batter up the cloudy highway
      where angels of anxiety
      careen through the trees
           and scream out of the engine.

We'd burn all night on the jackpine peak
      seen from Denver in the summer dark,
      forestlike unnatural radiance
           illuminating the mountaintop:

childhood youthtime age & eternity
      would open like sweet trees
      in the nights of another spring
           and dumbfound us with love,

for we can see together
      the beauty of souls
      hidden like diamonds
           in the clock of the world,

like Chinese magicians can
      confound the immortals
      with our intellectuality
           hidden in the mist,

in the Green Automobile
      which I have invented
      imagined and visioned
           on the roads of the world

more real than the engine
      on a track in the desert
      purer than Greyhound and
           swifter than physical jetplane.

Denver! Denver! we'll return
      roaring across the City & County Building lawn
      which catches the pure emerald flame
           streaming in the wake of our auto.

This time we'll buy up the city!
> I cashed a great check in my skull bank
> to found a miraculous college of the body
>> up on the bus terminal roof.

But first we'll drive the stations of downtown,
> poolhall flophouse jazzjoint jail
> whorehouse down Folsom
>> to the darkest alleys of Larimer

paying respects to Denver's father
> lost on the railroad tracks,
> stupor of wine and silence
>> hallowing the slum of his decades,

salute him and his saintly suitcase
> of dark muscatel, drink
> and smash the sweet bottles
>> on Diesels in allegiance.

Then we go driving drunk on boulevards
> where armies march and still parade
> staggering under the invisible
>> banner of Reality—

hurtling through the street
> in the auto of our fate
> we share an archangelic cigarette
>> and tell each other's fortunes:

fames of supernatural illumination,
> bleak rainy gaps of time,
> great art learned in desolation
>> and we beat apart after six decades . . .

and on an asphalt crossroad,
> deal with each other in princely
> gentleness once more, recalling
>> famous dead talks of other cities.

The windshield's full of tears,
        rain wets our naked breasts,
        we kneel together in the shade
                amid the traffic of night in paradise

and now renew the solitary vow
        we made each other take
        in Texas, once:
                I can't inscribe here. . . .

         •   •   •   •   •   •
         •   •   •   •   •   •

How many Saturday nights will be
        made drunken by this legend?
        How will young Denver come to mourn
                her forgotten sexual angel?

How many boys will strike the black piano
        in imitation of the excess of a native saint?
        Or girls fall wanton under his spectre in the high
                schools of melancholy night?

While all the time in Eternity
        in the wan light of his poem's radio
        we'll sit behind forgotten shades
                hearkening the lost jazz of all Saturdays.

Neal, we'll be real heroes now
        in a war between our cocks and time:
        let's be the angels of the world's desire
                and take the world to bed with us before we
                        die.

Sleeping alone, or with companion,
        girl or fairy sheep or dream,
        I'll fail of lacklove, you, satiety:
                all men fall, our fathers fell before,

but resurrecting that lost flesh
        is but a moment's work of mind:
        an ageless monument to love
                in the imagination:

memorial built out of our own bodies
        consumed by the invisible poem—
        We'll shudder in Denver and endure
                though blood and wrinkles blind our eyes.

So this Green Automobile:
        I give you in flight
        a present, a present
                from my imagination.

We will go riding
        over the Rockies,
        we'll go on riding
                all night long until dawn,

then back to your railroad, the SP
        your house and your children
        and broken leg destiny
                you'll ride down the plains

in the morning: and back
        to my visions, my office
        and eastern apartment
                I'll return to New York.

New York, May 22–25, 1953

Malest Cornifici Tuo Catullo

I'm happy, Kerouac, your madman Allen's
finally made it: discovered a new young cat,
and my imagination of an eternal boy
walks on the streets of San Francisco,
handsome, and meets me in cafeterias
and loves me. Ah don't think I'm sickening.
You're angry at me. For all of my lovers?
It's hard to eat shit, without having visions;
when they have eyes for me it's like Heaven.

San Francisco, 1955

from **Howl**

II

What sphinx of cement and aluminum bashed open their skulls
and ate up their brains and imagination?
Moloch! Solitude! Filth! Ugliness! Ashcans and unobtainable
dollars! Children screaming under the stairways! Boys
sobbing in armies! Old men weeping in the parks!
Moloch! Moloch! Nightmare of Moloch! Moloch the loveless!
Mental Moloch! Moloch the heavy judger of men!
Moloch the incomprehensible prison! Moloch the crossbone
soulless jailhouse and Congress of sorrows! Moloch whose
buildings are judgment! Moloch the vast stone of war!
Moloch the stunned governments!
Moloch whose mind is pure machinery! Moloch whose blood
is running money! Moloch whose fingers are ten armies!
Moloch whose breast is a cannibal dynamo! Moloch
whose ear is a smoking tomb!
Moloch whose eyes are a thousand blind windows! Moloch
whose skyscrapers stand in the long streets like endless
Jehovahs! Moloch whose factories dream and croak in the
fog! Moloch whose smokestacks and antennae crown the
cities!
Moloch whose love is endless oil and stone! Moloch whose
soul is electricity and banks! Moloch whose poverty is the
specter of genius! Moloch whose fate is a cloud of sexless
hydrogen! Moloch whose name is the Mind!
Moloch in whom I sit lonely! Moloch in whom I dream Angels!
Crazy in Moloch! Cocksucker in Moloch! Lacklove and
manless in Moloch!
Moloch who entered my soul early! Moloch in whom I am a
consciousness without a body! Moloch who frightened me
out of my natural ecstasy! Moloch whom I abandon!
Wake up in Moloch! Light streaming out of the sky!
Moloch! Moloch! Robot apartments! invisible suburbs! skele-
ton treasuries! blind capitals! demonic industries! spectral

nations! invincible mad-houses! granite cocks! monstrous bombs!

They broke their backs lifting Moloch to Heaven! Pavements, trees, radios, tons! lifting the city to Heaven which exists and is everywhere about us!

Visions! omens! hallucinations! miracles! ecstasies! gone down the American river!

Dreams! adorations! illuminations! religions! the whole boat-load of sensitive bullshit!

Breakthroughs! over the river! flips and crucifixions! gone down the flood! Highs! Epiphanies! Despairs! Ten years' animal screams and suicides! Minds! New loves! Mad generation! down on the rocks of Time!

Real holy laughter in the river! They saw it all! the wild eyes! the holy yells! They bade farewell! They jumped off the roof! to solitude! waving! carrying flowers! Down to the river! into the street!

from **Kaddish**

IV

O mother
what have I left out
O mother
what have I forgotten
O mother
farewell
with a long black shoe
farewell
with Communist Party and a broken stocking
farewell
with six dark hairs on the wen of your breast
farewell
with your old dress and a long black beard around the vagina
farewell

with your sagging belly
with your fear of Hitler
with your mouth of bad short stories
with your fingers of rotten mandolins
with your arms of fat Paterson porches
with your belly of strikes and smokestacks
with your chin of Trotsky and the Spanish War
with your voice singing for the decaying overbroken workers
with your nose of bad lay with your nose of the smell of the
    pickles of Newark
with your eyes
with your eyes of Russia
with your eyes of no money
with your eyes of false China
with your eyes of Aunt Elanor
with your eyes of starving India
with your eyes pissing in the park
with your eyes of America taking a fall
with your eyes of your failure at the piano
with your eyes of your relatives in California
with your eyes of Ma Rainey dying in an aumbulance
with your eyes of Czechoslovakia attacked by robots
with your eyes going to painting class at night in the Bronx
with your eyes of the killer Grandma you see on the horizon from
    the Fire-Escape
with your eyes running naked out of the apartment screaming into
    the hall
with your eyes being led away by policemen to an ambulance
with your eyes strapped down on the operating table
with your eyes with the pancreas removed
with your eyes of appendix operation
with your eyes of abortion
with your eyes of ovaries removed
with your eyes of shock
with your eyes of lobotomy
with your eyes of divorce
with your eyes of stroke
with your eyes alone

with your eyes
with your eyes
with your Death full of Flowers

V

Caw caw caw crows shriek in the white sun over grave stones
   in Long Island
Lord Lord Lord Naomi underneath this grass my halflife and
   my own as hers
caw caw my eye be buried in the same Ground where I stand
   in Angel
Lord Lord great Eye that stares on All and moves in a black
   cloud
caw caw strange cry of Beings flung up into sky over the waving
   trees
Lord Lord O Grinder of giant Beyonds my voice in a boundless
   field in Sheol
Caw caw the call of Time rent out of foot and wing an instant
   in the universe
Lord Lord an echo in the sky the wind through ragged leaves
   the roar of memory
caw caw all years my birth a dream caw caw New York the bus
   the broken shoe the vast highschool caw caw all Visions
   of the Lord
Lord Lord Lord caw caw caw Lord Lord Lord caw caw caw
   Lord

                    Paris, December 1957–New York, 1959

At Apollinaire's Grave

"... *voici le temps*
Où l'on connaîtra l'avenir
Sans mourir de connaissance"

I

I visited Père Lachaise to look for the remains of Apollinaire
the day the U.S. President appeared in France for the grand
conference of heads of state
so let it be the airport at blue Orly a springtime clarity in the
air over Paris
Eisenhower winging in from his American graveyard
and over the froggy graves at Père Lachaise an illusory mist as
thick as marijuana smoke
Peter Orlovsky and I walked softly thru Père Lachaise we both
knew we would die
and so held temporary hands tenderly in a citylike miniature
eternity
roads and streetsigns rocks and hills and names on everybody's
house
looking for the lost address of a notable Frenchman of the Void
to pay our tender crime of homage to his helpless menhir
and lay my temporary American Howl on top of his silent Cal-
ligramme
for him to read between the lines with Xray eyes of Poet
as he by miracle had read his own death lyric in the Seine
I hope some wild kidmonk lays his pamphlet on my grave for
God to read me on cold winter nights in heaven
already our hands have vanished from that place my hand
writes now in a room in Paris Git-le-Coeur
Ah William what grit in the brain you had what's death
I walked all over the cemetery and still couldn't find your grave
what did you mean by that fantastic cranial bandage in your
poems
O solemn stinking deathshead what've you got to say nothing
and that's barely an answer

You can't drive autos into a sixfoot grave tho the universe is
    mausoleum big enough for anything
the universe is a graveyard and I walk around alone in here
knowing that Apollinaire was on the same street 50 years ago
his madness is only around the corner and Genet is with us
    stealing books
the West is at war again and whose lucid suicide will set it all
    right
Guillaume Guillaume how I envy your fame your accomplish-
    ment for American letters
your Zone with its long crazy line of bullshit about death
come out of the grave and talk thru the door of my mind
issue new series of images oceanic haikus blue taxicabs in Mos-
    cow negro statues of Buddha
pray for me on the phonograph record of your former existence
with a long sad voice and strophes of deep sweet music sad and
    scratchy as World War I
I've eaten the blue carrots you sent out of the grave and Van
    Gogh's ear and maniac peyote of Artaud
and will walk down the streets of New York in the black cloak
    of French poetry
improvising our conversation in Paris at Père Lachaise
and the future poem that takes its inspiration from the light
    bleeding into your grave

II

Here in Paris I am your guest O friendly shade
the absent hand of Max Jacob
Picasso in youth bearing me a tube of Mediterranean
myself attending Rousseau's old red banquet I ate his violin
great party at the Bateau Lavoir not mentioned in the text-
    books of Algeria
Tzara in the Bois de Boulogne explaining the alchemy of the
    machineguns of the cuckoos
he weeps translating me into Swedish
well dressed in a violet tie and black pants
a sweet purple beard which emerged from his face like the moss
    hanging from the walls of Anarchism

he spoke endlessly of his quarrels with André Breton
whom he had helped one day trim his golden mustache
old Blaise Cendrars received me into his study and spoke wea-
    rily of the enormous length of Siberia
Jacques Vaché invited me to inspect his terrible collection of
    pistols
poor Cocteau saddened by the once marvelous Radiguet at his
    last thought I fainted
Rigaut with a letter of introduction to Death
and Gide praised the telephone and other remarkable inven-
    tions
we agreed in principle though he gossiped of lavender under-
    wear
but for all that he drank deeply of the grass of Whitman and
    was intrigued by all lovers named Colorado
princes of America arriving with their armfuls of shrapnel and
    baseball
Oh Guillaume the world so easy to fight seemed so easy
did you know the great political classicists would invade Mont-
    parnasse
with not one sprig of prophetic laurel to green their foreheads
not one pulse of green in their pillows no leaf left from their
    wars—Mayakovsky arrived and revolted.

III

Came back sat on a tomb and stared at your rough menhir
a piece of thin granite like an unfinished phallus
a cross fading into the rock 2 poems on the stone one Coeur
    Renversée
other Habituez-vous comme moi A ces prodiges que j'annonce
    Guillaume Apollinaire de Kostrowitsky
someone placed a jam bottle filled with daisies and a 5&10¢
    surrealist typist ceramic rose
happy little tomb with flowers and overturned heart
under a fine mossy tree beneath which I sat snaky trunk
summer boughs and leaves umbrella over the menhir and no-
    body there

Et quelle voix sinistre ulule Guillaume qu'es-tu devenu

his nextdoor neighbor is a tree

there underneath the crossed bones heaped and yellow cranium
     perhaps

and the printed poems Alcools in my pocket his voice in the
     museum

Now middleage footsteps walk the gravel

a man stares at the name and moves toward the crematory
     building

same sky rolls over thru clouds as Mediterranean days on the
     Riviera during war

drinking Apollo in love eating occasional opium he'd taken the
     light

One must have felt the shock in St. Germain when he went out
     Jacob & Picasso coughing in the dark

a bandage unrolled and the skull left still on a bed outstretched
     pudgy fingers the mystery and ego gone

a bell tolls in the steeple down the street birds warble in the
     chestnut trees

Famille Bremont sleeps nearby Christ hangs big chested and
     sexy in their tomb

my cigarette smokes in my lap and fills the page with smoke
     and flames

an ant runs over my corduroy sleeve the tree I lean on grows
     slowly

bushes and branches upstarting through the tombs one silky
     spiderweb gleaming on granite

I am buried here and sit by my grave beneath a tree

Paris, Winter–Spring 1958

Describe: The Rain on Dasaswamedh Ghat

Kali Ma tottering up steps to shelter tin roof, feeling her way
     to curb, around bicycle & leper seated on her way—to piss
     on a broom

left by the Stone Cutters who last night were shaking the street
    with Boom! of Stone blocks unloaded from truck
Forcing the blindman in his gray rags to retreat from his spot
    in the middle of the road where he sleeps & shakes under
    his blanket
Jai Ram all night telling his beads or sex on a burlap carpet
Past which cows donkeys dogs camels elephants marriage pro-
    cessions drummers tourists lepers and bathing devotees
step to the whine of serpent-pipes & roar of car motors around
    his black ears—
Today on a balcony in shorts leaning on iron rail I watched the
    leper who sat hidden behind a bicycle
emerge dragging his buttocks on the gray rainy ground by the
    glove-bandaged stumps of hands,
one foot chopped off below knee, round stump-knob wrapped
    with black rubber
pushing a tin can shiny size of his head with left hand (from
    which only a thumb emerged from leprous swathings)
beside him, lifting it with both ragbound palms down the curb
    into the puddled road,
balancing his body down next to the can & crawling forward
    on his behind
trailing a heavy rag for seat, and leaving a path thru the street
    wavering
like the Snail's slime track—imprint of his crawl on the muddy
    asphalt market entrance—stopping
to drag his can along stubbornly konking on the paved surface
    near the water pump—
Where a turban'd workman stared at him moving along—his
    back humped with rags—
and inquired why didn't he put his can to wash in the pump
    altarplace—and why go that way when free rice
Came from the alley back there by the river—As the leper
    looked up & rested, conversing curiously, can by his side
    approaching a puddle.
Kali had pissed standing up & then felt her way back to the
    Shop Steps on thin brown legs

her hands in the air—feeling with feet for her rag pile on the
stone steps' wetness—
as a cow busied its mouth chewing her rags left wet on the
ground for five minutes digesting
Till the comb-&-hair-oil-booth keeper woke & chased her
away with a stick
Because a dog barked at a madman with dirty wild black hair
who rag round his midriff & water pot in hand
Stopped in midstreet turned round & gazed up at the balconies,
windows, shops and city stagery filled with glum activity
Shrugged & said *Jai Shankar!* to the imaginary audience of
Me's,
While a white robed Baul Singer carrying his one stringed dried
pumpkin Guitar
Sat down near the cigarette stand and surveyed his new scene,
just arrived in the Holy City of Benares.

Benares, February 1963

Death News

*Visit to W.C.W. circa 1957, poets Kerouac Corso Orlovsky on
sofa in living room inquired wise words, stricken Williams
pointed thru window curtained on Main Street: "There's a lot of
bastards out there!"*

Walking at night on asphalt campus
road by the German Instructor with Glasses
W. C. Williams is dead he said in accent
under the trees in Benares; I stopped and asked
Williams is Dead? Enthusiastic and wide-eyed
under the Big Dipper. Stood on the Porch
of the International House Annex bungalow
insects buzzing round the electric light
reading the Medical obituary in *Time*.
"out among the sparrows behind the shutters"
Williams is in the Big Dipper. He isn't dead

as the many pages of words arranged thrill
with his intonations the mouths of meek kids
becoming subtle even in Bengal. Thus
there's a life moving out of his pages; Blake
also "alive" thru his experienced machines.
Were his last words anything Black out there
in the carpeted bedroom of the gabled wood house
in Rutherford? Wonder what he said,
or was there anything left in realms of speech
after the stroke & brain-thrill doom entered
his thoughts? If I pray to his soul in Bardo Thodol
he may hear the unexpected vibration of foreign mercy.
Quietly unknown for three weeks; now I saw Passaic
and Ganges one, consenting his devotion,
because he walked on the steely bank & prayed
to a Goddess in the river, that he only invented,
another Ganga-Ma. Riding on the old
rusty Holland submarine on the ground floor
Paterson Museum instead of a celestial crocodile.
Mourn O Ye Angels of the Left Wing! that the poet
of the streets is a skeleton under the pavement now
and there's no other old soul so kind and meek
and feminine jawed and him-eyed can see you
What you wanted to be among the bastards out there.

Benares, March 20, 1963

Kral Majales

And the Communists have nothing to offer but fat cheeks and
     eyeglasses and lying policemen
and the Capitalists proffer Napalm and money in green suit-
     cases to the Naked,
and the Communists create heavy industry but the heart is also
     heavy

and the beautiful engineers are all dead, the secret technicians
   conspire for their own glamour
in the Future, in the Future, but now drink vodka and lament
   the Security Forces,
and the Capitalists drink gin and whiskey on airplanes but let
   Indian brown millions starve
and when Communist and Capitalist assholes tangle the Just
   man is arrested or robbed or had his head cut off,
but not like Kabir, and the cigarette cough of the Just man
   above the clouds
in the bright sunshine is a salute to the health of the blue sky.
For I was arrested thrice in Prague, once for singing drunk on
   Narodni street,
once knocked down on the midnight pavement by a mustached
   agent who screamed out BOUZERANT,
once for losing my notebooks of unusual sex politics dream
   opinions,
and I was sent from Havana by plane by detectives in green
   uniform,
and I was sent from Prague by plane by detectives in Czechoslo-
   vakian business suits,
Cardplayers out of Cézanne, the two strange dolls that entered
   Joseph K's room at morn
also entered mine, and ate at my table, and examined my scrib-
   bles,
and followed me night and morn from the houses of lovers to
   the cafés of Centrum—
And I am the King of May, which is the power of sexual youth,
and I am the King of May, which is industry in eloquence and
   action in amour,
and I am the King of May, which is long hair of Adam and the
   Beard of my own body
and I am the King of May, which is Kral Majales in the Czecho-
   slovakian tongue,
and I am the King of May, which is old Human poesy, and
   100,000 people chose my name,
and I am the King of May, and in a few minutes I will land at
   London Airport,

and I am the King of May, naturally, for I am of Slavic parent-
age and a Buddhist Jew

who worships the Sacred Heart of Christ the blue body of
Krishna the straight back of Ram

the beads of Chango the Nigerian singing Shiva Shiva in a man-
ner which I have invented,

and the King of May is a middleeuropean honor, mine in the
XX century

despite space ships and the Time Machine, because I heard the
voice of Blake in a vision,

and repeat that voice. And I am King of May that sleeps with
teenagers laughing.

And I am the King of May, that I may be expelled from my
Kingdom with Honor, as of old,

To show the difference between Caesar's Kingdom and the
Kingdom of the May of Man—

and I am the King of May, tho' paranoid, for the Kingdom of
May is too beautiful to last for more than a month—

and I am the King of May because I touched my finger to my
forehead saluting

a luminous heavy girl trembling hands who said "one moment
Mr. Ginsberg"

before a fat young Plainclothesman stepped between our bod-
ies—I was going to England—

and I am the King of May, returning to see Bunhill Fields and
walk on Hampstead Heath,

and I am the King of May, in a giant jetplane touching Albion's
airfield trembling in fear

as the plane roars to a landing on the gray concrete, shakes &
expels air,

and rolls slowly to a stop under the clouds with part of blue
heaven still visible.

And *tho'* I am the King of May, the Marxists have beat me
upon the street, kept me up all night in Police Station, fol-
lowed me thru Springtime Prague, detained me in secret
and deported me from our kingdom by airplane.

Thus I have written this poem on a jet seat in mid Heaven.

May 7, 1965

Wales Visitation

White fog lifting & falling on mountain-brow
    Trees moving in rivers of wind
                    The clouds arise
  as on a wave, gigantic eddy lifting mist
    above teeming ferns exquisitely swayed
                        along a green crag
    glimpsed thru mullioned glass in valley raine—

Bardic, O Self, Visitacione, tell naught
  but what seen by one man in a vale in Albion,
    of the folk, whose physical sciences end in Ecology,
          the wisdom of earthly relations,
    of mouths & eyes interknit ten centuries visible
          orchards of mind language manifest human,
  of the satanic thistle that raises its horned symmetry
  flowering above sister grass-daisies' pink tiny
          bloomlets angelic as lightbulbs—

Remember 160 miles from London's symmetrical thorned tower
    & network of TV pictures flashing bearded your Self
  the lambs on the tree-nooked hillside this day bleating
  heard in Blake's old ear, & the silent thought of Wordsworth
                  in eld Stillness
  clouds passing through skeleton arches of Tintern Abbey—
  Bard Nameless as the Vast, babble to Vastness!

All the Valley quivered, one extended motion, wind
          undulating on mossy hills
  a giant wash that sank white fog delicately down red runnels
          on the mountainside
  whose leaf-branch tendrils moved asway
          in granitic undertow down—
and lifted the floating Nebulous upward, and lifted the arms of
                  the trees
    and lifted the grasses an instant in balance

and lifted the lambs to hold still
and lifted the green of the hill, in one solemn wave

A solid mass of Heaven, mist-infused, ebbs thru the vale,
a wavelet of Immensity, lapping gigantic through Llanthony
Valley,
the length of all England, valley upon valley under Heaven's ocean
tonned with cloud-hang,
—Heaven balanced on a grassblade.
Roar of the mountain wind slow, sigh of the body,
One Being on the mountainside stirring gently
Exquisite scales trembling everywhere in balance,
one motion thru the cloudy sky-floor shifting on the million feet
of daisies,
one Majesty the motion that stirred wet grass quivering
to the farthest tendril of white fog poured down
through shivering flowers on the mountain's head—

No imperfection in the budded mountain,
Valleys breathe, heaven and earth move together,
daisies push inches of yellow air, vegetables tremble,
grass shimmers green
sheep speckle the mountainside, revolving their jaws with empty
eyes,
horses dance in the warm rain,
tree-lined canals network live farmland,
blueberries fringe stone walls on hawthorn'd hills,
pheasants croak on meadows haired with fern—

Out, out on the hillside, into the ocean sound, into delicate gusts
of wet air,

Fall on the ground, O great Wetness, O Mother, No harm on your
body!
Stare close, no imperfection in the grass,
each flower Buddha-eye, repeating the story,
myriad-formed—
Kneel before the foxglove raising green buds, mauve bells drooped

doubled down the stem trembling antennae,
  & look in the eyes of the branded lambs that stare
    breathing stockstill under dripping hawthorn—
I lay down mixing my beard with the wet hair of the
                        mountainside,
  smelling the brown vagina-moist ground, harmless,
    tasting the violet thistle-hair, sweetness—
One being so balanced, so vast, that its softest breath
  moves every floweret in the stillness on the valley floor,
  trembles lamb-hair hung gossamer rain-beaded in the grass,
lifts trees on their roots, birds in the great draught
    hiding their strength in the rain, bearing same weight,

Groan thru breast and neck, a great Oh! to earth heart
      Calling our Presence together
  The great secret is no secret
    Senses fit the winds,
      Visible is visible,
  rain-mist curtains wave through the bearded vale,
    gray atoms wet the wind's kabbala
Crosslegged on a rock in dusk rain,
  rubber booted in soft grass, mind moveless,
  breath trembles in white daisies by the roadside,
    Heaven breath and my own symmetric
  Airs wavering thru antlered green fern
drawn in my navel, same breath as breathes thru Capel-Y-Ffn,
    Sounds of Aleph and Aum
      through forests of gristle,
  my skull and Lord Hereford's Knob equal,
      All Albion one.

What did I notice? Particulars! The
  vision of the great One is myriad—
smoke curls upward from ashtray,
  house fire burned low,
The night, still wet & moody black heaven
    starless
    upward in motion with wet wind.

July 29, 1967 (LSD)–August 3, 1967 (London)

Pentagon Exorcism

"No taxation without representation"

Who represents my body in Pentagon? Who spends
my spirit's billions for war manufacture? Who
levies the majority to exult unwilling in Bomb
Roar? *"Brainwash!"* Mind-fear! Governor's language!
"Military-Industrial-Complex!" President's language!
Corporate voices jabber on electric networks building
body-pain, chemical ataxia, physical slavery
to diaphanoid Chinese Cosmic-eye Military Tyranny
movie hysteria—Pay my taxes? No *Westmoreland* wants
to be Devil, others die for his General Power
sustaining hurt millions in house security
tuning to images on TV's separate universe where
peasant manhoods burn in black & white forest
villages—represented less than myself by Magic
Intelligence influence matter-scientists' *Rockefeller*
bank telephone war investment Usury Agency
executives jetting from *McDonnell Douglas* to *General
      Dynamics*
over smog-shrouded metal-noised treeless cities
patrolled by radio fear with tear gas, businessman!
Go spend your bright billions for this suffering!
Pentagon wake from planet-sleep! Apokatastasis!
Spirit Spirit Dance Dance Spirit Spirit Dance!
Transform Pentagon skeleton to maiden-temple O Phantom
Guevara! Om Raksa Raksa Hūṃ Hūṃ Hūṃ Phat Svaha!
Anger Control your Self feared Chaos, suffocation
body-death in Capitols caved with stone radar sentinels!
Back! Back! Back! Central Mind-machine Pentagon reverse
consciousness! Hallucination manifest! A million Americas
gaze out of man-spirit's naked Pentacle! Magnanimous
reaction to signal Peking, isolate Space-beings!

                                        Milan, September 29, 1967

On Neal's Ashes

Delicate eyes that blinked blue Rockies all ash
nipples, Ribs I touched w/ my thumb are ash
mouth my tongue touched once or twice all ash
bony cheeks soft on my belly are cinder, ash
earlobes & eyelids, youthful cock tip, curly pubis
breast warmth, man palm, high school thigh,
baseball bicept arm, asshole anneal'd to silken skin
all ashes, all ashes again.

August 1968

The Charnel Ground

> *. . . rugged and raw situations, and having accepted them as part*
> *of your home ground, then some spark of sympathy of compas-*
> *sion could take place. You are not in a hurry to leave such a place*
> *immediately. You would like to face the facts, realities of that*
> *particular world. . . .*
>
> From a commentary on THE SADHANA OF MAHAMUDRA,
> CHÖGYAM TRUNGPA, RINPOCHE

Upstairs Jenny crashed her car & became a living corpse, Jake
    sold grass, the white-bearded potbelly leprechaun silent
    climbed their staircase
Ex-janitor John from Poland averted his eyes, cheeks flushed
    with vodka, wine who knew what
as he left his groundfloor flat, refusing to speak to the inhabi-
    tant of Apt. 24
who'd put his boyfriend in Bellevue, calling police, while the
    artistic Buddhist composer
on sixth floor lay spaced out feet swollen with water, dying
    slowly of AIDS over a year—
The Chinese teacher cleaned & cooked in Apt. 23 for the ho-
    mosexual poet who pined for his gymnast

thighs & buttocks—Downstairs th' old hippie flower girl fell
    drunk over the banister, smashed her jaw—

her son despite moderate fame cheated of rocknroll money,
    twenty thousand people in stadiums

cheering his tattooed skinhead murderous Hare Krishna vege-
    tarian drum lyrics—

Mary born in the building rested on her cane, heavy-legged
    with heart failure on the second landing, no more able

to vacation in Caracas & Dublin—The Russian landlady's hus-
    band from concentration camp disappeared again—
    nobody mentioned he'd died—

tenants took over her building for hot water, she couldn't add
    rent & pay taxes, wore a long coat hot days

alone & thin on the street carrying groceries to her crooked
    apartment silent—

One poet highschool teacher fell dead mysterious heart dys-
    rhythmia, konked over

in his mother's Brooklyn apartment, his first baby girl a year
    old, wife stoical a few days—

their growling noisy little dog had to go, the baby cried—

Meanwhile the upstairs apartment meth head shot cocaine &
    yowled up and down

East 12th Street, kicked out of Christine's Eatery till police cor-
    nered him, 'top a hot iron steamhole

near Stuyvesant Town Avenue A telephone booth calling his
    deaf mother—sirens speed the way to Bellevue—

past whispering grass crack salesman jittering in circles on East
    10th Street's

southwest corner where art yuppie come out of the overpriced
    Japanese Sushi Bar—& they poured salt into potato soup
    heart failure vats at KK's Polish restaurant

—Garbage piled up, nonbiodegradable plastic bags emptied by
    diabetic sidewalk homeless

looking for returnable bottles recycled dolls radios half-eaten
    hamburgers—thrown-away Danish—

On 13th Street the notary public sat in his dingy storefront,
    driver's lessons & tax returns prepared on old metal
    desks—

Sunnysides crisped in butter, fries & sugary donuts passed over
    the luncheonette counter next door—
The Hispanic lady yelled at the rude African-American behind
    the Post Office window
"I waited all week my welfare check you sent me notice I was
    here yesterday
I want to see the supervisor bitch dont insult me refusing to
    look in—"
Closed eyes of Puerto Rican wino lips cracked skin red
    stretched out
on the pavement, naphtha backdoor open for the Korean fam-
    ily dry cleaners at the 14th Street corner—
Con Ed workmen drilled all year to bust electric pipes 6 feet
    deep in brown dirt
so cars bottlenecked wait minutes to pass the M14 bus stopped
    mid-road, heavy dressed senior citizens step down in red
    rubble
with Reduced Fare Program cards got from grey city Aging De-
    partment offices downtown up the second flight by eleva-
    tors don't work—
News comes on the radio, they bomb Baghdad and the Garden
    of Eden again?
A million starve in Sudan, mountains of eats stacked on docks,
    local gangs & U.N.'s trembling bureaucrat officers sweat
    near the equator arguing over
wheat piles shoved by bulldozers—Swedish doctors ran out of
    medicine—The Pakistan taxi driver
says Salman Rushdie must die, insulting the Prophet in fic-
    tions—
"No that wasn't my opinion, just a character talking like in a
    poem no judgment"—
"Not till the sun rejects you do I," so give you a quarter by the
    Catholic church 14th St. you stand half drunk
waving a plastic glass, flush-faced, live with your mother a
    wounded look on your lips, eyes squinting,
receding lower jaw sometimes you dry out in Bellevue, most
    days cadging dollars for sweet wine
by the corner where Plump Blindman shifts from foot to foot

showing his white cane, rattling coins in a white paper cup
some weeks
where girding the subway entrance construction sawhorses
painted orange
guard steps underground—And across the street the NYCE
bank machine cubicle door sign reads
Not in Operation as taxis bump on potholes asphalt mounded
at the crossroad when red lights change green
& I'm on my way uptown to get a CAT scan liver biopsy, visit
the cardiologist,
account for high blood pressure, kidneystones, diabetes, misty
eyes & dysesthesia—
feeling lack in feet soles, inside ankles, small of back, phallus
head, anus—
Old age sickness death again come round in the wink of an
eye—
High school youth the inside skin of my thighs was silken
smooth tho nobody touched me there back then—
Across town the velvet poet takes Darvon N, Valium nightly,
sleeps all day kicking methadone
between brick walls sixth floor in a room cluttered with col-
lages & gold dot paper scraps covered
with words: "The whole point seems to be the idea of giving
away the giver."

August 19, 1992

After Lalon

I

It's true I got caught in
            the world
When I was young Blake
            tipped me off
Other teachers followed:
Better prepare for Death

Don't get entangled with
       possessions
That was when I was young,
     I was warned
Now I'm a Senior Citizen
and stuck with a million
       books
a million thoughts a million
        dollars a million
          loves
How'll I ever leave my body?
Allen Ginsberg says, I'm
     really up shits creek

II

I sat at the foot of a
       Lover
       and he told me everything
Fuck off, 23 skidoo,
      watch your ass,
      watch your step
exercise, meditate, think
     of your temper—
Now I'm an old man and
     I won't live another
20 years maybe not another
     20 weeks,
maybe the next second I'll
     be carried off to
       rebirth
   the worm farm, maybe it's
     already happened—
How should I know, says
    Allen Ginsberg
Maybe I've been dreaming
     all along—

III

It's 2 A.M. and I got to
          get up early
and taxi 20 miles to satisfy
          my ambition—
How'd I get into this fix,
this workaholic show-
          biz meditation market?
If I had a soul I sold it
          for pretty words
If I had a body I used
          it up spurting my essence
If I had a mind it got
          covered with Love—
If I had a spirit I forgot
          when I was breathing
If I had speech it was
          all a boast
If I had desire it went
          out my anus
If I had ambitions to
          be liberated
how'd I get into this
          wrinkled person?
With pretty words, Love essences,
          breathing boasts, anal
          longings, famous crimes?
What a mess I am, Allen Ginsberg.

IV

Sleepless I stay up &
          think about my Death
—certainly it's nearer
          than when I was ten
                    years old
and wondered how big the
          universe was—

If I dont get some rest I'll die faster
If I sleep I'll lose my
            chance for salvation—
asleep or awake, Allen
    Ginsberg's in bed
        in the middle of the night.

    V

4 A.M.

Then they came for me,
        I hid in the toilet stall
They broke down the toilet door
        It fell in on an innocent boy
Ach the wooden door fell
        in on an innocent kid!
I stood on the bowl & listened,
        I hid my shadow,
they shackled the other and
        dragged him away
in my place—How long can
        I get away with this?
Pretty soon they'll discover
        I'm not there
They'll come for me again, where
        can I hide my body?
Am I myself or some one else
        or nobody at all?
Then what's this heavy flesh this
        weak heart leaky kidney?
Who's been doing time
        for 65 years
in this corpse? Who else went
        into ecstasy besides me?
Now it's all over soon,
        what good was all that come?
Will it come true? Will
        it really come true?

VI

I had my chance and lost it,
many chances & didn't
    take them seriously enuf.
Oh yes I was impressed, almost
    went mad with fear
I'd lose the immortal chance,
    One lost it.
Allen Ginsberg warns you
    dont follow my path
    to extinction

March 31, 1992

PETER ORLOVSKY

||||||||||||||||||||||||||||||||||||||||||||||||||||||||||||||||||||||||||||||||||||||||||||||||||||||||||||||||||

PETER ORLOVSKY was born into a family of Russian immigrants on the Lower East Side of New York City in 1933. Drafted into the U.S. Army in 1953, he told his lieutenant that "an army is an army against love" and was deployed as a medic in a San Francisco hospital. He met the painter Robert La-Vigne, who introduced him in 1954 to Allen Ginsberg. Orlovsky appears in various Kerouac novels as the constant companion of Ginsberg, but he also gained a reputation as a poet in his own right. In 1961–62, Orlovsky traveled with Ginsberg to India, where they met up with Gary Snyder and Joanne Kyger. Kyger's *Japan and India Journals* details the trip with wry, irritable accounts of Orlovsky's experiments with opium. On returning to the U.S., Orlovsky took charge of the gardens at Ginsberg's communal farmhouse in Cherry Valley, New York. He was Allen Ginsberg's companion for four decades. Orlovsky is the author of the underground classic *Clean Asshole Poems and Smiling Vegetable Songs*, first published in 1978 by City Lights.

Dream May 18, 1958

In a dream I bought a
church something like $80 a mo.
It had a very haunted like
backyard—an old church
with sacradness inside—
I dont remember the rest
of the dream—lost—
in the wake of morning but
I bought a church in my
dream—I wish I bought the church
for a piece of my finger, or a heavenly
spirit in my tit.
Oh Russia, Russia, Russia, Russia.
Look what I saw—on 58 St. & 8 Ave—
in a red covered brick room house
whare yellow window shades
hand curles to their grey parted
curtains—behind a dusty window
Lenin sat in a masters chair
but looks with a masters face
beard and all eyes to the street—
And look, look, at his face—
Looking at the bubbley
Housing development across the
street—and in my old age
I will be sitting next to him—
for I too will sit & look with my eyes
on the street—

1958 NYC

Collaboration: Letter to Charlie Chaplin

Our Dear Friend Charles:

Love letter for you. We are one happey poet & one unhappey poet in India which makes 2 poets. We would like come visit you when we get thru India to tickle yr feet. Further more King in New York is great picture,—I figure it will take about 10 yrs before it looks funny in perspective. Every few years we dream in our sleep we meat you.

Why dont you go ahead & make another picture & fuck everybody. If you do could we be Extras. We be yr Brownies free of charge.

Let us tell you about Ganesha. He is elephant-faced god with funney fat belley human body. Everyone in India has picture of him in their house. To think of him brings happey wisdom success that he gives after he eats his sweet candey. He neither exists nor does not exist. Because of that he can conquer aney demon. He rides around on a mouse.& has 4 hands. We salute yr comedy in his name.

Do you realize how maney times we have seen yr pictures in Newark & cried in the dark at the roses. Do you realize how maney summers in Coney Island we sat in open air theatre & watched you disguised as a lamp-shade in scratchey down stairs eternity. You even made our dead mothers laugh. So, remember everything is alright. We await your next move & the world still depends on yr *next move*.

What else shall we say to you before we all die? If everything we feel could be said it would be very beautiful. Why didn't we ever do this before? I guess the world seems so vast, its hard to find the right moment to forget all about his shit & wave hello from the other side of the earth. But there is certainly millions & millions of people waveing hello to you silently all over the windows, streets & movies. Its only life waveing to its self.

Tell Michael to read our poems too if you ever get them. Again we say you got that personal tickle-tuch we like-love.

Shall we let it go at that?
NO, we still got lots more room on the page—we still to emp-
tey our hearts. Have you read Louis Ferdinand Celine?—hes
translated into english from French—Celine vomits Rasberries.
He wrote the most Chaplin-esque prose in Europe & he has a
bitter mean sad uggly eternal comical soul enough to make you
cry.

You could make a great picture about the Atom Bomb!

Synops:

a grubby old janitor with white hair who cant get the
air-raid drill instructions right & goes about his own
lost business in the basement in the midst of great inter-
national air-raid emergencies, sirens, kremlin riots, fly-
ing rockets, radios screaming, destruction of the earth.
He comes out the next day, he cralls out of the pile of
human empire state building bodies, & the rest of the
picture, a hole hour the janitor on the screen alone
makeing believe he is being sociable with nobody there,
haveing a beer at the bar with invisible boys, reading
last years newspapers, & ending looking blankly into
the camera with the eternal aged Chaplin-face looking
blankly, raptly into the eyes of the God of Solitude.

There is yr fitting final statement Sir Chaplin,
you will save the world if ya make it—but yr
final look must be so beautiful that it doesn't
matter if the world is saved or not.

Okay I guess we can end it now. Forgive us if you knew it all
before. Okay

Love & Flowers
Peter Orlovsky, Allen Ginsberg

1961 Bombay

Dick Tracy's Yellow Hat

Dick Tracy's yellow Hat & Blacksuit
   always running thro doors
    fingering leaves for telephone ears
     He's in a jam this time
      but at the bottom of the page
sooner or latter comes the brave end—
I have the Prooff to Prove Dick died
    say 25,000 times—
     & all the ex Killies are living in
      his mansion House as like in
       a wax museum.

The colors are bright & fine
    a white restaurant floor
    a pale orange street—pure flat
    never a bumpy road in this city—
all the tears even of yesteryears
   have that shape of raindrop or fingernail.

Of course Dick moves into the mardern world
   with the same nife cut pencle face
    what a sharp Kiss he must give his wife
& I never saw His finger prints
& his shoes look like their made of cement.
If I had my way I'd give Dickey
   a real crime to solve
 to face the crime of life
his badge melt like a candle—
   his gun to shoot watter at
    two wilted leaves on the
         house porch—
Many nights have Orphan Annie's
   dog kept me warm
    & her Golden Hair must be saved under
   the dark sky—

Nov. 1959 NYC

Snail Poem

Make my grave shape of heart so like a flower be free aired
    & handsome felt.
Grave root pillow, tung up from grave & wigle at
    blown up clowd.
Ear turnes close to underlayer of green felt moss & sound
    of rain dribble thru this layer
      down to the roots that will tickle my ear.
Hay grave, my toes need cutting so file away
    in sound curve or
Garbage grave, way above my head, blood will soon
    trickle into my ear—
      no choise but the grave, so cat & sheep are daisey
      turned.
Train will tug my grave, my breath hueing gentil vapor
    between weel & track.
So kitten string & ball, jumpe over this mound so
    gently & cutely
So my toe can curl & become a snail & go curiousely
    on its way.

1958 NYC

I Dream of St. Francis

St Francias came to me alive last night & tole me
some strange things—he said everybody is green & trees
are blue & hills are wheelbarrows turned inside out—that
a tree is a cane & the eyes grow old because of tears spilt
because of the Tokay Sun—& that life is much more
than a charming bracelet—he said life is more like a
Chinese tea pot—a big one for lots of mouths—then
he came closer to me & almost through his eyes into mine
& he said All the Saints of old were all right but they were

not good enough because they dident feel enough faith & love
in man to carry out his own individual life—

St Francias is at different times all over my body—
some times—like above me he is in my mind & heart—
other times he is in my stocking & I walk on him &
how it hurts us both—other times he is in my left pocket
& I take him out to show to little children
who laugh when I talk or look or make faces—one time
he was under my arm, & I scratched him away—he
got in my hair too & my finger nails are all broken
because he cralled in there—& when I was sleeping last night
he ran all over my hand with his chizel & hammer,
carving lines—

1957 NYC

DIANE DI PRIMA

||||||||||||||||||||||||||||||||||||||||||||||||||||||||||||||||||||||||||||||||||||||||||||||||||||||||||||||||||||||||||||||||||||||||

DIANE DI PRIMA was born in 1934 and grew up in New York City. She dropped out of Swarthmore College to become a writer and lived in Greenwich Village, holding down a variety of jobs, consorting with artists, musicians, and poets. LeRoi Jones and his wife, Hettie, published di Prima's first book in 1958. She was active in the Poets' Theatre in New York and in the late sixties moved to San Francisco, where she raised five children, living in various communal situations, writing, and pursuing studies in politics, music, mythology, and religion. She also spent time in Timothy Leary's Psychedelic community in Millbrook, New York. In 1962 she encountered the Zen teacher Suzuki Roshi: "I sat because he sat. To know his mind. It was the first time in my twenty-eight years that I had encountered another human being and felt trust. It blew my tough, sophisticated young-artist's mind." After Suzuki Roshi's death, di Prima was accepted as a student by Chögyam Trungpa Rinpoche in 1983. Di Prima was a founding faculty member of the Poetics Program at New College in San Francisco, along with Robert Duncan, and was one of the early founding "mothers" of the Jack Kerouac School of Disembodied Poetics. She received a Lifetime Achievement Award in poetry from the National Poetry Association in 1993. Di Prima's books include the incendiary *Revolutionary Letters,* several volumes of memoirs, such as *Recollections of My Life as a Woman*, and many collections of poetry, including *Loba*.

Song For Baby-O, Unborn

Sweetheart
when you break thru
you'll find
a poet here
not quite what one would choose.

I won't promise
you'll never go hungry
or that you won't be sad
on this gutted
breaking
globe

but I can show you
baby
enough to love
to break your heart
forever

Short Note on the Sparseness of the Language

wow man I said
when you tipped my chin and fed
on headlong spit my tongue's libation fluid

and wow I said when we hit the mattressrags
and wow was the dawn: we boiled the coffeegrounds
in an unkempt pot

wow man I said the day you put me down
(only the tone was different)
wow man oh wow   I took my comb
and my two books and cut and that was that

The Practice of Magical Evocation

The female is fertile, and discipline
(contra naturam) only
                confuses her
                        —Gary Snyder

i am a woman and my poems
are woman's: easy to say
this.   the female is ductile
and
        (stroke after stroke)
built for masochistic
calm.   The deadened nerve
is part of it:
awakened sex, dead retina
fish eyes;   at hair's root
minimal feeling

and pelvic architecture functional
assailed inside & out
(bring forth)   the cunt gets wide
and relatively sloppy
bring forth men children only
                        female
                        is
                        ductile

woman, a veil thru which the fingering Will
twice torn
twice torn
            inside & out
the flow
what rhythm add to stillness
what applause?

Montezuma

to give it away, give it up, before they take it from us.
not to go down fighting.

the hard part comes later
to see the women taken, the young men maimed
the city
no city is built twice
the long wall down at Athens, the olive trees
                    five hundred years of tillage
burning. "not these but men"
i.e., mourn
            not these

and yet no city is ever built again

For the Dead Lecturer

> *We must convince the living*
> *that the dead*
> *cannot sing.*
> >   —LeRoi Jones

THE DEAD CAN SING
and do
muttering thru beards of old vanilla
malteds, soft shoe
loving, the tin noises of cheap refrigerators.
I have heard you creaking
over the roof at night to steal my books
coming in thru the telephone wires
just when my head
was empty
When Milarepa & other Tantric wisdom
was clambering thru my skull

suddenly again your bumpy face
in my arms
the rags of your winter clothes
hitting my broken windows
(who else would have stolen the Poems of
John Skelton
of Tu Fu
or Thomas Traherne
Who else left that aroma
of pot & sweat, tobacco smoke & beer
((tears))
on my sofa?)
You dead sing now, thru your eyes,
they push up jade trees
they start
out of the skull of your daughter
asleep in my arms
and why not talk of these things
are we less faithful than bisons
or giraffes?

I'll tangle my crest with yours, like scorpions
and kill you for love
I'll kill you yet
so your song can fill my life.

Poem in Praise of My Husband (Taos)

I suppose it hasn't been easy living with me either,
with my piques, and ups and downs, my need for privacy
leo pride and weeping in bed when you're trying to sleep
and you, interrupting me in the middle of a thousand poems
did I call the insurance people? the time you stopped a poem
in the middle of our drive over the nebraska hills and
into colorado, odetta singing, the whole world singing in me
the triumph of our revolution in the air

me about to get that down, and you
you saying something about the carburetor
so that it all went away

but we cling to each other
as if each thought the other was the raft
and he adrift alone, as in this mud house
not big enough, the walls dusting down around us, a fine dust
     rain
counteracting the good, high air, and stuffing our nostrils
we hang our pictures of the several worlds:
new york college, and san francisco posters,
set out our japanese dishes, chinese knives
hammer small indian marriage cloths into the adobe
we stumble thru silence into each other's gut

blundering thru from one wrong place to the next
like kids who snuck out to play on a boat at night
and the boat slipped from its moorings, and they look at the
     stars
about which they know nothing, to find out
where they are going

Tassajara, 1969

Even Buddha is lost in this land
the immensity
takes us all with it, pulverizes, & takes us in

Bodhidharma came from the west.
Coyote met him

Fragmented Address to the FBI

O do you in fedora or trenchcoat bear record
Of the elusive days, date & hour
The subway journeys to forgotten loves
(Do you indeed have them forever, name & picture)
The old phone numbers, whose rhythm no longer
Sings for us, descriptions of long dead cars?
O gentle chroniclers of our rainbow lives
Blessed laborers in the labyrinthine archive
Recording angels who will consign to fire
Name & form, body & papers while we
Rise singing above the trees

Letter to Jeanne (at Tassajara)

dry heat of the Tassajara canyon
moist warmth of San Francisco summer
bright fog reflecting sunrise as you
step out of September zendo
heart of your warmth, my girl, as you step out
into your vajra pathway, glinting
like your eyes turned sideways at us
your high knowing 13-year-old
wench-smile, flicking your thin
ankles you trot toward Adventure
all sizes & shapes, O may it be various
for you as for me it was, sparkle
like dustmotes at dawn in the back
of grey stores, like the shooting stars
over the Hudson, wind in the Berkshire pines

O you have landscapes dramatic like mine
never was, uncounted caves

to mate in, my scorpio, bright love
like fire light up your beauty years
on these new, jagged hills

American Indian Art: Form and Tradition

Were we not fine
were we not all fine
in our buckskin coats, the quillwork, the
buttons & beads?
Were we not fine
were we not all fine

O they have hung our
empty shirts in their cold
marble halls. They have
labeled our baskets, lighted
our masks, disassembled our pipes
in glass cases.

       (We flashed in those colors
thru the dark woods over the dun plains
in the harsh desert)
          Where
do they hang our breath? our
bright glance, where is our song now
our sorrow?

Walker Art Center, Minneapolis

To the Unnamed Buddhist Nun Who Burned Herself to Death on the Night of June 3, 1966

Outside your temple wall. Stone or wood, I can't
quite see the detail; under this last full moon
which I did see. Moon of this June, unearthly light
heavy with potency, the air filled with the smells
and buzzing of springtime

you with your shaved head and can
of kerosene. Under what driving form
of ecstasy? I pray to taste it once

your soaked robe chilly in the spring night wind

> "Oh nun, is it hot in there?"
> "Only a stupid person like yourself would ask
> such a question."

Brief Wyoming Meditation

I read
Sand Creek massacre: White Antelope's scrotum
      became tobacco pouch
for Colorado Volunteer;
I see
destitute prairie: short spiny grass & dusty wind
& all for beef too expensive to eat;
I remember
at least two thirds of you voted for madman Nixon
were glad to bomb the "gooks" in their steamy jungle
& I seek
  I seek
  I seek

the place where your nature meets mine,
      the place where we touch

    nothing lasts long
    nothing,
            but earth
    & the mountains

I Fail as a Dharma Teacher

I don't imagine I'll manage to express Sunyata
in a way that all my students will know & love
or present the 4 Noble Truths so they look delicious
& tempting as Easter candy. My skillful means
is more like a two by four banging on the head
of a reluctant diver
I then go in and save—
what pyrotechnics!

Alas this life I can't be kind and persuasive
slip the Twelve-part Chain off hundreds of shackled
housewives
present the Eight-fold Path like the ultimate roadmap
at all the gas stations in samsara

But, oh, my lamas, I want to
how I want to!
Just to see your old eyes shine in this Kaliyuga
stars going out around us like birthday candles
your Empty Clear Luminous and Unobstructed
Rainbow Bodies
swimming in and through us like transparent fish.

Ave

O lost moon sisters
crescent in hair, sea underfoot do you wander
in blue veil, in green leaf, in tattered shawl do you wander
with goldleaf skin, with flaming hair do you wander
on Avenue A, on Bleecker Street do you wander
on Rampart Street, on Fillmore Street do you wander
with flower wreath, with jeweled breath do you wander

    footprints
       shining mother of pearl
               behind you
   moonstone eyes
      in which the crescent moon

with gloves, with hat, in rags, in fur, in beads
under the waning moon, hair streaming in black rain
wailing with stray dogs, hissing in doorways
shadows you are, that fall on the crossroads, highways

jaywalking do you wander
spitting do you wander
mumbling and crying do you wander
aged and talking to yourselves
with roving eyes do you wander
hot for quick love do you sander
weeping your dead

           naked you walk
           swathed in long robes you walk
           swaddled in death shroud you walk
           backwards you walk

                hungry
                hungry
                hungry

shrieking I hear you
singing I hear you
cursing I hear you
praying I hear you

you lie with the unicorn
you lie with the cobra
you lie in the dry grass
you lie with the yeti
you flick long cocks of satyrs with your tongue

you are armed
you drive chariots
you tower above me
you are small
you cower on hillsides
out of the winds

pregnant you wander
barefoot you wander
battered by drunk men you wander

you kill on steel tables
you birth in black beds
        fetus you tore out stiffens in snow
        it rises like new moon
        you moan in your sleep

digging for yams you wander
looking for dope you wander
playing with birds you wander
chipping at stone you wander

I walk the long night seeking you
I climb the sea crest seeking you
I lie on the prairie, batter at stone gates
calling your names

you are coral
you are lapis and turquoise
your brain curls like shell
you dance on hills

>   hard-substance-woman you whirl
>   you dance on subways
>   you sprawl in tenements
>   children lick at your tits

you are the hills, the shape and color of mesa
you are the tent, the lodge of skins, the hogan
the buffalo robes, the quilt, the knitted afghan
you are the cauldron and the evening star
you rise over the sea, you ride the dark

I move within you, light the evening fire
I dip my hand in you and eat your flesh
you are my mirror image and my sister
you disappear like smoke on misty hills
you lead me thru dream forest on horseback
large gypsy mother, I lean my head on your back

I am you
and I must become you
I have been you
and I must become you
I am always you
I must become you

>   *ay-a*
>   *ay-a ah*
>   *ay-a*
>   *ay-a ah ah*
>   *maya ma maya ma*
>   *om star mother ma om*
>   *maya ma ah*

Abyss

It really irks me to think I'm afraid of heights
will probably never hike in the Himalayas
And it's unlikely I'll come to know Singapore
as well as I know Manhattan

Then there's the drugs I haven't taken yet
ibogaine, ketamine—who knows what comes next?
Will my aging body stand for it all? Don't think so.

When I think of the alphabets they won't decipher
before I'm outta here—secret geometrical magics
the dharma lore of ancient Africa

I've never laid eyes on the Gobi desert!
Found the last remaining Wends!
Spoken in tongues in a tent on a summer night

So many tropical forests to explore! the birds! the flowers!
The house I grew up in!
The white dog with a hole in his side!
Or was it a whale?
And that reminds me—spear-fishing on the ice
is probably beyond me too
Like life in Chicago w/bodies in the basement

I'll never sing Turandot, play the bass clarinet
or master the art of tatting.
won't live long enough for colloquial Tibetan.

I won't be the abbess of a monastery,
freak out the psychic next door, or walk
in a formal garden. I might not even
learn to belly-dance, or marry a bear
like the girl in that Indian story.

The worst is I might not tell all the people I love
how much I love them.
Or send them boxes of chocolate.
Or paint my toenails iridescent green
tho there's no excuse
for neglecting that little chore.

I haven't yet eaten croissants in Quebec
Or spent the winter solstice in Iceland
Or woven a tapestry based on the phases
of the moon.

I won't be a Shinto princess in a Kami shrine
on a gloomy shore w/three rocks & one ancient pine
Or an Ainu girl pulling mussels off the rocks
her skirt tucked into her belt.

Death Sunyata Chant:
A Rite for Passing Over

> *Everything is illusion*
> *but I am confident that all is well.*
> —"Hidden adept" of Tibet,
> quoted by Sogyal Rinpoche

If there is a Pure Land
we release the spirit
send it flying
into the Buddha's heart

Everything is illusion

If there are angels
will they carry you
singing
into the Presence?

I am confident

If the flesh is light & the fire
is a lover
If the ashes are scattered at sea
on the wind or planted in the earth
If all the five elements
are Wisdom Dakinis

and I am confident that all is well

what shape
    size
    glaze
will you take
in the potter's hands?
what realm
emerge in?

If the paths of the bardo are glorious
or frightening
if the light & sound is deafening
overwhelming
everything is illusion

If there is only extinction
& total dark
If we cycle thru forms throughout
the galaxy
If we must now return to Sirius
continue our Evolution
I am confident
that all is well

If you will be judged by a bureaucratic god
or wear golden shoes in the golden fields of the Lord
or carry to death yr guilt at kinky sex

If the faces you hallucinate *are* a last judgement
Everything is illusion

the bodhisattvas
    adepts
the magickal teachers
    lotus paradises
     pearly gates
& all the realms of Satan

the name of confusion & the name of wisdom
both blow away on the wind

the night of Brahma lasts a thousand aeons
the worlds are born & die
        sixty times a second
Valhalla & the land of the Ghost Dancers
the spiral journeys under other stars
all shift & fade
flicker & re-emerge

they are all
an ancestral Dream Time

do you see?

the black air
that rattles in the back of yr throat
is transparent
a window on an unspeakable
energy dance

       vortex of Isis
         Shiva
         Hayagriva
         Olokun

the ambrosia of Kali is just this bitter taste
bile at the back of the the tongue

awareness focuses as the vision fades

> *everything is illusion*
> *but I am confident*
> *that all is well—*

Rant

You cannot write a single line w/out a cosmology
a cosmogony
laid out, before all eyes

there is no part of yourself you can separate out
saying, this is memory, this is sensation
this is the work I care about, this is how I
make a living

it is whole, it is a whole, it always was whole
you do not "make" it so
there is nothing to integrate, you are a presence
you are an appendage of the work, the work stems from
hangs from the heaven you create

every man / every woman carries a firmament inside
& the stars in it are not the stars in the sky

w/out imagination there is no memory
w/out imagination there is no sensation
w/out imagination there is no will, desire

history is a living weapon in yr hand
& you have imagined it, it is thus that you
"find out for yourself"

history is the dream of what can be, it is
the relation between things in a continuum

of imagination
what you find out for yourself is what you select
out of an infinite sea of possibility
no one can inhabit yr world

yet it is not lonely,
the ground of imagination is fearlessness
discourse is video tape of a movie of a shadow play
but the puppets are in yr hand
your counters in a multidimensional chess
which is divination
                    & strategy

the war that matters is the war against the imagination
all other wars are subsumed in it.

the ultimate famine is the starvation
of the imagination

it is death to be sure, but the undead
seek to inhabit someone else's world

the ultimate claustrophobia is the syllogism
the ultimate claustrophobia is "it all adds up"
nothing adds up & nothing stands in for
anything else

THE ONLY WAR THAT MATTERS IS THE WAR AGAINST
    THE IMAGINATION
THE ONLY WAR THAT MATTERS IS THE WAR AGAINST
    THE IMAGINATION
THE ONLY WAR THAT MATTERS IS THE WAR AGAINST
    THE IMAGINATION

ALL OTHER WARS ARE SUBSUMED IN IT

There is no way out of the spiritual battle
There is no way you can avoid taking sides
There is no way you can *not* have a poetics
no matter what you do: plumber, baker, teacher

you do it in the consciousness of making
or not making yr world
you have a poetics: you step into the world
like a suit of readymade clothes

or you etch in light
your firmament spills into the shape of your room
the shape of the poem, of yr body, of yr loves

A woman's life / a man's life is an allegory

Dig it

There is no way out of the spiritual battle
the war is the war against the imagination
you can't sign up as a conscientious objector

the war of the worlds hangs here, right now, in the balance
it is a war for this world, to keep it
a vale of soul-making

the taste in all our mouths is the taste of our power
and it is bitter as death

bring yr self home to yrself, enter the garden
the guy at the gate w/the flaming sword is yrself

the war is the war for the human imagination
and no one can fight it but you / & no one can fight it for you

The imagination is not only holy, it is precise
it is not only fierce, it is practical
men die everyday for the lack of it,
it is vast & elegant

JOHN WIENERS

||||||||||||||||||||||||||||||||||||||||||||||||||||||||||||||||||||||||||||||||||||||||||||||||||||

JOHN WIENERS was born in 1934 in Milton, Massachusetts. In the autumn of 1954, after graduating from Boston College, he heard the poet Charles Olson deliver a reading and enrolled at Black Mountain College, a renowned experimental college in North Carolina where Olson taught. Wieners returned to Boston the following year and published *Measure,* which ran work by Black Mountain poets. In 1958, Wieners moved to San Francisco, where he consorted with painter Robert LaVigne, poet Robert Duncan, and other writers, bohemians, artists, drug addicts, and wanderers. Auerhahn Press published the first book of his own poems, *The Hotel Wentley Poems.* Wieners returned to the East Coast in 1960. He was active at the Poets' Theatre in Cambridge as an actor, a stage manager, and a playwright. In 1965, Wieners enrolled for graduate work at the State University of New York in Buffalo, worked as a teaching fellow and continued his relationship with Olson-inspired "Projectivist" writers, which resulted in a book in their Curriculum of the Soul Series, *Women.* In 1970 he moved to Boston and worked in education cooperatives, political action committees, and with gay activist groups. He died on March 1, 2002. He received many awards during his writing career and was a member of the Academy of American Poets. His papers are housed at University of Delaware, Kent State, and University of Connecticut.

A poem for vipers

I sit in Lees. At 11:40 PM with
Jimmy the pusher. He teaches me
Ju Ju. Hot on the table before us
shrimp foo yong, rice and mushroom
chow yuke. Up the street under the wheels
of a strange car is his stash—The ritual.
We make it. And have made it.
For months now together after midnight.
Soon I know the fuzz will
interrupt, will arrest Jimmy and
I shall be placed on probation. The poem
does not lie to us. We lie under
its law, alive in the glamour of this hour
able to enter into the sacred places
of his dark people, who carry secrets
glassed in their eyes and hide words
under the coats of their tongue.

                              6.16.58

A poem for museum goers

I walk down a long
passage way with a
red door waiting open.

It is Edvard Munch.
Turn right turn
And I see my sister

hanging on the wall,
heavy breasts and hair
Tied to a tree in the garden

with the full moon
are the ladies of the street.
Whipped for whoring.

Their long hair binds them,

They have lain long
hours in bed, blood
on their mouths, arms
reaching down for
ground not given them.

They are enveloped
in pain. Bah.
There is none. Munch

knew it. Put the
Shriek in their ears
to remove it from his own.

Open thy mouth, tell us
the landscape you have
escaped from,
                    Fishing
boats are in the bay, no
outgoing tides for you
who he anchored to
                            Hell.

Even here the young lovers
cast black shadows.
Nets are down.

Huge seasnakes
squirm on shore
taking away even
the beach from us.

Move on. Moonlight

I see the garden women
in their gravy days
when hair hung golden or

black to the
floor & the walls
were velvet.

An old sailor his face like wood
his chin splintered
by many shipwrecks
keeps their story
in his eyes. How the house
at the top of the drive
held them all, and their lovers,

with Munch the most
obsessed. His face
carved by knife blades.

Lover leaves lover,
1896, 62 years
later, the men
sit, paws and
jagged depths
under their heads,

Now the season of
the furnished room. Gone
the Grecian walls & the
cypress trees,
plain planks and spider
webs, a bed

only big enough for one,
it looks like a
casket. Death

death on every
wall, guillotined
and streaming in
flames.

                    6.21.58

A poem for the insane

The 2nd afternoon I come
back to the women of Munch.

Models with god over—
their shoulders, vampires,

the heads are down and
blood is the water-
                    color
they use to turn on.

The story is not done.
There is one wall
left to walk. Yeah—

Afterwards—Nathan,
gone, Big Eric busted,
Swanson down. It is

right, the Melancholy
on the Beach. I do not
                    split
but hang on the Demon

Tree, while shadows drift
around me. Until at last
there is left only the

Death Chamber. Family Reunion
in it. Rocking chairs and
who is the young man

who sneaks out thru
the black curtain, away
from the bad bed.

Yeah stand now
on the new road, with the
huge mountain on your

right out of the mist
the Bridge before me,
the woman waiting

with no mouth, waiting
for me to kiss it on.
I will. I will walk with

my eyes up on you for
ever. We step into
the Kiss, 1897.

The light streams.
 Melancholy carries
a red sky and our dreams

are blue boats
no one can bust or
blow out to sea.

We ride them
and Tingel-Tangel
in the afternoon.

                    6.23.58

Act #2

For Marlene Dietrich

I took love home with me,
we fixed in the night and
sank into a stinging flash.

¼ grain of love
          we had,
2 men on a cot, a silk
cover and a green cloth
over the lamp.
          The music was just right.
I blew him like a symphony,
     it floated and
          he took me
down the street and
          left me here.
3 AM. No sign.

     only a moving van
     up Van Ness Avenue.

Foster's was never like this.

I'll walk home, up the
          same hills we
               came down.
He'll never come back,
          there'll be no horse
               tomorrow nor pot
tonight to smoke till dawn.

He's gone and taken
my morphine with him
Oh Johnny. Women in
     the night moan yr. name

6.19.59

A Poem for Trapped Things

This morning with a blue flame burning
this thing wings its way in.
Wind shakes the edges of its yellow being.
Gasping for breath.
Living for the instant.
Climbing up the black border of the window.
Why do you want out.
I sit in pain.
A red robe amid debris.
You bend and climb, extending antennae.

I know the butterfly is my soul
grown weak from battle.

A Giant fan on the back of
                    a beetle.
A caterpillar chrysalis that seeks
a new home apart from this room.

And will disappear from sight
at the pulling of invisible strings.
Yet so tenuous, so fine
   this thing is, I am
   sitting on the hard bed, we could
         vanish from sight like the puff
            off an invisible cigarette.
Furred chest, ragged silk under
         wings beating against the glass

      no one will open.

The blue diamonds on your back
are too beautiful to do
            away with.

I watch you
> all morning
>> long.
With my hand over my mouth.

A Poem for Painters

> Our age bereft of nobility
How can our faces show it?
I look for love.
> My lips stand out
dry and cracked with want
>> of it.
>> Oh it is well.

Again we go driven by forces
we have no control over. Only
>> in the poem
comes an image—that we rule
> the line by the pen
in the painter's hand one foot
>> away from me.
Drawing the face
> and its torture.
That is why no one dares tackle it.
Held as they are in the hands
>> of forces they
> cannot understand.
>> That despair
is on my face and shall show
in the fine lines of any man.

I had love once in the palm of my hand.
> See the lines there.
>> How we played
its game, are playing now

in the bounds of white and heartless fields.
　　　Fall down on my head,
love, drench my flesh in the streams
　　　　　of fine sprays. Like
　　　　　　　French perfume
　　　so that I light up as
　　　　　　morning glorys and
I am showered by the scent
　　　of the finished line.

　　　　　　No circles
but that two parallels do cross
　　　And carry our souls and
bodies together as the planets
　　　Showing light on the surface
　　　　　　of our skin, knowing
　　　that so much flows through
　　　　　　the veins underneath.
The checks puffed with it.
　　　Our pockets full.

　　　2

Pushed on by the incompletion
　　　of what goes before me
I hesitate before this paper
　　　scratching for the right words.
Paul Klee scratched for seven years
　　　on smoked glass to develop
　　　his line, Lavigne says: Look
at his face! he who has spent
　　　all night drawing mine.

The sun
also rises on the rooftops
　　　beginning with violet.
I begin in blue knowing what's cool.

3

My middle name is Joseph and I
walk beside an ass on the way to
what Bethlehem, where a new babe is born.
  Not the second hand of Yeats but
first prints on a cloudy windowpane.

4

America, you boil over

The cauldron scalds.
Flesh is scarred.
Eyes shot.

The street aswarm with
vipers and heavy armed bandits.
There are bandages on the wounds
but blood flows unabated.
     Oh stop
    up the drains.
   We are run over.

5

Let us stay with what we know.
That love is my strength, that
I am overpowered by it:
     Desire
      that too
is on the face: gone stale.
When green was the bed my love
and I laid down upon.
Such it is, heart's complaint,
You hear upon a day in June.
And I see no end in view
when summer goes, as it will,
upon the roads, like singing
companions across the land.

South of Mission, Seattle,
over the Sierra Mountains,
the Middle West and Michigan,
moving east again, easy
coming into Chicago and
the cattle country, calling
to each other over canyons,
careful not to be caught
at night, they are still out,
the destroyers, and down
into the South, familiar land,
lush places, blue mountains
of Carolina, into Black Mountain
and you can sleep out, or
straight across into states

I cannot think of their names
this nation is so large, like
our hands, our love it lives
with no lover, looking only
for the beloved, back home
into the heart, New York,
New England, Vermont, green
mountains and Massachusetts
my city, Boston and the sea
again to smell what this calm
ocean cannot tell us. The seasons.
Only the heart remembers
and records in the words

6

At last. I come to the last defense.

My poems contain no
wilde beestes, no
lady of the lake, music
of the spheres, or organ chants.

Only the score of a man's
struggle to stay with
what is his own, what
lies within him to do.

Without which is nothing.
And I come to this
knowing the waste,
leaving the rest up to love
and its twisted faces,
my hands claw out at
only to draw back from the
blood already running there.

My Mother

talking to strange men on the subway,

doesn't see me when she gets on,

  at Washington Street
but I hide in a booth at the side

  and watch her worried, strained face—
 the few years she has got left.
 Until at South Station

 I lean over and say:
I've been watching you since you got on.
  She says in an artificial
   voice: Oh, for Heaven's sake!

 as if heaven cared.

But I love her in the underground
 and her gray coat and hair
sitting there, one man over from me
  talking together between the wire grates of a cage.

The Acts of Youth

And with great fear I inhabit the middle of the night
What wrecks of the mind await me, what drugs
to dull the senses, what little I have left,
what more can be taken away?

The fear of travelling, of the future without hope
or buoy. I must get away from this place and see
that there is no fear without me: that it is within
unless it be some sudden act or calamity

to land me in the hospital, a total wreck, without
memory again; or worse still, behind bars. If
I could just get out of the country. Some place
where one can eat the lotus in peace.

For in this country it is terror, poverty awaits; or
am I a marked man, my life to be a lesson
or experience to those young who would trod
the same path, without God

unless he be one of justice, to wreak vengeance
on the acts committed while young under un-
due influence or circumstance. Oh I have
always seen my life as drama, patterned

after those who met with disaster or doom.
Is my mind being taken away me.
I have been over the abyss before. What
is that ringing in my ears that tells me

all is nigh, is naught but the roaring of the winter wind.
Woe to those homeless who are out on this night.
Woe to those crimes committed from which we
can walk away unharmed.

So I turn on the light
And smoke rings rise in the air.
Do not think of the future; there is none.
But the formula all great art is made of.

Pain and suffering. Give me the strength
to bear it, to enter those places where the
great animals are caged. And we can live
at peace by their side. A bride to the burden

that no god imposes but knows we have the means
to sustain its force unto the end of our days.
For that is what we are made for; for that
we are created. Until the dark hours are done.

And we rise again in the dawn.
Infinite particles of the divine sun, now
worshipped in the pitches of the night.

With Meaning

Rise, shining martyrs
over the multitudes
for the season of migration
between earth and heaven.

Rise shining martyrs
cut down in fire
and darkness,
speeding past light
straight through imagination's park.

In the smart lofts on West Newton St.
or the warehouse district of S.F., come,
let us go back
to bequeathed memory

of Columbus Ave., or the beach
at the end of Polk St.,
where Jack Spicer went,
or Steve Jonas' apts.
all over town

from Beacon Hill to St. Charles,
without warning how they went.
The multitude of martyrs,
staring out of

town houses now on Delaware Ave.
in the gray mist
of traffic circles, taking LSD
then not holding up
to rooming houses, Berkeley and motorcycles.

Books of poems all we had
to bound the frustration
of leaving them behind
in Millbrook mornings, on the swing

with Tambimuttu, exercising his solar plexus
during conversation. Each street
contains its own time of
other decades, recollected
after the festival, carefully

as so many jewels
to brush aside for
present occupation.
A printing press by the Pacific,

a Norman cottage in the east,
dancing to Donovan, in Pucci pajamas,
or perhaps prison, past imagination's plain,
with Saturday night sessions in the tombs, oh yes
rise shining martyrs, out of the movie house's matinee

on Long Island, to your love walking by
in the sun. Over the multitudes,
shortripping. And backyard swimming pools
of Arizona or Pacific Palisades,

in the canyons of L.A.
plus the journeys over oceans
and islands, to metropolis
spreadeagled the earth.
Yes rise shining martyrs

out of your graves, tell us
what to do, read your poems
under springtime moonlight.
Rise and salvage our century.

Children of the Working Class

to Somes

from incarceration, Taunton State Hospital, 1972

gaunt, ugly deformed

broken from the womb, and horribly shriven
at the labor of their forefathers, if you check back

scout around grey before actual time
their sordid brains don't work right,
pinched men emaciated, piling up railroad ties and highway
ditches
blanched women, swollen and crudely numb
ered before the dark of dawn

scuttling by candlelight, one not to touch, that is, a signal panic
thick peasants after *the* attitude

at that time of their century, bleak and centrifugal
they carry about them, tough disciplines of copper
        Indianheads.

there are worse, whom you may never see, non-crucial around
the
spoke, these you do, seldom
locked in Taunton State Hospital and other peon work farms
drudge from morning until night, abandoned within destitute
crevices odd clothes
intent on performing some particular task long has been far
removed
there is no hope, they locked-in key's; housed of course

and there fed, poorly
off sooted, plastic dishes, soiled grimy silver knives and forks,
stamped Department of Mental Health spoons
but the unshrinkable duties of any society
produces its ill-kempt, ignorant and sore idiosyncrasies.

There has never been a man yet, whom no matter how wise
can explain how a god, so beautiful he can create
the graces of formal gardens, the exquisite twilight sunsets
in splendor of elegant toolsmiths, still can yield the horror of

dwarfs, who cannot stand up straight with crushed skulls,
diseases on their legs and feet unshaven faces and women,
worn humped backs, deformed necks, hare lips, obese arms
distended rumps, there is not a flame shoots out could ex-
tinguish the torch of any liberty's state infection.

1907, My Mother was born, I am witness t-
o the exasperation of gallant human beings at g-
od, priestly fathers and Her Highness, Holy Mother the Church
persons who felt they were never given a chance, had n-
o luck and were flayed at suffering.

They produced children with phobias, manias and depression,
they cared little for their own metier, and kept watch upon
others, some chance to get ahead

Yes life was hard for them, much more hard than for any blo
ated millionaire, who still lives on
their hard-earned monies. I feel I shall
have to be punished for writing this,
that the omniscient god is the rich one,
cared little for looks, less for Art,
still kept weekly films close for the
free dishes and scandal hot. Some how
though got cheated in health and upon
hearth. I am one of them. I am witness
not to Whitman's vision, but instead the
poorhouses, the mad city asylums and re-
lief worklines. Yes, I am witness not to
God's goodness, but his better or less scorn.

The First of May, The Commonwealth of State Massachusetts, 1972

WILLIAM S. BURROUGHS

||||||||||||||||||||||||||||||||||||||||||||||||||||||||||||||||||||||||||||||||||||||||||||||||||||||||||||||||||||||||||||||||||||||||||||||||||||||

WILLIAM S. BURROUGHS was born in 1914 in St. Louis, Missouri. He graduated in anthropology from Harvard, lived briefly in Chicago, and subsequently moved to New York. In 1943 he met Allen Ginsberg, then a student at Columbia College. Ginsberg, Kerouac, and various friends looked up to Burroughs as a sage elder and teacher, skilled in the ways of dope and the criminal life, as well as a mighty intellectual visionary and social critic. Burroughs married Joan Vollmer, and the two set out for places more hospitable to drug dependency, ending up in Mexico City, where Burroughs wrote his first book, *Junky*. After accidentally shooting his wife, Burroughs insisted he had been invaded by a hostile Ugly Spirit. "I have had no choice but to write my way out." He traveled through South America in search of the shamanic hallucinogen *yage* and then headed for Tangiers. There he lived alone and wrote. Burroughs's letters to Ginsberg and Kerouac inspired them to visit him in Tangiers. When they got there, they found hundreds of wild, disconnected pages of writing and set about compiling them into a book. Kerouac dubbed the manuscript *Naked Lunch*. It was banned from the *Chicago Review* by the University of Chicago but appeared as a book in 1958. U.S. obscenity trials ensued, which were finally decided in favor of the publisher, Grove Press. Living in Paris with writer and painter Brion Gysin, Burroughs explored the "cut-up" method of composition and the emergence of a "Third Mind" through collaboration. The result was *The Soft Machine, The Ticket That Exploded,* and *Nova Express.* Burroughs's terrible visions of the techno-police state have influenced a myriad of writers, artists, and musicians. He died on August 7, 1997, and was buried in St. Louis with his hat, his cane, his gun, his Moroccan vest, and a joint of marijuana. *Last Words: The final Journals of William S. Burroughs* was published in 2001.

My Legs *Señor*

attic room and window my ice skates on the wall
the Priest could see the bathroom pale yellow wood panels
toilet young legs shiny black leg hairs
"It is my legs, *señor.*"
luster of stumps rinses his lavender horizon
feeling the boy groan and what it meant
face of a lousy kid on the doctor's table
I was the shadow of the waxing evenings and strange
    windowpanes.
I was the smudge and whine of missed times in the reflected sky
points of polluted water under his lavender horizon
    windowpane
smudge scrawled by some boy cold lost marbles in the room
the doctor's shabby table . . . his face . . .
boy skin spreads to something else.
"CHRIST WHAT'S INSIDE?" he screams.
flesh and bones rose tornado
"THAT HURTS."
I was the smudge and whine of missed legs shiny black leg hairs
silver paper in the wind frayed sounds of a distant city.

from **Naked Lunch**

Benway

So I am assigned to engage the services of Doctor Benway for Islam Inc.

Dr. Benway had been called in as advisor to the Freeland Republic, a place given over to free love and continual bathing. The citizens are well adjusted, co-operative, honest, tolerant and above all clean. But the invoking of Benway indicates all is not well behind that hygienic façade: Benway is a manipulator and coordinator of symbol systems, an expert on all phases of interrogation, brainwashing and control. I have not seen Benway since his precipitate departure from Annexia, where his assignment had been T.D.—Total Demoralization. Benway's first act was to abolish concentration camps, mass arrest and, except under certain limited and special circumstances, the use of torture.

"I deplore brutality," he said. "It's not efficient. On the other hand, prolonged mistreatment, short of physical violence, gives rise, when skillfully applied, to anxiety and a feeling of special guilt. A few rules or rather guiding principles are to be borne in mind. The subject must not realize that the mistreatment is a deliberate attack of an anti-human enemy on his personal identity. He must be made to feel that he deserves *any* treatment he receives because there is something (never specified) horribly wrong with him. The naked need of the control addicts must be decently covered by an arbitrary and intricate bureaucracy so that the subject cannot contact his enemy direct."

Every citizen of Annexia was required to apply for and carry on his person at all times a whole portfolio of documents. Citizens were subject to be stopped in the street at any time; and the Examiner, who might be in plain clothes, in various uniforms, often in a bathing suit or pyjamas, sometimes stark naked except for a badge pinned to his left nipple, after checking each paper, would stamp it. On subsequent inspection the

WILLIAM S. BURROUGHS   165

citizen was required to show the properly entered stamps of the last inspection. The Examiner, when he stopped a large group, would only examine and stamp the cards of a few. The others were then subject to arrest because their cards were not properly stamped. Arrest meant "provisional detention"; that is, the prisoner would be released if and when his Affidavit of Explanation, properly signed and stamped, was approved by the Assistant Arbiter of Explanations. Since this official hardly ever came to his office, and the Affidavit of Explanation had to be presented in person, the explainers spent weeks and months waiting around in unheated offices with no chairs and no toilet facilities.

Documents issued in vanishing ink faded into old pawn tickets. New documents were constantly required. The citizens rushed from one bureau to another in a frenzied attempt to meet impossible deadlines.

All benches were removed from the city, all fountains turned off, all flowers and trees destroyed. Huge electric buzzers on the top of every apartment house (everyone lived in apartments) rang the quarter hour. Often the vibrations would throw people out of bed. Searchlights played over the town all night (no one was permitted to use shades, curtains, shutters or blinds).

No one ever looked at anyone else because of the strict law against importuning, with or without verbal approach, anyone for any purpose, sexual or otherwise. All cafés and bars were closed. Liquor could only be obtained with a special permit, and the liquor so obtained could not be sold or given or in any way transferred to anyone else, and the presence of anyone else in the room was considered *prima facie* evidence of conspiracy to transfer liquor.

No one was permitted to bolt his door, and the police had pass keys to every room in the city. Accompanied by a mentalist they rush into someone's quarters and start "looking for it."

The mentalist guides them to whatever the man wishes to hide: a tube of vaseline, an enema, a handkerchief with come on it, a weapon, unlicensed alcohol. And they always submitted the suspect to the most humiliating search of his naked person on which they make sneering and derogatory comments. Many a latent homosexual was carried out in a straitjacket when they planted vaseline in his ass. Or they pounced on any object. A pen wiper or a shoe tree.

"And what is this supposed to be for?"

"A pen wiper, he says."

"I've heard everything now."

"I guess this is all we need. Come on, you."

After a few months of this the citizens cowered in corners like neurotic cats.

Of course the Annexia police processed suspected agents, saboteurs and political deviants on an assembly line basis. As regards the interrogation of suspects, Benway has this to say:

"While in general I avoid the use of torture—torture locates the opponent and mobilizes resistance—the threat of torture is useful to induce in the subject the appropriate feeling of helplessness and gratitude to the interrogator for withholding it. And torture can be employed to advantage as a penalty when the subject is far enough along with the treatment to accept punishment as deserved. To this end I devised several forms of disciplinary procedure. One was known as The Switchboard. Electric drills that can be turned on at any time are clamped against the subject's teeth; and he is instructed to operate an arbitrary switchboard, to put certain connections in certain sockets in response to bells and lights. Every time he makes a mistake the drills are turned on for twenty seconds. The signals are gradually speeded up beyond his reaction time. Half an hour on the switchboard and the subject breaks down like an overloaded thinking machine.

"The study of thinking machines teaches us more about the brain than we can learn by introspective methods. Western man is externalizing himself in the form of gadgets. Ever pop coke in the mainline? It hits you right in the brain, activating connections of pure pleasure. The pleasure of morphine is in the viscera. You listen down into yourself after a shot. But C is electricity through the brain, and the C yen is of the brain alone, a need without body and without feeling. The C-charged brain is a berserk pinball machine, flashing blue and pink lights in electric orgasm. C pleasure could be felt by a thinking machine, the first stirrings of hideous insect life. The craving for C lasts only a few hours, as long as the C channels are stimulated. Of course the effect of C could be produced by an electric current activating the C channels. . . .

"So after a bit the channels wear out like veins, and the addict has to find new ones. A vein will come back in time, and by adroit vein rotation a junky can piece out the odds if he don't become an oil burner. But brain cells don't come back once they're gone, and when the addict runs out of brain cells he is in a terrible fucking position.

"Squatting on old bones and excrement and rusty iron, in a white blaze of heat, a panorama of naked idiots stretches to the horizon. Complete silence—their speech centers are destroyed—except for the crackle of sparks and the popping of singed flesh as they apply electrodes up and down the spine. White smoke of burning flesh hangs in the motionless air. A group of children have tied an idiot to a post with barbed wire and built a fire between his legs and stand watching with bestial curiosity as the flames lick his thighs. His flesh jerks in the fire with insect agony.

"I digress as usual. Pending more precise knowledge of brain electronics, drugs remain an essential tool of the interrogator in his assault on the subject's personal identity. The barbiturates are, of course, virtually useless. That is, anyone who can be broken down by such means would succumb to the puerile methods used in an American precinct. Scopolamine is often effective in dissolving resistance, but it impairs the memory: an agent might be prepared to reveal his secrets but quite unable to remember them, or cover story and secret life info might be inextricably garbled. Mescaline, harmaline, LSD6, bufotenine, muscarine successful in many cases. Bulbocapnine induces a state approximating schizophrenic catatonia . . . instances of automatic obedience have been observed. Bulbocapnine is a back-brain depressant probably putting out of action the centers of motion in the hypothalamus. Other drugs that have produced experimental schizophrenia—mescaline, harmaline, LSD6—are backbrain stimulants. In schizophrenia the backbrain is alternately stimulated and depressed. Catatonia is often followed by a period of excitement and motor activity during which the nut rushes through the wards giving everyone a bad time. Deteriorated schizos sometimes refuse to move at all and spend their lives in bed. A disturbance of the regulatory function of the hypothalamus is indicated as the 'cause' (causal thinking never yields accurate description of metabolic process—limitations of existing language) of schizophrenia. Alternate doses of LSD6 and bulbocapnine—the bulbocapnine potentiated with curare—give the highest yield of automatic obedience.

"There are other procedures. The subject can be reduced to deep depression by administering large doses of benzedrine for several days. Psychosis can be induced by continual large doses of cocaine or demerol or by the abrupt withdrawal of barbiturates after prolonged administration. He can be addicted by dihydro-oxy-heroin and subjected to withdrawal (this compound should be five times as addicting as heroin, and the withdrawal proportionately severe).

"There are various 'psychological methods,' compulsory psychoanalysis, for example. The subject is requested to free-associate for one hour every day (in cases where time is not of the essence). 'Now, now. Let's not be negative, boy. Poppa call nasty man. Take baby walkabout switchboard.'

"The case of a female agent who forgot her real identity and merged with her cover story—she is still a fricoteuse in Annexia—put me onto another gimmick. An agent is trained to deny his agent identity by asserting his cover story. So why not use psychic jiu-jitsu and go along with him? Suggest that his cover story is his identity and that he has no other. His agent identity becomes unconscious, that is, out of his control; and you can dig it with drugs and hypnosis. You can make a square heterosex citizen queer with this angle . . . that is, reinforce and second his rejection of normally latent homosexual trends—at the same time depriving him of cunt and subjecting him to homosex stimulation. Then drugs, hypnosis, and—" Benway flipped a limp wrist.

"Many subjects are vulnerable to sexual humiliation. Nakedness, stimulation with aphrodisiacs, constant supervision to embarrass subject and prevent relief of masturbation (erections during sleep automatically turn on an enormous vibrating electric buzzer that throws the subject out of bed into cold water, thus reducing the incidence of wet dreams to a minimum). Kicks to hypnotize a priest and tell him he is about to consummate a hypostatic union with the Lamb—then steer a randy old sheep up his ass. After that the Interrogator can gain complete hypnotic control—the subject will come at his whistle, shit on the floor if he but say Open Sesame. Needless to say, the sex humiliation angle is contraindicated for overt homosexuals. (I mean let's keep our eye on the ball here and remember the old party line . . . never know who's listening in.) I recall this one kid, I condition to shit at sight of me. Then I wash his ass and screw him. It was real tasty. And he was a lovely fellah too. And some times a subject will burst into boyish tears because he can't keep from ejaculate when you screw him. Well, as you can plainly see, the possibilities are endless like meandering paths in a great big beautiful garden. I was just scratching that lovely surface when I am purged by Party Poops. . . . Well, 'son cosas de la vida.' "

I reach Freeland, which is clean and dull my God. Benway is directing the R.C., Reconditioning Center. I drop around, and "What happened to so and so?" sets in like: "Sidi Idriss 'The Nark' Smithers crooned to the Senders for a longevity serum. No fool like an old queen." "Lester Stroganoff Smuunn—'El Hassein'—turned himself into a Latah trying to perfect A.O.P., Automatic Obedience Processing. A martyr to the industry . . ." (Latah is a condition occurring in South East Asia. Otherwise sane, Latahs compulsively imitate every motion once their attention is attracted by snapping the fingers or calling sharply. A form of compulsive involuntary hypnosis. They sometimes injure themselves trying to imitate the motions of several people at once.)

"Stop me if you've heard this atomic secret. . . ."

Benway's face retains its form in the flash bulb of urgency, subject at any moment to unspeakable cleavage or metamorphosis. It flickers like a picture moving in and out of focus.

"Come on," says Benway, "and I'll show you around the R.C."

We are walking down a long white hall. Benway's voice drifts into my consciousness from no particular place . . . a disembodied voice that is sometimes loud and clear, sometimes barely audible like music down a windy street.

"Isolated groups like natives of the Bismarck Archipelago. No overt homosexuality among them. God damned matriarchy. All matriarchies anti-homosexual, conformist and prosaic. Find yourself in a matriarchy walk don't run to the nearest frontier. If you run, some frustrate latent queer cop will likely shoot you. So somebody wants to establish a beach head of homogeneity in a shambles of potentials like West Europe and U.S.A.? Another fucking matriarchy, Margaret Mead notwithstanding . . . Spot of bother there. Scalpel fight with a colleague in the operating room. And my baboon assistant leaped on the patient and tore him to pieces. Baboons always attack the weakest party in an altercation. Quite right too. We must never forget our glorious simian heritage. Doc Browbeck was party inna second part. A retired abortionist and junk pusher (he was a veterinarian actually) recalled to service during the manpower shortage. Well, Doc had been in the hospital kitchen all morning goosing the nurses and tanking up on coal gas and Klim—and just before the operation he sneaked a double shot of nutmeg to nerve himself up."

(In England and especially in Edinburgh the citizens bubble coal gas through Klim—a horrible form of powdered milk tasting like rancid chalk—and pick up on the results. They hock everything to pay the gas bill, and when the man comes around to shut it off for the non-payment, you can hear their screams for miles. When a citizen is sick from needing it he says "I got the klinks" or "That old stove climbing up my back."

Nutmeg. I quote from the author's article on narcotic drugs in the *British Journal of Addiction*: "Convicts and sailors sometimes have recourse to nutmeg. About a tablespoon is swallowed with water. Result vaguely similar to marijuana with side effects of headache and nausea. There are a number of narcotics of the nutmeg family in use among the Indians of South America. They are usually administered by sniffing a dried powder of the plant. The medicine men take these noxious substances and go into convulsive states. Their twitchings and mutterings are thought to have prophetic significance.")

"I had a Yage hangover, me, and in no condition to take any of Browbeck's shit. First thing he comes on with I should start the incision from the back instead of the front, muttering some garbled nonsense about being sure to cut out the gall bladder it would fuck up the meat. Thought he was on the farm cleaning a chicken. I told him to go put his head back in the oven, whereupon he had the effrontery to push my hand severing the patient's femoral artery. Blood spurted up and blinded the anesthetist, who ran out through the halls screaming. Browbeck tried to knee me in the groin, and I managed to hamstring him with my scalpel. He crawled about the floor stabbing at my feet and legs. Violet, that's my baboon assistant—only woman I ever cared a damn about—really wigged. I climbed up on the table and poise myself to jump on Browbeck with both feet and stomp him when the cops rushed in.

"Well, this rumble in the operating room, 'this unspeakable occurrence' as the Super called it, you might say was the blow off. The wolf pack was closing for the kill. A crucifixion, that's the only word for it. Of course I'd made a few 'dumheits' here and there. Who hasn't? There was the time me and the anesthetist drank up all the ether and the patient came up on us, and I was accused of cutting the cocaine with Saniflush. Violet did it actually. Had to protect her of course. . . .

"So the wind-up is we are all drummed out of the industry. Not that Violet was a *bona fide* croaker, neither was Browbeck for that matter, and even my own certificate was called in question. But Violet knew more medicine than the Mayo Clinic. She had an extraordinary intuition and a high sense of duty.

"So there I was flat on my ass with no certificate. Should I turn to another trade? No. Doctoring was in my blood. I managed to keep up my habits performing cutrate abortions in subway toilets. I even descended to hustling pregnant women in

the public streets. It was positively unethical. Then I met a great
guy, Placenta Juan the After Birth Tycoon. Made his in slunks
during the war. (Slunks are underage calves trailing afterbirths
and bacteria, generally in an unsanitary and unfit condition. A
calf may not be sold as food until it reaches a minimum age of
six weeks. Prior to that time it is classified as a slunk. Slunk
trafficking is subject to a heavy penalty.) Well, Juanito con-
trolled a fleet of cargo boats he register under the Abyssinian
flag to avoid bothersome restrictions. He gives me a job as
ship's doctor on the S.S. *Filiarisis,* as filthy a craft as ever sailed
the seas. Operating with one hand, beating the rats offa my
patient with the other and bedbugs and scorpions rain down
from the ceiling.

"So somebody wants homogeneity at this juncture. Can do
but it costs. Bored with the whole project, me. . . . Here we
are. . . . Drag Alley."

Benway traces a pattern in the air with his hand and a door
swings open. We step through and the door closes. A long ward
gleaming with stainless steel, white tile floors, glass brick walls.
Beds along one wall. No one smokes, no one reads, no one
talks.

"Come and take a close look," says Benway. "You won't
embarrass anybody."

I walk over and stand in front of a man who is sitting on his
bed. I look at the man's eyes. Nobody, nothing looks back.

"IND's," says Benway, "Irreversible Neural Damage. Over-
liberated, you might say . . . a drag on the industry."

I pass a hand in front of the man's eyes.

"Yes," says Benway, "they still have reflexes. Watch this."
Benway takes a chocolate bar from his pocket, removes the
wrapper and holds it in front of the man's nose. The man sniffs.
His jaws begin to work. He makes snatching motions with his
hands. Saliva drips from his mouth and hangs off his chin in
long streamers. His stomach rumbles. His whole body writhes
in peristalsis. Benway steps back and holds up the chocolate.
The man drops to his knees, throws back his head and barks.
Benway tosses the chocolate. The man snaps at it, misses,
scrambles around on the floor making slobbering noises. He

crawls under the bed, finds the chocolate and crams it into his mouth with both hands.

"Jesus! These ID's got no class to them."

Benway calls over the attendant who is sitting at one end of the ward reading a book of J. M. Barrie's plays.

"Get these fucking ID's outa here. It's a bring down already. Bad for the tourist business."

"What should I do with them?"

"How in the fuck should I know? I'm a scientist. A *pure* scientist. Just get them outa here. I don't hafta look at them is all. They constitute an albatross."

"But what? Where?"

"Proper channels. Buzz the District Coordinator or whatever he calls himself . . . new title every week. Doubt if he exists."

Doctor Benway pauses at the door and looks back at the IND's. "Our failures," he says. "Well, it's all in the day's work."

"Do they ever come back?"

"They don't come back, won't come back, once they're gone," Benway sings softly. "Now this ward has some inna-rest."

The patients stand in groups talking and spitting on the floor. Junk hangs in the air like a grey haze.

"A heart-warming sight," says Benway, "those junkies standing around waiting for the Man. Six months ago they were all schizophrenic. Some of them hadn't been out of bed for years. Now look at them. In all the course of my practices, I have never seen a schizophrenic junky, and junkies are mostly of the schizo physical type. Want to cure anybody of anything, find out who doesn't have it. So who don't got it? Junkies don't got it. Oh, incidentally, there's an area in Bolivia with no psychosis. Right sane folk in them hills. Like to get in there, me, before it is loused up by literacy, advertising, TV and drive-ins. Make a study strictly from metabolism: diet, use of drugs and alcohol, sex, etc. Who cares what they think? Same nonsense everybody thinks, I daresay.

"And why don't junkies got schizophrenia? Don't know yet. A schizophrenic can ignore hunger and starve to death if he isn't fed. No one can ignore heroin withdrawal. The fact of addiction imposes contact.

"But that's only one angle. Mescaline, LSD6, deteriorated adrenalin, harmaline can produce an approximate schizophrenia. The best stuff is extracted from the blood of schizos; so schizophrenia is likely a drug psychosis. They got a metabolic connection, a Man Within you might say.

"In the terminal stage of schizophrenia the backbrain is permanently depressed, and the front brain is almost without content since the front brain is only active in response to backbrain stimulation.

"Morphine calls forth the antidote of backbrain stimulation similar to schizo substance. (Note similarity between withdrawal syndrome and intoxication with Yage or LSD6.) Eventual result of junk use—especially true of heroin addiction where large doses are available to the addict—is permanent backbrain depression and a state much like terminal schizophrenia: complete lack of affect, autism, virtual absence of cerebral event. The addict can spend eight hours looking at a wall. He is conscious of his surroundings, but they have no emotional connotation and in consequence no interest. Remembering a period of heavy addiction is like playing back a tape recording of events experienced by the front brain alone. Flat statements of external events. 'I went to the store and bought some brown sugar. I came home and ate half the box. I took a three grain shot etc.' Complete absence of nostalgia in these memories. However, as soon as junk intake falls below par, the withdrawal substance floods the body.

"If all pleasure is relief from tension, junk affords relief from the whole life process, in disconnecting the hypothalamus, which is the center of psychic energy and libido.

"Some of my learned colleagues (nameless assholes) have suggested that junk derives its euphoric effect from direct stimulation of the orgasm center. It seems more probable that junk suspends the whole cycle of tension, discharge and rest. The orgasm has no function in the junky. Boredom, which always indicates an undischarged tension, never troubles the addict.

He can look at his shoe for eight hours. He is only roused to action when the hourglass of junk runs out."

At the far end of the ward an attendant throws up an iron shutter and lets out a hog call. The junkies rush up grunting and squealing.

"Wise guy," says Benway. "No respect for human dignity. Now I'll show you the mild deviant and criminal ward. Yes, a criminal is a mild deviant here. He doesn't deny the Freeland contract. He merely seeks to circumvent some of the clauses. Reprehensible but not too serious. Down this hall . . . We'll skip wards 23, 86, 57 and 97 . . . and the laboratory."

"Are homosexuals classed as deviants?"

"No. Remember the Bismarck Archipelago. No overt homosexuality. A *functioning* police state needs no police. Homosexuality does not occur to anyone as conceivable behaviour. . . . Homosexuality is a *political* crime in a matriarchy. No society tolerates overt rejection of its basic tenets. We aren't a matriarchy here, *Insh'allah.* You know the experiment with rats where they are subject to this electric shock and dropped in cold water if they so much as move at a female. So they all become fruit rats and that's the way it is with the etiology. And shall such a rat squeak out, 'I'm queah and I luuuuuuuuve it' or 'Who cut yours off, you two-holed freak?' 'twere a square rat so to squeak. During my rather brief experience as a psychoanalyst—spot of bother with the Society—one patient ran amok in Grand Central with a flame thrower, two committed suicide and one died on the couch like a jungle rat (jungle rats are subject to die if confronted suddenly with a hopeless situation). So his relations beef and I tell them, 'It's all in the day's work. Get this stiff outa here. It's a bring down for my live patients'—I noticed that all my homosexual patients manifested strong unconscious heterosex trends and all my hetero patients unconscious homosexual trends. Makes the brain reel, don't it?"

"And what do you conclude from that?"

"Conclude? Nothing whatever. Just a passing observation."

We are eating lunch in Benway's office when he gets a call.

"What's that? . . . Monstrous! Fantastic! . . . Carry on and stand by."

He puts down the phone. "I am prepared to accept immediate assignment with Islam Incorporated. It seems the electronic brain went berserk playing six-dimensional chess with the Technician and released every subject in the R.C. Leave us adjourn to the roof. Operation Helicopter is indicated."

From the roof of the R.C. we survey a scene of unparalleled horror. IND's stand around in front of the café tables, long streamers of saliva hanging off their chins, stomachs noisily churning, others ejaculate at the sight of women. Latahs imitate the passers-by with monkey-like obscenity. Junkies have looted the drugstores and fix on every street corner. . . . Catatonics decorate the parks. . . . Agitated schizophrenics rush through the streets with mangled, inhuman cries. A group of P.R.'s— Partially Reconditioned—have surrounded some homosexual tourists with horrible knowing smiles showing the Nordic skull beneath in double exposure.

"What do you want?" snaps one of the queens.

"We want to *understand* you."

A contingent of howling simopaths swing from chandeliers, balconies and trees, shitting and pissing on passers-by. (A simopath—the technical name for this disorder escapes me—is a citizen convinced he is an ape or other simian. It is a disorder peculiar to the army, and discharge cures it.) Amoks trot along cutting off heads, faces sweet and remote with a dreamy half smile. . . . Citizens with incipient Bang-utot clutch their penises and call on the tourists for help. . . . Arab rioters yipe and howl, castrating, disembowelling, throw burning gasoline. . . . Dancing boys strip-tease with intestines, women stick severed genitals in their cunts, grind, bump and flick it at the man of their choice. . . . Religious fanatics harangue the crowd from helicopters and rain stone tablets on their heads, inscribed with meaningless messages. . . . Leopard Men tear people to pieces with iron claws, coughing and grunting. . . . Kwakiutl Cannibal Society initiates bite off noses and ears. . . .

A coprophage calls for a plate, shits on it and eats the shit, exclaiming, "Mmmm, that's my rich substance."

A battalion of rampant bores prowls the streets and hotel lobbies in search of victims. An intellectual avant-gardist—"Of course the only writing worth considering now is to be found in scientific reports and periodicals"—has given someone a bulbocapnine injection and is preparing to read him a bulletin on "the use of neo-hemoglobin in the control of multiple degenerative granuloma." (Of course, the reports are all gibberish he has concocted and printed up.)

His opening words: "You look to me like a man of intelligence." (Always ominous words, my boy . . . When you hear them stay not on the order of your going but go at once.)

An English colonial, assisted by five police boys, has detained a subject in the club bar: "I say, do you know Mozambique?" and he launches into the endless saga of his malaria. "So the doctor said to me, 'I can only advise you to leave the area. Otherwise I shall bury you. This croaker does a little undertaking on the side. Piecing out the odds you might say, and throwing himself a spot of business now and then." So after the third pink gin when he gets to know you, he shifts to dysentery. "Most extraordinary discharge. More or less of a white yellow color like rancid jism and stringy you know."

An explorer in sun helmet has brought down a citizen with blow gun and curare dart. He administers artificial respiration with one foot. (Curare kills by paralyzing the lungs. It has no other toxic effect, is not, strictly speaking, a poison. If artificial respiration is administered the subject will not die. Curare is eliminated with great rapidity by the kidneys.) "That was the year of the rindpest when everything died, even the hyenas. . . . So there I was completely out of K.Y. in the headwaters of the Baboons asshole. When it came through by air drop my gratitude was indescribable. . . . As a matter of fact, and I have never told this before to a living soul—elusive blighters"—his voice echoes through a vast empty hotel lobby in 1890 style, red plush, rubber plants, gilt and statues—"I was the only white man ever initiated into the infamous Agouti Society, witnessed and participated in their unspeakable rites."

(The Agouti Society has turned out for a Chimu Fiesta. (The Chimu of ancient Peru were much given to sodomy and occasionally staged bloody battles with clubs, running up several hundred casualties in the course of an afternoon.) The youths, sneering and goosing each other with clubs, troop out to the field. Now the battle begins.

Gentle reader, the ugliness of that spectacle buggers description. Who can be a cringing pissing coward, yet vicious as a purple-assed mandril, alternating these deplorable conditions like vaudeville skits? Who can shit on a fallen adversary who, dying, eats the shit and screams with joy? Who can hang a weak passive and catch his sperm in mouth like a vicious dog? Gentle reader, I fain would spare you this, but my pen hath its will like the Ancient Mariner. Oh Christ what a scene is this! Can tongue or pen accommodate these scandals? A beastly young hooligan has gouged out the eye of his confrere and fuck him in the brain. "This brain atrophy already, and dry as grandmother's cunt."

He turns into Rock and Roll hoodlum. "I screw the old gash—like a crossword puzzle what relation to me is the outcome if it outcome? My father already or not yet? I can't screw you, Jack, you is about to become my father, and better 'twere to cut your throat and screw my mother playing it straight than fuck my father or *vice versa mutatis mutandis* as the case may be, and cut my mother's throat, that sainted gash, though it be the best way I know to stem her word horde and freeze her asset. I mean when a fellow be caught short in the switches and don't know is he to offer up his ass to 'great big daddy' or commit a torso job on the old lady. Give me two cunts and a prick of steel and keep your dirty finger out of my sugar bum what you think I am a purple-assed reception already fugitive from Gibraltar? Male and female castrated he them. Who can't distinguish between the sexes? I'll cut your throat you white mother fucker. Come out in the open like my grandchild and meet thy unborn mother in dubious battle. Confusion hath fuck his masterpiece. I have cut the janitor's throat quite by mistake of identity, he being such a horrible fuck like the old man. And in the coal bin all cocks are alike."

So leave us return to the stricken field. One youth hath pene-
trate his comrade, whilst another youth does amputate the
proudest part of that cock's quivering beneficiary so that the
visiting member projects to fill the vacuum nature abhors and
ejaculate into the Black Lagoon where impatient piranha snap
up the child not yet born nor—in view of certain well estab-
lished facts—at all likely.)

Another bore carries around a suitcase full of trophies and
medals, cups and ribbons: "Now this I won for the Most Inge-
nious Sex Device Contest in Yokohama. (Hold him, he's des-
perate.) The Emperor gave it to me himself and there were tears
in his eyes, and the runners-up all castrated theirselves with
harakiri knives. And I won this ribbon in a Degradation Con-
test at the Teheran meeting of Junkies Anonymous."

"Shot up my wife's M.S. and her down with a kidney stone
big as the Hope Diamond. So I give her half a Vagamin and tell
her, "You can't expect too much relief. . . . Shut up awready. I
wanta enjoy my medications.' "

"Stole an opium suppository out of my grandmother's ass."

The hypochondriac lassoes the passer-by and administers a
straitjacket and starts talking about his rotting septum: "An
awful purulent discharge is subject to flow out . . . just wait till
you see it."

He does a strip tease to operation scars, guiding the reluctant
fingers of a victim. "Feel that suppurated swelling in my groin
where I got the lymphogranulomas. . . . And now I want you
to palpate my internal haemorrhoids."

(The reference is to lymphogranuloma, "climactic buboes."
A virus venereal disease indigenous to Ethiopia. "Not for noth-
ing are we known as feelthy Ethiopians," sneers an Ethiopian
mercenary as he sodomizes Pharaoh, venomous as the King's
cobra. Ancient Egyptian papyrus talk all the time about them
feelthy Ethiopians.

So it started in Addis Ababa like the Jersey Bounce, but these
are modern times, One World. Now the climactic buboes swell
up in Shanghai and Esmeraldas, New Orleans and Helsinki,
Seattle and Capetown. But the heart turns home and the disease
shows a distinct predilection for Negroes, is in fact the white-

haired boy of white supremacists. But the Mau Mau voodoo men are said to be cooking up a real dilly of a VD for the white folks. Not that Caucasians are immune: five British sailors contracted the disease in Zanzibar. And the Dead Coon County, Arkansas ("Blackest Dirt, Whitest People in the U.S.A.— Nigger, Don't Let The Sun Set On You Here") the County Coroner come down with the buboes fore and aft. A vigilante committee of neighbours apologetically burned him to death in the Court House privy when his interesting condition came to light. "Now, Clem, just think of yourself as a cow with the aftosa." "Or a poltroon with the fowl pest." "Don't crowd too close, boys. His intestines is subject to explode in the fire." The disease in short arm hath a gimmick for going places unlike certain unfortunate viruses who are fated to languish unconsummate in the guts of a tick or a jungle mosquito, or the saliva of a dying jackal slobbering silver under the desert moon. And after an initial lesion at the point of infection the disease passes to the lymph glands of the groin, which swell and burst in suppurating fissures, drain for days, months, years, a purulent stringy discharge streaked with blood and putrid lymph. Elephantiasis of the genitals is a frequent complication, and cases of gangrene have been recorded where the amputation *in medio* of the patient from the waist down was indicated but hardly worth while. Women usually suffer secondary infection of the anus. Males who resign themselves up for passive intercourse to infected partners like weak and soon to be purple-assed baboons, may also nourish a little stranger. Initial proctitis and the inevitable purulent discharge—which may pass unnoticed in the shuffle—is followed by stricture of the rectum requiring intervention of an apple corer or its surgical equivalent, lest the unfortunate patient be reduced to fart and shit in his teeth giving rise to stubborn cases of halitosis and unpopularity with all sexes, ages and conditions of *homo sapiens*. In fact a blind bugger was deserted by his seeing eye police dog—copper at heart. Until quite recently there was no satisfactory treatment. "Treatment is symptomatic"—which means in the trade there is none. Now many cases yield to intensive therapy with aureomycin, terramycin and some of the newer molds. However a certain appreciable percentage remain refractory as mountain gorillas. . . . So, boys, when those hot licks play over your balls and prick and dart up your ass like an invisible blue blow torch of orgones, in the words of I. B. Watson, *Think*. Stop panting and start palpating . . . and if you palpate a bubo draw yourself back in and say in a cold nasal whine: "You think I am inna-rested to contact your horrible old condition? I am not inna-rested at all.")

Rock and Roll adolescent hoodlums storm the streets of all nations. They rush into the Louvre and throw acid in the Mona Lisa's face. They open zoos, insane asylums, prisons, burst water mains with air hammers, chop the floor out of passenger plane lavatories, shoot out lighthouses, file elevator cables to one thin wire, turn sewers into the water supply, throw sharks and sting rays, electric eels and candiru into swimming pools (the candiru is a small eel-like fish or worm about one-quarter inch through and two inches long patronizing certain rivers of ill repute in the Greater Amazon Basin, will dart up your prick or your asshole or a woman's cunt *faute de mieux,* and hold himself there by sharp spines with precisely what motives is not known since no one has stepped forward to observe the cand-iru's life-cycle *in situ*), in nautical costumes ram the *Queen Mary* full speed into New York Harbor, play chicken with pas-senger planes and busses, rush into hospitals in white coats car-rying saws and axes and scalpels three feet long; throw paralyt-ics out of iron lungs (mimic their suffocations flopping about on the floor and rolling their eyes up), administer injections with bicycle pumps, disconnect artificial kidneys, saw a woman in half with a two-man surgical saw, they drive herds of squeal-ing pigs into the Curb, they shit on the floor of the United Na-tions and wipe their ass with treaties, pacts, alliances.

By plane, car, horse, camel, elephant, tractor, bicycle and steam roller, on foot, skis, sled, crutch and pogo-stick the tour-ists storm the frontiers, demanding with inflexible authority asylum from the "unspeakable conditions obtaining in Free-land," the Chamber of Commerce striving in vain to stem the debacle: "Please to be restful. It is only a few crazies who have from the crazy place outbroken."

The Cut-up Method of Brion Gysin

At a surrealist rally in the 1920s Tristan Tzara the man from nowhere proposed to create a poem on the spot by pulling words out of a hat. A riot ensued wrecked the theater. André Breton expelled Tristan Tzara from the movement and grounded the cut-ups on the Freudian couch.

In the summer of 1959 Brion Gysin painter and writer cut newspaper articles into sections and rearranged the sections *at random*. "Minutes to Go" resulted from this initial cut-up experiment. "Minutes to Go" contains unedited unchanged cut-ups emerging as quite coherent and meaningful prose.

The cut-up method brings to writers the collage, which has been used by painters for fifty years. And used by the moving and still camera. In fact all street shots from movie or still cameras are by the unpredictable factors of passersby and juxtaposition cut-ups. And photographers will tell you that often their best shots are accidents . . . writers will tell you the same. The best writing seems to be done almost by accident but writers until the cut-up method was made explicit—all writing is in fact cut-ups; I will return to this point—had no way to produce the accident of spontaneity. You cannot *will* spontaneity. But you can introduce the unpredictable spontaneous factor with a pair of scissors.

The method is simple. Here is one way to do it. Take a page. Like this page. Now cut down the middle and across the middle. You have four sections: 1 2 3 4 . . . one two three four. Now rearrange the sections placing section four with section one and section two with section three. And you have a new page. Sometimes it says much the same thing. Sometimes something quite different—cutting up political speeches is an interesting exercise—in any case you will find that it says something and something quite definite. Take any poet or writer you fancy. Here, say, or poems you have read over many times. The words have lost meaning and life through years of repetition. Now take the poem and type out selected passages. Fill a page with excerpts. Now cut the page. You have a new poem. As many poems as you like. As many Shakespeare Rimbaud poems as you like. Tristan Tzara said: "Poetry is for everyone." And André Breton called him a cop and expelled him from the movement. Say it again: "Poetry is for everyone." Poetry is a place and it is free to all cut up Rimbaud and you are in Rimbaud's place. Here is a Rimbaud poem cut up.

"Visit of memories. Only your dance and your voice house. On the suburban air improbable desertions . . . all harmonic pine for strife.

"The great skies are open. Candor of vapor and tent spitting blood laugh and drunken penance.

"Promenade of wine perfume opens slow bottle.

"The great skies are open. Supreme bugle burning flesh children to mist."

Cut-ups are for everyone. Anybody can make cut-ups. It is experimental in the sense of being *something to do*. Right here write now. Not something to talk and argue about. Greek philosophers assumed logically that an object twice as heavy as another object would fall twice as fast. It did not occur to them to push the two objects off the table and see how they fall. Cut the words and see how they fall. Shakespeare Rimbaud live in their words. Cut the word lines and you will hear their voices. Cut-ups often come through as code messages with special meaning for the cutter. Table tapping? Perhaps. Certainly an improvement on the usual deplorable performance of contacted poets through a medium. Rimbaud announces himself, to be followed by some excruciatingly bad poetry. Cut Rimbaud's words and you are assured of good poetry at least if not personal appearance.

All writing is in fact cut-ups. A collage of words read heard overheard. What else? Use of scissors renders the process explicit and subject to extension and variation. Clear classical prose can be composed entirely of rearranged cut-ups. Cutting and rearranging a page of written words introduces a new dimension into writing enabling the writer to turn images in cinematic variation. Images shift sense under the scissors smell images to sound sight to sound sound to kinesthetic. This is where Rimbaud was going with his color of vowels. And his "systematic derangement of the senses." The place of mescaline hallucination: seeing colors tasting sounds smelling forms.

The cut-ups can be applied to other fields than writing. Dr. Neumann in his *Theory of Games and Economic Behavior* introduces the cut-up method of random action into game and military strategy: assume that the worst has happened and act accordingly. If your strategy is at some point determined . . . by random factor your opponent will gain no advantage from knowing your strategy since he cannot predict the move. The cut-up method could be used to advantage in processing scientific data. How many discoveries have been made by accident? We cannot produce accidents to order. The cut-ups could add new dimension to films. Cut gambling scene in with a thousand gambling scenes all times and places. Cut back. Cut streets of the world. Cut and rearrange the word and image in films. There is no reason to accept a second-rate product when you can have the best. And the best is there for all. "Poetry is for everyone" . . .

Now here are the preceding two paragraphs cut into four sections and rearranged:

ALL WRITING IS IN FACT CUT-UPS OF GAME AND ECONOMIC BEHAVIOR OVERHEARD? WHAT ELSE? ASSUME THAT THE WORST HAS HAPPENED EXPLICIT AND SUBJECT TO STRATEGY IS AT SOME POINT CLASSICAL PROSE. CUTTING AND REARRANGING FACTOR YOUR OPPONENT WILL GAIN INTRODUCES A NEW DIMENSION YOUR STRATEGY. HOW MANY DISCOVERIES SOUND TO KINESTHETIC? WE CAN NOW PRODUCE ACCIDENT TO HIS COLOR OF VOWELS. AND NEW DIMENSION TO FILMS CUT THE SENSES. THE PLACE OF SAND. GAMBLING SCENES ALL TIMES COLORS TASTING SOUNDS SMELL STREETS OF THE WORLD. WHEN YOU CAN HAVE THE BEST ALL: "POETRY IS FOR EVERYONE" DR NEUMANN IN A COLLAGE OF WORDS READ HEARD INTRODUCED THE CUT-UP SCISSORS RENDERS THE PROCESS GAME AND MILITARY STRATEGY, VARIATION CLEAR AND ACT ACCORDINGLY. IF YOU POSED ENTIRELY OF REARRANGED CUT DETERMINED BY RANDOM A PAGE OF WRITTEN

WORDS NO ADVANTAGE FROM KNOWING INTO WRITER PREDICT THE
MOVE. THE CUT VARIATION IMAGES SHIFT SENSE ADVANTAGE IN
PROCESSING TO SOUND SIGHT TO SOUND. HAVE BEEN MADE BY ACCI-
DENT IS WHERE RIMBAUD WAS GOING WITH ORDER THE CUT-UPS
COULD "SYSTEMATIC DERANGEMENT" OF THE GAMBLING SCENE IN
WITH A TEA HALLUCINATION: SEEING AND PLACES. CUT BACK. CUT
FORMS. REARRANGE THE WORD AND IMAGE TO OTHER FIELDS THAN
WRITING.

Cold Lost Marbles

my ice skates on a wall
luster of stumps washes his lavender horizon
he's got a handsome face of a lousy kid
rooming houses dirty fingers
whistled in the shadow
"Wait for me at the detour."
river . . . snow . . . someone vague faded in a mirror
filigree of trade winds
cold white as lace circling the pepper trees
the film is finished
memory died when their photos weather worn points of
polluted water under the trees in the mist shadow of
boys by the daybreak in the peony fields cold lost
marbles in the room carnations three ampoules of
morphine little blue-eyed twilight grins between his
legs yellow fingers blue stars erect boys of sleep
have frozen dreams for I am a teenager pass it on
flesh and bones withheld too long yes sir *oui oui*
craps last map . . . lake . . . a canoe . . . rose tornado in
the harvest brass echo tropical jeers from Panama
City night fences dead fingers you in your own body
around and maybe a boy skin spreads to something
else on Long Island the dogs are quiet.

"What Washington? What Orders?"

Old Sarge: "All right you Limey has-been I'm going to say it country simple. You have been taken over like a Banana Republic. Your royal family is nothing but a holograph picture projected by the CIA. What is its purpose? Well what is the purpose of the Pope for you Catholics good and bad standing with John 23 like a good soldier in the presence of your captain. Any way you slice it it's a grovel operation the way we like to see them I mean what we are doing while the Pope and the other Holies keep the marks paralyzed with grovel rays is one of mysteries you cannot understand the mercy of God we don't intend to be here when this shithouse goes up maybe I'm talking too much about private things family matters you might say and that's what we call the good old CIA the Family. When the prodigal son creeps back disillusioned from Peking.

Information known.

Expel barbarian.

Well the Family will forgive him if he is sincere in his hear on a lie detector . . .

"Well we're going to take you back."

The old ham fixes him with blue eyes like steel in sunlight.

"Just don't ever let us down again."

From here to eternity the old game of war. Where would the Family be without it? So we can whittle off a little something to keep the royal family projected in Limey Land can't we now? So the Queen needs more money? Well humm call a story conference . . . Just how are we slanting this B.J.?"

B.J. (Doodling muscle boys) . . . "Nothing new. Just keep it going. They do need more money otherwise they will go down in the same spiral as everybody else and they wouldn't be the royal family any more could wind up in a semidetached in Darlington. They are supposed to be a supernatural family religious figures in fact and the more potent in that they are not acknowledged as such. Just ask an upper-class English about the royal family and he goes all huffy and vague

"It's not important . . . "

"Who *cares* about Philip."

"Can't stand that chap Tony."

"But you want the royal family to continue as such?"

(B.J. bulges a jockstrap)

"Well uh yes we are a *monarchy* . . . excuse me . . ."

"What about this million a year?"

"We're all together in this . . . couldn't abolish titles and keep the royal family . . . We've had to take cuts . . . Why shouldn't they take a cut too . . ."

Mutiny in the ranks? . . . (He doodles a boy pealing off plastic tits) It could come to that . . . (He doodles a boy looking at another boy's ass. A light bulb attached to his head lights up) . . . So why not put the royal family in a Darlington semidetached on a middle-class income and let them prove themselves in a TV serial . . .

Philip and the Queen are doing all right. She is known as Queen to all the nabors where she runs a small grocery shop. Every customer receives the same gracious smile and quick inquiry as to the family she is good at remembering things like that and keeping a line moving at the same time she learned that shaking millions of hands. Philip sells ecology equipment to factories . . . Good at his work and believes in it . . . strong middle-class message there Charles is a successful pop singer. Why they all get knighted in the end one way or another and the wind-up is back in Buckingham stronger than ever . . .

CIA Black: "Don't you think there is some limit somewhere to what people will stand still for? Suppose the ecology equipment doesn't work? Suppose the Queen's gracious smile is reserved for her white customers she has eyes for Enoch Powell and flying saucers . . . Suppose Bonny Prince Charlie . . ."

"For Chrisakes we're building them up not down . . . the *Family* . . ."

"All right call in the special effects boys and give them supernatural powers . . ."

"Never go too far in any direction is the basic rule on which Limey Land is built. The Queen stabilizes the whole sinking shithouse . . ."

"I tell you anything that is not going forward is going out
. . . You know what we can do with special do with the word.
Talk about the power in an atom. All hate all fear all pain all
death all sex is in the word. The word was a killer virus once.
It could become a killer virus again. The word is too hot to
handle so we sit on our ass waiting for the pension. But some-
body is going to pick up that virus and use it . . . *Virus B-
23* . . ."

"Aw we got the Shines cooled back with Che Guevara in a
19th-century set . . ."

"Is that right? And you got the Tiddlywinks cooled too? You
can cool anybody else who gets ideas? You going to cool this
powder keg with your moth-eaten Queen? I tell you anybody
could turn it loose. You all know how basically simple it is . . .
Sex word and image cut in with death word and image . . ."

"Yeah *we* could do it."

"But what about Washington? Our orders?"

"Just one test tube and SPUT . . . What Washington? What
orders?"

My Face

Let me say at the outset that I have for many years been
concerned with the possibility of taking over a young body I
would wake up stretch and look in the mirror the lookout dif-
ferent just enough of the other thoughts and feelings left to
make it really new you understand a dream old and banal as
the fountain of youth so on this day I left the house on Ladue
Road. After the death of my father the grounds have gone
down and the garden is overgrown with weeds. On this day I
walked out and was not particularly surprised to find things
changed as if a new landscape had been substituted for the old
like a film backdrop. Walking at random I came around three
in the afternoon to an inn of sorts something between an En-
glish pub and a company cafeteria. There was a small bar with
fireplace but the dining room was like a barn with zinc-topped

tables. This room was almost empty here and there a few people drinking tea and reading newspapers. However the tables were all set as if many more were expected. I sat down and noticed that the sugar was grey and the tableware had the greasy black feel common to jails, orphanages, mental hospitals or other institution canteens. There was only one waiter and he immediately engaged my attention. He was about 19 years old with thin red hands and wrists. His face was splashed with red and his hair was sandy. He must be called Pinkie I decided. He showed me a menu on white paper splashed with gravy and I ordered roast lamb and mashed potatoes. It was as I recall quite tasteless. After the meal I called him to the table and with an assurance unknown to me ordinarily asked if he would be interested to aid me in an experiment he would be paid of course in any case he could decide for himself after we had discussed the details and where could we be private for a few minutes after he had finished work. He said that he was finished now and we could talk in his room. He led the way up stairs with worn red carpeting and brass strips. Room 18 on the top floor. Bleakly clear in the afternoon light an unmade bed, tarnished mirror over a washstand, a hot plate, a cup half-full of cold coffee in which floated the remains of a cigarette butt. He motioned me to a chair sat down on the bed and pulled a package of cigarettes from his shirt pocket. He lit one for himself and blew out the smoke.

"All right. Let's have it."

I explained that as soon as I saw him I had realized he was the person I was supposed to meet the one who could help me in an experiment of transference which would be of benefit to both of us perhaps of incalculable benefit but in all fairness not without danger.

"You mean we change places like?"

"Something like that . . ."

"Well what's the pay-off?"

I told him that I was prepared to pay him an immediate retainer of one hundred dollars but that much larger sums would be involved in the event of success, perhaps incalculable sums.

I handed him five twenty-dollar bills which he shoved into his pocket without comment.

One thinks of such operations as involving electrical apparatus from a Frankenstein film, unknown drugs, bizarre sexual practices. It was nothing like that. I knew what to do and the apparatus was in my head, a triangle of light the apex of which extended about three feet and fitted into his head precisely at the source point. I felt a click and shift of outlines. The waiter was lying on his back head on the grimy pillow. I took off his shoes and covered him with a pink blanket. I walked over to the mirror. My movements seemed to require almost no effort. I was looking at my face in the mirror my new face. It was not exactly Pinkie's face nor mine. In fact I would hesitate to say that it was a face at all. Only the eyes were noticeable and these had a curious droop not unlike the eyes of a drug addict except that there was power and purpose in them. I saw also a red tie that I had not been wearing. Out on the stairs I hardly felt the worn carpet under my feet. The restaurant was deserted. I stepped in and suddenly the plates on the nearest table were whipped away as if by a great wind and crashed against the opposite wall. For a moment the Chinese cook appeared in the doorway. He looked at me, said one word in Chinese and closed the door. Again. As I proceeded through the restaurant crockery and silverware was swept from the tables on both sides of my path. I opened the side door and stepped out into a cobblestone alley. The day had been clear when I arrived at the inn. Now there were a few clouds in the sky. I had not reached the main road before the clouds had gathered and the sky darkened. As I stepped out of the alley rain fell in torrents. I don't know how long I walked around in the rain. Later much later I was looking into the mirror again rain dripping from my coat. I could see only the red tie and the drooping eyes. I turned toward the bed. Pinkie was still there under the blanket. I walked over and looked at him. I pulled the blanket back and felt a sudden pang in the heart and a prickling sensation at the back of my neck. He was thinner much thinner the ribs clearly visible under his open shirt. He opened his eyes and sat up. Then he said two words which I cannot bring myself to repeat.

Later we were outside in the road. He was silent now and sullen.

"I will see you soon" I said.

He just nodded looking down at the cobblestones. Walking with difficulty stumbling on the stairs I found my way back to the room. When I woke up it was four in the afternoon. You understand his room chair by the bed three cigarettes in a shirt pocket garden outside in the afternoon light. I splashed some water on my face my new face and went downstairs. Standing in the stuffy little bar were two well-dressed men. They called me over.

"I am Lord Bothby and this is Doctor Harrison." We shook hands. "We would like to talk to you for a few minutes."

I said "All right" without enthusiasm. We sat down at a table by the cold fireplace. The two men ordered Scotch and I had a pint of bitters.

"I will come straight to the point" said Lord Bothby.

"You see we know who you are."

"In that case you know more than I do."

"Exactly. You need our help."

"To do what exactly?"

"You may not realize the importance of the discovery you have made the uh success of your preliminary experiment. It is in your power to shape the entire future of this planet."

"Does it have a future?"

"That will depend on you . . . whether you are willing to accept expert guidance and do what is necessary. You must be prepared to lay aside all preconceptions of a sentimental nature."

In a flash I saw the emaciated body of the waiter under a torn pink blanket and realized that as the "experiments" continued the body would be always more drained. And then?

As if anticipating my thought Lord Bothby said "When the present subject is no longer serviceable we will know where to find another. The power must be guided."

I almost said "If you know so much more than I do why do you need me?" However I had already perceived that Lord Bothby and Doctor Harrison were nothing but film extras and

I might see his lordship a few days from now behind the bar of some pub and the learned doctor driving a hack. Looking past them I glimpsed a far flung organization with unlimited funds and well-trained ruthless agents. I would do well to exercise caution. I thanked them for their interest and promised to consider carefully what they had told me and to meet them here on Friday afternoon. Afterward I took my leave and went to the kitchen where I told the Chinese cook I would be taking the day off. He just nodded without looking around. I knew I would find Pinkie in my house on Ladue Road. He was sitting in the downstairs living room reading a science-fiction magazine. He greeted me apathetically. I had hoped he would prove an ally against the two agents and the organization they represented. In this I was disappointed. He listened to my account without interest shrugged and lit a cigarette. A wave of depression and horror swept over me.

"Look Pinkie I don't want to go on with this. There must be a way back. I'd be willing to reverse roles anything you like."

"I don't know anything about it" he said sullenly. "It was your idea not mine." After a meal of tinned beans and tea we went to the upstairs bedroom where my father died and made love. I remember it was dim and sad like making love to an empty body. Looking up at the dark ceiling lit occasionally by the headlights of passing cars phrases in my mind flat trite phrases from some old science-fiction magazine. "They called me. Doctor Harrison." Shook hands without enthusiasm looked sullenly at the floor turned abruptly away lighting a cigarette far flung organization ruthless agents unlimited funds you may not realize the importance of the Chinese preliminary experiments greeted me without interest in the gathering shadows incalculable sums the grimy pillow I took my leave. The last word is written lost voice whispering in the living room that night of stale cigarette smoke a moment palpable in the air years later I remember London the grimy stations and the tracks your name remains as the human structure not a word is mine I have no words left breathing old pulp magazines in the living dust of the dead Gods lonely fringes of a remote galaxy a million light-years away the pale skies fall apart T.B. waiting at the next stop spit blood at dawn is it later I remember London grimy pants open I pulled at my face in the mirror my new face agony to remember the words "Too Late." Don't you understand overgrown with weeds a long time. Do you begin to see there is no face there in the tarnished mirror? I was waiting there pale character in someone else's writing they called me years later your name remains breathing in these trite phrases. T.B. waiting at the next stop pale emaciated body of the waiter. Remember the boy who used to whistle? bleakly clear the suburban gardens mirror over a cheap chest of drawers. I was waiting there. "They called me. Doctor Harrison." Led the way up. Head on a grimy pillow phantom voice whispering in the living room. "Too late." Agony to remember the old human structure dim buildings overgrown with vines.

I remember a room where the lights wouldn't turn on and later in Mexico City I see myself on a street looking at him as if trying to focus to remember who the stranger was standing under a dusty tree thin boy ruffled brown hair light blue eyes blank factual I remember London grimy pants open stairs worn red carpeting the smell of oranges and I could see his pants were sticking up between his legs far pale sun the wind ruffled brown hair a colored photograph and something written . . . "*Vuelvete y aganchete*" . . . I let myself go limp inside blank factual he slid it in out through the little dusty window pale light over worn-out hills the old broken point of origin St Louis Missouri smell of sickness in the room head on the grimy pillow a million light-years away there was nothing for me to do his head on a pillow spit blood at dawn.

"They called me. Doctor Harrison."

Remember what hope feels like I was sitting by the bed the last words face very pale breathing into the mirror . . .

Then he said something: your name

Pulled the blanket up: my face

And there he is again walking around some day later across the street smiled round the corner so long ago the old grey corner blurred sadness in his eyes the corner shop I was walking behind him at the corner said something . . . one word . . . no dice flickered across his good bye his mouth a little open there looking for a name it is getting dark boy burglar spots the door open.

"Abrupt question brought me Mister."

Desolate thin blue overcoat far to go a street sadness in his eyes looking for a name . . .

Click of distant heels . . .

from My Education

I am involved in some fraudulent scheme in Canada to market some drug to cure alcoholism. The company chairman is reading into a telephone or microphone. "We are at war. We are under siege." Nobody about in this great empty building . . . dusty and dirty but large. I have been promised $128 to write some blurb for the company. I say: "I haven't been paid!" Then a woman comes into my room that opens off a large hall and gives me $500, she says. It looks like stage money. I can't even find any numbers on the lower-denomination, one-dollar bills. Figure I better ask the bank if the note is genuine before I try to cash it.

Meanwhile the police have arrived in huge vans, high as two house stories, and everyone crowds to the window, looking down onto the street. Looks like Lower Broadway seen from a second-floor loft. Brion says: "Well, we can stay here for a hundred and five dollars per month and the directors will beat any charges, because they are Elliots."

He needs to conserve his Sek. They call it "ammo" here. The Sek has to be pure or it won't discharge. Essential to avoid the deadly distractions: sentimentality which is secondhand affect, "made in Hollywood" self-glorification. Then he starts saying: "Looka me! Looka me!" You have to look fast. He won't be there long. Like waving around a .25 in a room full of .45s. The survivor doesn't want to be looked at. Doesn't want to be seen. By the time he is close enough to be seen, there won't be anybody to see him.

I harbor deep distaste for scientists. Give me a worldly cultured priest any day, and twice on Sunday . . . and not some timorous old beastie, cowering in the eternal lavatory of a dead universe.

"Dreams mean nothing," Crick croaks, "just neural housecleaning. The quicker we forget our dreams the better." He's telling me *my* dreams, where I get my best sets and characters, are meaningless. Meaningless to whom, exactly? They can't even think straight. As if "meaning" floats about in a vacuum, with no relation to time, place, or person. Science is as riddled with underlying dogmas and outright falsifications as Catholicism. More so, in fact. The most basic dogma is that the human will cannot possibly produce any physical effects. "No death wish can ever be effective." No? Anybody who keeps his eyes open sees people wished to death all the time.

"No one seriously says that the rituals of a shaman can produce any changes in the weather." Quote is from an article in *New York Times*. Don't recall writer or subject. He has obviously swallowed the implicit dogma hook, line, and blinkers. I have seen weather magic. I have even performed weather magic.

It follows from the above-mentioned dogma that ESP *must* be invalid. One scientist said he would never believe in telepathy, no matter what evidence he was offered. John Wheeler takes up arms against ESP, complaining that he has enough trouble observing his fucking photons without ESP buzzing around his ears, and signals transmitted faster than the speed of light.

That nothing can exceed the speed of light is another scientific dogma, more hallowed and inviolate and immaculate than the Immaculate Conception or the Holy Ghost. So I flick a switch and a light goes on or off, ten light-years away. "Impossible to exceed the speed of light." Don't have to. Simple matter of synchronicity. After all, we've come a ways since the Rothschilds got dirty rich from signals reflected on mirrors across the channel to France. One is way beyond such primitive cause-

and-effect modes of communication. In fact, the whole concept of communication is antiquated.

Another inviolate dogma is mortality. "The only thing that gives dignity and meaning to life is death," said an English physicist. He's shoving it down all our throats, not "from my viewpoint" or "my opinion," but THE ONLY. The Hallowed Mould, or you might call it the Immaculate Rot.

This English one I read in a book review years ago, and here is John Wheeler, only yesterday: "There is no picture without a frame. No life without death." Same song, but not so clearly stated. Perhaps Wheeler did not have the advantage of a classical education.

What have I done in my life? Scratched a few surfaces. Not ready to be framed yet.

Severe pain last night and this morning. Left side, down the left arm and up into the jaw. Classical heart attack symptoms, but a previous attack was diagnosed by Dr. Gray as emphysema . . . a bubble bursting in the lung. Painful, but not dangerous. However, Dr. Gray misdiagnosed James' classic appendicitis. Fortunately, Michael got him to the emergency room in time. So I think it is time to seek a second opinion. Will call the other doctor tomorrow.

I have been to a concert with Kerouac and others. What others? Where? I can't remember. What time is it? Six o'clock? Have I had breakfast?

A large dusty room like a löft. Sitting now at a table. Some strawberries and sugar on a plate. A shift, a bag on the table. I extract a chocolate-covered confection shaped like a scarab, two inches long and an inch thick. I bite into it. The inside is white, creamy, with a taste of coconut, marzipan, opera cream, inhumanly delicious with a tingle of glancing sweetness. I know I can eat the whole bag and then want more more more, consumed by insatiable craving. I can sit there and eat and eat until the toothsome tangy cream dissolves my teeth and bones down to a churning, slobbering maw of ravening hunger.

A rowboat in a lake or a lagoon. The water is gray and dead calm, slick as glass but still the boat is moving further and further out until I can barely see the shore. There must be a current like a surface river. Gray sky now, and gray water to the horizon.

Find myself in ancient Rome talking to Cicero, who complains that the situation is unstable and dangerous. He would prefer a little peace. He has a long nose, like a figure in a painting I did yesterday, and I notice now that the figure, which is black on white, has a suggestion of a toga.

There is a room where no females are allowed. This is a permanent location, you might say, no females in here ever—and when I go in, I am leaving the whole male/female world forever. Eternal farewells. There is a serving bar between this room and the area where I am. Some women are sitting there, and I say: "Stand aside!"

They do, and I climb over the bar, but behind me I can hear other female voices saying that they do not agree to my departure. The room into which I have climbed is small like the kitchen here. But there is a door beyond. The voices still complaining from the outside area.

A series of my paintings is based on the mystery of the *Mary Celeste*. The brigantine *Mary Celeste* was sighted under full sail off the Azores in 1872. A boarding party found the ship deserted. (One lifeboat and the ship's compass were missing.) The cargo of alcohol was untouched. The ship left Halifax for Lisbon with a crew of thirteen. The captain's wife was on board. The *Mary Celeste* was towed to Gibraltar, where a board of inquiry was held.

A number of theories were advanced. Pirates? Then why was the cargo untouched? Alcohol, as cooking fuel, is readily saleable in the area: Spain, Portugal, Morocco. Sea monsters? Egotism? Perhaps alien abduction? After reading *Communion* and *Breakthrough* by Whitley Strieber, I became seriously interested in alien landings and abductions. I visited him and spent a weekend at his cabin. After talking with him and his secretary and reading the *Communion Newsletters*, I was convinced that the aliens, or whatever they are, are a real phenomenon. The abductions, in several accounts, involved sexual contacts. Indeed, that would seem to be their purpose.

AMIRI BARAKA

||||||||||||||||||||||||||||||||||||||||||||||||||||||||||||||||||||||||||||||||||||||||||||||||||||||||||||||||||||||||||||||||||||

AMIRI BARAKA (LeRoi Jones) was born in 1934 in Newark, New Jersey. He grew up in Newark's industrial wasteland, attended Howard University in Washington, D.C., and did a stint with the U.S. Air Force before settling in Greenwich Village in the late fifties. In a blaze of activity he wrote poetry, a novel, short fiction, music reviews, cultural criticism, and plays. In 1964 his play *Dutchman* won the Obie Award, and in 1965 he published *Blues People,* a landmark study of the social origin of the blues. He edited *Yugen* magazine and founded Totem Press, which published early books by Philip Whalen, Gary Snyder, Frank O'Hara, Jack Kerouac, Allen Ginsberg, and a range of other bohemian and Beat poets. After the assassination of Malcolm X in 1965, Baraka moved to Harlem, and founded the Black Arts Repertory Theatre. The next year he returned to Newark to found Spirit House Movers Congress of Afrikan People and Jihad and People's War Press. Influenced by African nationalism and the Sunni Islam of Malcolm X, he was given the religious name he has used since that time. A tireless "cultural worker," Baraka is always on the edge of a politics that is being shaped by art—too far ahead of the politicians for them to understand. The FBI has for decades kept a meticulous file on his activities. His poetry, incendiary social critiques, and writings on music all work to define the Marxist-Leninist Third World Socialism he aligns himself with.

In 2002 Baraka was named New Jersey's third poet laureate. However, his poem "Somebody Blew Up America" suggested Israel had foreknowledge of the 2001 terrorist attack on the World Trade Center and led to a furious controversy in the state. Demands for Baraka's resignation failed, as did attempts to fire him, but in 2003 the state legislature removed him by eliminating the poet laureate post.

Preface to a Twenty Volume Suicide Note

(for Kellie Jones, born 16 May 1959)

Lately, I've become accustomed to the way
The ground opens up and envelopes me
Each time I go out to walk the dog.
Or the broad edged silly music the wind
Makes when I run for a bus . . .

Things have come to that.

And now, each night I count the stars,
And each night I get the same number.
And when they will not come to be counted,
I count the holes they leave.

Nobody sings anymore.

And then last night, I tiptoed up
To my daughter's room and heard her
Talking to someone, and when I opened
The door, there was no one there . . .
Only she on her knees, peeking into

Her own clasped hands.

1957

State/meant

The Black Artist's role in America is to aid in the destruction of America as he knows it. His role is to report and reflect so precisely the nature of the society, and of himself in that society, that other men will be moved by the exactness of his rendering and, if they are black men, grow strong through this moving, having seen their own strength, and weakness; and if they are white men, tremble, curse, and go mad, because they will be drenched with the filth of their evil.

The Black Artist must draw out of his soul the correct image of the world. He must use this image to band his brothers and sisters together in common understanding of the nature of the world (and the nature of America) and the nature of the human soul.

The Black Artist must demonstrate sweet life, how it differs from the deathly grip of the White Eyes. The Black Artist must teach the White Eyes their deaths, and teach the black man how to bring these deaths about.

> We are unfair, and unfair.
> We are black magicians, black art
> s we make in black labs of the heart.
>
> The fair are
> fair, and death
> ly white.
>
> The day will not save them
> and we own
> the night.

1965

from Cuba Libre

Preface

If we live all our lives under lies, it becomes difficult to see *anything* if it does not have anything to do with these lies. If it is, for example, true or, say, honest. The idea that things of this nature continue to exist is not ever brought forward in our minds. If they do, they seem, at their most sympathetic excursion, monstrous untruths. Bigger lies than our own. I am sorry. There are things, elements in the world, that continue to exist, for whatever time, completely liberated from our delusion. They press us also, and we, of course, if we are to preserve the sullen but comfortable vacuum we inhabit, must deny that anyone else could possibly tolerate what we all agree is a hellish world. And for me to point out, assuming I am intrepid enough, or, all right, naïve enough to do so, i.e., that perhaps it is just this miserable subjection to the fantastic (in whatever fashion, sphere, or presence it persists) that makes your/our worlds so hellish, is, I admit, presumption bordering on insanity. But it is certainly true . . . whether I persist or no . . . or whether you believe (at least the words) or continue to stare off into space. It's a bad scene either way.

(What I Brought to the Revolution)

A man called me on a Saturday afternoon some months ago and asked if I wanted to go to Cuba with some other Negroes, some of whom were also writers. I had a house full of people that afternoon and since we had all been drinking, it seemed pretty silly for me to suddenly drop the receiver and say, "I'm going to Cuba," so I hesitated for a minute, asking the man just why would we (what seemed to me to be just "a bunch of Negroes") be going. For what purpose? He said, "Oh, I thought that since you were a poet you might like to know what's *really* going on down there." I had never really thought of anything in that particular light. Being an American poet, I suppose, I thought my function was simply to talk about everything as if I knew . . . it had never entered my mind that I might really like to find out for once what was actually happening someplace else in the world.

In Memory of Radio

Who has ever stopped to think of the divinity of Lamont
    Cranston?
(Only Jack Kerouac, that I know of: & me.
The rest of you probably had on WCBS and Kate Smith,
Or something equally unattractive.)

What can I say?
It is better to have loved and lost
Than to put linoleum in your living rooms?

Am I a sage or something?
Mandrake's hypnotic gesture of the week?
(Remember, I do not have the healing powers of Oral
    Roberts . . .
I cannot, like F. J. Sheen, tell you how to get saved & *rich!*
I cannot even order you to gaschamber satori like Hitler or
    Goody Knight

& Love is an evil word.
Turn it backwards/see, see what I mean?
An evol word. & besides
who understands it?
I certainly wouldn't like to go out on that kind of limb

Saturday mornings we listened to *Red Lantern* & his undersea
    folk.
At 11, *Let's Pretend*/& we did/& I, the poet, still do, Thank
    God!

What was it he used to say (after the transformation, when he
    was safe

& invisible & the unbelievers couldn't throw stones?) "Heh,
     heh, heh,
Who knows what evil lurks in the hearts of men? The Shadow
     knows."

O, yes he does
O, yes he does.
An evil word it is,
This Love.

Hymn for Lanie Poo

> *Vous êtes de faux Négres*
> —Rimbaud

O,
these wild trees
will make charming wicker baskets,
the young woman
the young black woman
the young black beautiful woman
said
          These wild-assed trees
          will make charming
          wicker baskets.

(now, I'm putting words in her mouth . . . tch)

1

All afternoon
we watched the cranes
humping each other
                    dropped
                    our shadows
                    onto the beach
and covered them over with sand.

Beware the evil sun . . .
turn you black

turn your hair

crawl your eyeballs

rot your teeth.

All afternoon
we sit around
near the edge of the city
                    hacking open
                    crocodile skulls
                    sharpening our teeth.

The god I pray to
got black boobies
got steatopygia

make faces in the moon
make me a greenpurple &
maroon winding sheet.
                    I wobble to
                    the edge of the water
give my horny yell
& 24 elephants
stomp out of the subway
with consecrated hardons.

(watch out for that evil sun
turn you black)
                    My fireface

my orange
and fireface
squat by the flames.
She had her coming out party

with 3000 guests
from all parts of the country.
Queens, Richmond, Togoland, The Cameroons;
A white hunter, very unkempt,
with long hair,
whizzed in on the end of a vine.
(spoke perfect english too.)

"Throw on another goddamned Phoenecian,"
I yelled, really getting with it.

John Coltrane arrived with an Egyptian lady.
he played very well.

"Throw on another goddamned Phoenecian."

We got so drunk (Hulan Jack
brought his bottle of Thunderbird),
nobody went hunting
the next morning.

    2

o,
don't be shy honey.
we all know
these wicker baskets
would make wild-assed trees.

Monday, I spent most of the day hunting.
Knocked off about six, gulped down a cou-
ple of monkey foreskins, then took in a
flick. Got to bed early.

Tuesday, same thing all day. (Caught a
mangy lioness with one tit.) Ate.
Watched television for awhile. Read the
paper, then hit the sack.

Wednesday, took the day off.
Took the wife and kids to the games.
Read Garmanda's book, "14 Tribes of
Ambiguity," didn't like it.

Thursday, we caught a goddamn ape.
Must've weighed about 600 pounds.
We'll probably eat ape meat for the
rest of the month. Christ, I hate
ape meat.

Friday, I stayed home with a supposed
cold. Goofed the whole day trying to
rethatch the roof. Had a run in with
the landlord.

We spent the weekend at home.
I tried to get some sculpting done,
but nothing came of it. It's impos-
sible to be an artist and a bread
winner at the same time.
Sometimes I think I oughta chuck
the whole business.

  3

The firemasons parade.

(The sun is using this country
as a commode.

Beware the sun, my love.)

The firemasons are very square.
They are supposed to be a civic
and fraternal organization, but
all they do is have parades and
stay high. They also wear funny

looking black hats, which are
round and have brims. The fire-
masons are cornballs.

4

Each morning
I go down
to Gansevoort St.
and stand on the docks.
I stare out
at the horizon
until it gets up
and comes to embrace
me. I
make believe
it is my father.
This is known
as genealogy.

5

We came into the
silly little church
shaking our wet raincoats
on the floor.
It wasn't water,
that made the raincoats
wet.
>   The preacher's
>   conning eyes
>   fired when he saw
>   the way I walked to-
>   wards him; almost
>   throwing my hips out
>   of whack.
>   He screamed,

He's wet with the blood of the lamb!!

And everybody
got real happy.

6

(die schwartze Bohemien)

They laught,

and religion was something

he fount in coffee shops, by God.

It's not that I got enything

against cotton, nosiree, by God

It's just that . . .
                    Man lookatthatblonde
                                        whewee!

I think they are not treating us like

Mr. Lincun said they should
                            or Mr. Gandhi

For that matter. By God.

                    ZEN

is a bitch! Like "Bird" was,
                            Cafe Olay

for me, Miss.

                    But white cats can't swing . . .

Or the way this guy kept patronizing me—

like he was Bach or somebody
                            Oh, I knew

John Kasper when he hung around with shades . . .

She's a painter, Man.

It's just that it's such a drag to go

Way uptown for Bar B Cue,
By God . . .

How much?

7

About my sister.
>   (O, generation revered
>   above all others.
>   O, generation of fictitious
>   Ofays
>   I revere you . . .
>   You are all so beautiful)

my sister drives a green jaguar
my sister has her hair done twice a month
my sister is a school teacher
my sister took ballet lessons
my sister has a fine figure: never diets
my sister doesn't like to teach in Newark
    because there are too many colored
    in her classes
my sister hates loud shades
my sister's boy friend is a faggot music teacher
    who digs Tschaikovsky
my sister digs Tschaikovsky also
it is because of this similarity of interests
that they will probably get married.
>   Smiling & glad/in
>   the huge & loveless
>   white anglo sun/of
>   benevolent step
>   mother America.

1957

Crow Jane

"Crow Jane, Crow Jane, don't hold your head so high,
You realize, baby, you got to lay down and die."
—Mississippi Joe Williams

For Crow Jane
     Mama Death.

For dawn, wind
off the river. Wind
and light, from
the lady's hand. Cold
stuff, placed against
strong man's lips. Young gigolo's
of the 3rd estate. Young ruffians
without no homes. The wealth
is translated, corrected, a
dark process, like thought, tho
it provide a landscape
with golden domes.

               'Your people
without love.' And life
rots them. Makes a silence
blankness in every space
flesh thought to be. (First light,
is dawn. Cold stuff
to tempt a lover. Old lady
of flaking eyes. Moon lady
of useless thighs.

Crow Jane's Manner.

          Is some pilgrimage
to thought. Where she goes, in fairness,
"nobody knows." And then, without love,
returns to those wrinkled stomachs
ragged bellies / of young ladies
gone with seed. Crow

will not have. Dead virgin
of the mind's echo. Dead lady
of thinking, back now, without
the creak of memory.

                  Field is yellow. Fils dead
(Me, the last . . . black lip hung
in dawn's gray wind. The last,
for love, a taker, took my kin.

Crow. Crow. Where
you leave my
other boys?

Crow Jane In High Society.

                   (Wipes
her nose
on the draperies. Spills drinks
fondles another man's
life. She is looking
for alternatives. Openings
where she can lay all
this greasy talk
on somebody. Me, once. Now
I am her teller.

                (And I tell
her symbols, as the grey movement
of clouds. Leave
grey movements
of clouds. Leave, always,
more.

Where is she? That she
moves without light. Even
in our halls. Even with
our laughter, lies, dead drunk

in a slouch hat famous king.
                              Where?

To come on so.

Crow Jane The Crook.

Of the night
of the rain, she
reigned, reined, her
fat whores and horse.

(A cloud burst,
and wet us. The mountain
split, and burned us. We thought
we were done.

                    Jane.
Wet lady of no image. We
thought, you had left us. Dark
lady, of constant promise. We
thought
you had gone.

    2

My heart is cast in bitter
metal. Condiments, spices
all the frustration of earth.
that has so much more desire

than resolution. Want than pleasure.
Oh, Jane. (Her boat bumps at the
ragged
shore. Soul of the ocean, go out,
return.
Oh, Jane, we thought you had gone.

The dead lady canonized.

               (A thread
of meaning. Meaning light. The quick
response. To breath, or the virgins
sick odor against the night.

               (A trail
of objects. Dead nouns, rotted faces
propose the night's image. Erect
for that lady, a grave of her own.

               (The stem
of the morning, sets itself, on
each window (of thought, where it
goes. The lady is dead, may the Gods,

               (those others
get our forgiveness. And Damballah, kind father,
sew up
her bleeding hole.

from **Wise/Whys/y's**

Wise 5

    Breaks
    Baby Dodds

I overheard the other night
standing by the window
of the big house

a nigra say, through an alabaster
mask, "the first negro
was a white man."

Slanty red darts angulate the darkness
my hands got cold, my head was sweaty

like a mystery
story
like a gospel
hymn
like the tales
of the
wizards
and the life
of the gods

I did not know
who my father
was

I only barely
knew
my mother

But I knew something that night
about a negro
something even
the tv cant wash
away

I fount out something
about the negro

the wind may blow
the train dont come
the mayor might belch
his mistress might gain weight

But I fount out something that night
about the negro
& the world
got clear

you can hurray all you want to
you can kiss an elephants ass

But I fount out something
that night, before I slid
back to the field hands quarters
I fount out somthing
about
the magic
of slavery

& I vowed not to be
a slave
no more

Wise 6

> *Jimmy's Blues*
> Grachan Moncur III

Has we come far?

We has come far.

How we got there

How we got where?

Who we talkin bout?

What they name?

Oh, the slave peepas
you the slave peepas

Who the slave peepas
Just the same.

Struggle in dark, come down
the road. Knew your life
your sorrow. Knew your singing
in the dark. Knew the whip

that scarred you. And the century
change, alright, alright, the
years go by in light in darkness

there's white peepa voice behind my air
claim I should be free. They peepas hang out
in the north somewhere, dont need no bread
from the big house man. They voice hang
in the air.

But thas alright, alright wit me.
I preciate all of that.

Thas alright, alright wit me
But I been gone, naw, I been gone

my shape look like black on black
and fading

Wise 7

> *The Four Man*
> "Papa" Jo Jones

Back in the forest

the maroons laid

outraged by slavery, & split

from it, when the bombs burst

across the air, and fire tore

mens hearts, they knew some new

joint change was upon the time

and so emerged, a gun in one hand,

something funky, in the other.

Wise 8

Mojo Hand
Lightnin Hopkins

From the country
to the city, we left
where things
were pretty—to get away from
the klansmen, and race freaks who
hung with the Slavemasters' cause
who could not believe in democracy
who would not let life be beautiful
who howled moon shadows screaming
for the primitive. Who climbed the trees
for past centuries, hollering for caves
and blood. From the country, to the city
we left where things were
pretty. Got city life, got city bred
wanted rights and services (get to that,
we thought) when all the time
it coulda been better, when all the time
new cdda been, built cdda been, progress
cdda been, and all the great notes of peace
all the great notes of peace
    all that
        cdda
            been

Wise 9

God Don't Never Change
Rev. Pearly Brown

our war
was for
liberation
to end
slave times

now war
is over
we free
they say

who they
who say
what free
gone be?

there are cities
we can go to

there are cities
of light and newing

So what these faces laws hover
these swine wind law death people
these death time rebs return to crow
these slavemaster corpse leap off the flo
these sheet face coward monster haints
these death word carriers and slave lovers

there was war
before
be war
again
died before
will die again

but not gon' die
not gon' leave
not gon' cry too long
not gon' grieve
free is who we are and be
love who what will lift us we
struggle love struggle—against primitive death
while you walking round
spirit death tie you down
slave death and servant death and let me work for us to be

Wise 10

> *Do, Lord, Remember Me*
> Rev. R. Wilkins

So in 1877 the lie grew
we all knew
the heart dead
the lie instead

They talked blood
They put on hoods
They paid for murder
They closed the books

No democracy
No light
primitive times
returned

across the road
the horse men prowled
American guns for African American lives

You'll never vote
you'll never grow

you'll never never never
be free   never
be free
          never
be free
          never
          never
          never
                              Enter Booker T.

Rough Hand Dreamers (Wise 11)

Milneburg Joys
Jelly Roll Morton
          "I, myself, happen to be the Creator
          (of Jazz) in the year 1902."
                    —JRM (Fernande LaMenthe)

You was a country folk, on the
land. Farmers before farmers
founders of cities, ile ife,*
where the world began. Was creator
of university, I trumpet timbuctoo
because I cannot bear to think
you think Banneker was wilder
than the breed. It was the women
conceived of familiar cows and
architecture. Yon drummers know
how they are hide curers & musicians.

Now they enter the cities to enter future
reality. Now death, now blood, now hooded
criminals, resistance in its human dimension
like electric theories, post all abrahams.

*Ile Ife was an ancient holy Yoruba city.

What was it we wanted = Ourselves!
And why? We had been inside others being alive
for nothing
and worked to death
    our murders
    were circuses
    our murderers
    something like
    clowns

A *farmer come to the city (Wise 12)*

    High Society
    "Old" George Lewis

dirt growing in his mind
songs black land come in to
curl your poetry blind.
Banjo
waves and sinking bones
play eyes on sky
blood music

heaven people
say see heaven
they seeing
up side down

now they say we fought for evil
took our guns, the wise ones hid, say you
never was to be here
you never was to be

kept to edge of city
alleys behind the bossman's
house. got a job, you got a space,
you got a bond to heal your face

changed from slave
to convict, gone
from lazy to vagrant
jail lost boy in sleep
jail house/plantation moan
jail, was how they changed it
we
vote among roaches

Wise 13

>   *Mr. Pinetop's Boogie*
>   Pinetop Smith

And now you know
how "ghettoes"
grow

$$\diagdown \mid \diagup$$
— SCREAM —
$$\diagup \mid \diagdown$$

(you knew
(how ghettoes)
grew?   )

(Reality
for "you"
is minstrelsy.)

When Miles Split

Someone called me and said you died, Miles. Yeh, that cold. Here in North America, with all the other bullshit we putup with. You know. I know you know. Knew. And still know, where ever you is.

I'm one of yr children, actually, for all the smoke and ignorant mimmyjimmies . . . you know / I can say that. I was one of yr children / you got a buncha children man, more than you probably dug on the serious side. Not innocent ass fans. But the school of the world you created from inside the world's head. You gotta buncha children brother. I still am. Will be. In some important ways. For instance, I will never take no shit. Yr legacy. I will never believe anybody can tell me shit. Unless they are something I can feel. Like Aretha said. Something I can feel. You were that. I cd feel you, I cd be you when I was a little boy, up the street with the trumpet bag. I wanted to be in that music. I wanted to be that hip, that out, that whatever it was I felt you were. I wanted to be that. All my life.

What it was was the place and the time. But it was you describing it with your feeling. For me that place was New ark, where we grew, and then here you come so hip. I cd dig that I needed to be that, but more, I knew, I was that. I was with you in that fingering, that slick turn and hang of the whole self and horn. And the sound. I had never been in that place, there wasn't no such place in Newark, before.

I mean I never thought of the shit you made me think with *Godchild.* I never thought of nothing before like *Venus De Milo.* There was nothing in my life like that before you brother. And then the persona, what it all spelled. Yeh, I wanted to look like that. That green shirt and rolled up sleeves on *Milestones.* That cap and seersucker on *Dig* I always wanted to look like that. And be able to play *Green Dolphin Street* or *Autumn Leaves* or *Walkin* or *Blue Haze* or *Round Bout Midnight,* or yeh yeh yeh yeh hey, even the mammy jammin *Surrey With The Fringe On Top,* as whatever he wanted, as tiny lyric, or cooler than thou, hot pointillist funkmares, cubist, expressionist, impressionist, inhabiting your being into a plane of omniscient downness (dig that!)

It was the self of us all the way without anything but our saying, our breath, night times, or walking where we was. We could be whole and separate from any dumb shit. We could be the masters, the artists, the diggenist knowers, the suave, the new, the masters.

This is what art doos. Your voice, that out sharp growl. That was how art should dig itself to be talking. *So What* is probably a prayer in the future.

I held my horn like that, and rolld my body like an ark of music, just looking at things. The cool placement of emotion.

The information. I carried that consciously. No one could put me down, I was Miles child. His man. somehow. anyway.

And then each change, stage, was a path I wd walk. When I heard you as a little boy. Then went to see you. You was me alright. You was one of the few I could let be me.

Now some motherfucker wannta tell me you outta here. No. No. Miles. Why. You left. So right away I figure none of the shit still here is cool. But dig, Dizzy and Max is still here. So that's the pain. And I know I dig you. I know I carry *Dr. Jackle* in my speech. And *Godchild* and *Miles Ahead* and *Kinda Blue* and even *Porgy and Bess,* somethin Gershwin cdnt do.

Cause no one was that tender, that touching the where touch cd ultimately is.

They taking all the Giants. You. Trane. Duke. Monk. Billie. Your whole band is dead, man. Paul. Philly Joe. Cannonball. John. Red. Your whole band. and what does that do to us, but leave us on the shore watching the waves, and trying to write music from that regular funk.

But what it says is that our youth is gone. That we are the adult. What that? That you have it in yr hand now, to do. That if it will go, this life, this memory and history, this desire for freedom and a world family. That's its on you.

Like I dug, when Philly Joe hattd up. On us. If we are the ones. If it is to be, something other than the savages and bush mens. Then we got to. The giants. Our fathers and mothers. Sassy split last year. Monk. Count. LTD. If it is to go then we are the goers. The comers. In that whole sound and thought. That life that makes the blues. That makes the dark hip, the roll and rumble. Yeh. Then if, all that long two hundred centuries of slick, is to be on bein. Then we are the only carriers.

I cd dig the way you walked and held that horn. That gorgeous chilling sweet sound. That's the music you wanted playing when you was coming in a joint or just lookin up at the sky w/ yr baby by yo side. That mixture of America and Remerica and them Changes, them blue Africa magic chants. So I am a carrier. I got the stick. I aint stopping. If you, whoever else you tapped, then them too.

Headline the Giants are murdered. Then we got it. All of

those who finally must dig, dont say it brother, truth and beauty. But who am I talkin to if you split, Miles, Man, and what the fuck is there to listen to? (OK, everything.)

Except you did leave jabillion ultra hip notes, 70 billion swift blue cool phrases. And how many millions of unheard dig'its, them nasty nasty silences right in the middle of the shit. Bee-bee beep beeppp., ba dee da dee da . . .

So what about it, like they say in the tradition, what about it, is Miles and them, John, Duke, Monk, Sassy all, the giants, does it mean our shit is over with? I know about the records and shit. I'm not talking about that. Does it mean, with the crazies vampin and now even some things look like regular nig-gers can break out with bushy tongues. Where before with your cool Boplicity in our heads it was somehow not only soft yet sharp yet gentle but like a weapon against such square shit as most of the rest of America is. That all of you giant figures that we emulate and listen to and hear and visualize night after night inside our heads, from the nightclubs, the concert halls, the bars, the records, the t.v. . . . is this, your death, like some hideous omen of our own demise, and I mean everybody here, not just niggers, cause if we go, this whole playhouse go up in smoke.

No, I mean either this death is the beginning of death in cut time, or it means that one earth has turned and another begun. One age, one era, one being. Listening to you now, and know-ing that whole of change you went through, from life to life, from music to music, from revelation to revelation, even evolu-tion can be dissolution or devolution.

But you was Bop when you got here, flyin w/the human headed soul Ba, Bird, the doped up revolutionary. Next, you was Cool. It was like your own creation yet, of course, very Presidential. Then you got with Philly and them for the harder Bop and then got Ball, the Dis Heah and Dat Dere of we funky story. Then you sic'ed the straight out vision monster on us Trane, in that perfect wonderful all time classical hydrogen bomb and switch blade band. Let us all always be able to hear *Straight No Chaser* anytime we want to.

I know the last few years I heard you and saw you dressed

up all purple and shit, it did scare me. All that loud ass rock and roll I wasnt in to most of it, but look brother I heard *Tutu* and *Human Nature* and *D Train*. I heard you one night behind the Apollo for Q, and you was bashin like the you we knew, when you used to stand coiled like a blue note and play everything the world meant, and be in charge of the shit too. I'll always remember you like that Miles, and yr million children will too. With that messed up poppa stoppa voice, I know you looken up right now and say (growl) So What?

The Next Evening
9/29/1991

LAWRENCE FERLINGHETTI

||||||||||||||||||||||||||||||||||||||||||||||||||||||||||||||||||||||||||||||||||||||||||||||||||||||||||||||||||||||||||||||||||||||||||||||

LAWRENCE FERLINGHETTI was born in 1919 in Yonkers, New York. He graduated from the Sorbonne, Paris, where he studied on the G.I. Bill. In an astute business move, Ferlinghetti set up City Lights with Peter Marin in San Francisco, modeled on the bookshops of Paris; it was the first bookshop in the United States devoted exclusively to paperback books. City Lights quickly became a publishing house as well, its Pocket Poet series publishing Kenneth Rexroth, Robert Duncan, Denise Levertov, Gregory Corso, Jack Kerouac, Allen Ginsberg, Gary Snyder, and much modern European poetry in translation. When the publication of Ginsberg's *Howl* drew down the wrath of the authorities, Ferlinghetti attended the obscenity trials and wrote about it for *Evergreen Review* in 1957. Ferlinghetti has worked tirelessly on the political front. He championed Castro's revolution, visiting Cuba in 1960, then visited Nicaragua two decades later as a sympathetic investigator of the Sandinista revolution. He continues to publish cutting-edge poets and writers through City Lights and also paints. In 1994, a street in San Francisco's North Beach was renamed Via Ferlinghetti in his honor. In 1998 he was named Poet Laureate of San Francisco. In 2003 he was awarded the Robert Frost Memorial Medal and the Author's Guild Lifetime Achievement Award, and he was elected to the prestigious American Academy of Arts and Letters. Ferlinghetti's book, *A Coney Island of the Mind* (1958), is one of the best-selling books of poetry ever published.

Pound at Spoleto

I walked into a loge in the Teatro Melisso, the lovely Renaissance salle where the poetry readings and the chamber concerts were held every day of the Spoleto Festival, and suddenly saw Ezra Pound for the first time, still as a mandarin statue in a box in a balcony at the back of the theatre, one tier up from the stalls. It was a shock, seeing only a striking old man in a curious pose, thin and long haired, aquiline at 80, head tilted strangely to one side, lost in permanent abstraction. . . . After three younger poets on stage, he was scheduled to read from his box, and there he sat with an old friend (who held his papers) waiting. He regarded the knuckles of his hands, moving them a very little, expressionless. Only once, when everyone else in the full theatre applauded someone on stage, did he rouse himself to clap, without looking up, as if stimulated by sound in a void. . . . After almost an hour, his turn came. Or after a life. . . . Everyone in the hall rose, turned and looked back and up at Pound in his booth, applauding. The applause was prolonged and Pound tried to rise from his armchair. A microphone was partly in the way. He grasped the arms of the chair with his bony hands and tried to rise. He could not and he tried again and could not. His old friend did not try to help him. Finally she put a poem in his hand, and after at least a minute his voice came out. First the jaw moved and then the voice came out, inaudible. A young Italian pulled the mike up very close to his face and held it there and the voice came over, frail but stubborn, higher than I had expected, a thin, soft monotone. The hall had gone silent at a stroke. The voice knocked me down, so soft, so thin, so frail, so stubborn still. I put my head on my arms on the velvet sill of the box. I was surprised to see a single tear drop on my knee. The thin, indomitable voice went on. I went blind from the box, through the back door of it, into the empty corridor of the theatre where they still sat turned to him, went down and out, into the sunlight, weeping. . . .

Up above the town
                    by the ancient aqueduct
    the chestnut trees
                    were still in bloom
        Mute birds
                    flew in the valley
                                far below
        The sun shone
                    on the chestnut trees
        and the leaves
                turned in the sun
        and turned and turned and turned
            And would continue turning
    His voice
                went on
                    and on
                            through the leaves. . . .

Ladakh Buddhess Biker

The Ladakh Buddhess is watching me
with her witchy eyes
on the corner of Columbus & Broadway
A gold button on her temple
between the eyes with the blue pupils
her eyes with blue eyebrows
not designed to blink
her eyelids like fenders
on old Oldsmobiles
her corneas red and blue
as if from loving & weeping too much
over our samsara
Eternally feminist
her headlight eyes beam at me
as if the sight of me
might make her finally

lower those heavy lids
I notice now she's seated on
a huge hog called Harley
her leather legs hugging its body
in a retro lotus position
Suddenly the traffic light changes
and she roars off still unblinking
through the late late traffic
of our Kali Yuga age

Cro-Magnons

Cro-Magnons carried stones for books
And a flat dark stone I came upon
was one in which I read
the carbon copy histories
of creepy man
in the fine print of fossils pressed
between the stone's aged pages
the first syllables of recorded time
made into burning messages
about the first decline and fall
and the dissent of species

so that
when I cracked it open I surprised
the shadow of a lizard on the steps
of an Alexandrian branch library
burning on the broken stone
in a bright daze of sunlight
And in a flicker of that lizard's loose tongue
in one cooled instant of carbonized time
deciphered eternity

Third World Calling

This loud morning
    sensed a small cry in
      the news
          paper
      caught somewhere on
       an inner page
           I
    decide to travel for lunch &
    end up in an automat
        White House Cafeteria
looking thru a little window
  put a nickle in the slot
    and out comes
          fried rice
Taking a tour
  of the rest of that building
  I hear a small cry
    beyond the rice paddies
      between floors where
        the escalator sticks
and remember last night's dream of
  attending my own funeral
  at a drive-in mortuary
  not really believing
    I was that dead
  Someone throwing rice
      All the windows dry
Tipped the coffin open & laughed
          into it
    and out falls
      old funnyface
       myself
      the bargain tragedian
  with a small cry

followed by sound of Che Guevara singing
   in the voice of Fidel

Far over the Perfume River
                    the clouds pass
      carrying small cries
The monsoon has set in
               the windows weep

     I
      back up to
           the Pentagon
   on a flatbed truck
and unload the small brown bodies
        fresh from the blasted fields!

Baseball Canto

Watching baseball
sitting in the sun
eating popcorn
reading Ezra Pound
and wishing Juan Marichal
would hit a hole right through
the Anglo-Saxon tradition
in the First Canto
and demolish the barbarian invaders
When the San Francisco Giants take the field
and everybody stands up to the National Anthem
with some Irish tenor's voice
piped over the loudspeakers
with all the players struck dead in their places
and the white umpires like Irish cops
in their black suits and little black caps
pressed over their hearts
standing straight and still

like at some funeral of a blarney bartender
and all facing East
as if expecting some Great White Hope
or the Founding Fathers
to appear on the horizon
like 1066 or 1766 or all that
But Willie Mays appears instead
in the bottom of the first
and a roar goes up
            as he clouts the first one into the sun
                and takes off
                    like a footrunner from Thebes
        The ball is lost in the sun
                and maidens wail after him
                    but he keeps running
                        through the Anglo-Saxon epic
And Tito Fuentes comes up
        looking like a bullfighter
        in his tight pants and small pointed shoes

And the rightfield bleachers go mad
        with chicanos & blacks & Brooklyn beerdrinkers
            "Sweet Tito! Sock it to heem, Sweet Tito!"
And Sweet Tito puts his foot in the bucket
            and smacks one that don't come back at all
            and flees around the bases
        like he's escaping from the United Fruit Company
        as the gringo dollar beats out the Pound
            and Sweet Tito beats it out
            like he's beating out usury
            not to mention fascism and anti-semitism
And Juan Marichal comes up
    and the chicano bleachers go loco again
        as Juan belts the first fast ball
            out of sight
                and rounds first and keeps going
        and rounds second and rounds third
                        and keeps going

and hits pay-dirt
to the roars of the grungy populace
As some nut presses the backstage panic button
for the tape-recorded National Anthem again
to save the situation
but it don't stop nobody this time
in their revolution round the loaded white bases
in this last of the great Anglo-Saxon epics
in the *Territorio Libre* of baseball

A River Still To Be Found

Stoned &

singing Indian scat

with Ravi Shankar

(as if we knew him)

his sitar like a boat

by the 'river of life'

that flows on & on

into 'eternity'

Time itself a boat

upon that river

Slow distant figures

drawing barges

along those banks

the small drum a pulse

beating slow

under the skin

And our bodies

still in time—

transported—

dreamt eternal

by the Ganges

a river

still to be found

in the interior

of America

from Work-in-Progress

And Pablo Neruda
            that Chilean omnivore of poetry
            who wanted to
                    put everything in
                        and take nothing out
                            (of his *Canto General*)
        said to me in Cuba Libre Hilton 1959
                            'I love your wide open poetry'
        by which he meant a certain kind of
                    poesia norteamericana

and its rebel band who
rose over the rooftops of
tenement boneyards
intent on making out
And made out of madness
a hundred years of beatitude

'So boring I'm snoring'
cried Joe Public
before *they* came along
and busted out the sides
of Poetry Chicago
and various New Yorkerish
poetasters
out of their Westchester cradles
endlessly rocking
on the Times Square Shuttle
between the Times Book Review
and the Algonquin
while lady critics and professors
moaned about poetic pederasts
at Columbia
They cruised Times Square and America
and cruised into history
'waving genitals and manuscripts'
And tuned their holy unholy voices
to a wide open society
that didn't yet exist
And so jump-started
the stalled merrygoround
of American ecstasy
left along East River's
echoing shores
after Old Walt stepped off
Brooklyn Ferry
into the heart of America

JOANNE KYGER

||||||||||||||||||||||||||||||||||||||||||||||||||||||||||||||||||||||||||||||||||||||||||||||||||||||||||||||||||

JOANNE KYGER was born in 1934. She moved to San Francisco's North Beach in 1957, where she was actively involved with Robert Duncan, Jack Spicer, and other writers of the San Francisco Renaissance. Her first book, *The Tapestry and the Web,* was published by Don Allen. In 1960 she traveled to Japan, where she married Gary Snyder. She belonged to the American expatriate scene in Kyoto, which included poets Cid Corman, Clayton Eshleman, Will Petersen, members of the First Zen Institute, Ruth Fuller Sasaki, the scholar Burton Watson, and others. Kyger traveled to India with Snyder, Ginsberg, and Orlovsky. She returned to San Francisco in 1964, spent periods of time in New York City, and settled in the late sixties in the fishing village of Bolinas, north of San Francisco Bay. A longtime student of Buddhism, Kyger developed a dry, witty, incisive form of poetry, drawn from daily journal writing practices, among other sources. The poems include studies of California history and natural history, observations of weather, readings in a range of subjects, and the odd comings and goings of neighbors and friends. She has taught at New College of San Francisco's Poetics program and is a regular teacher at Naropa University's Jack Kerouac School. In 2006 she received a Lifetime Achievement Award from Small Press Traffic. Kyger has been an active citizen of her Bolinas community, editing the *Hearsay News,* teaching workshops, organizing readings and study groups, and taking on environmental issues. She has been generous to and supportive of younger writers for decades.

The Maze

I saw the
dead bird on the sidewalk
his neck uncovered
and prehistoric

At seven in the morning
my hair was bound
against the fish in the air
who begged for the ocean
I longed for their place

Behind the
tall thin muslin of the curtain
we could see his shadow
knocking
and we waited
not stirring
crouched by the fireplace
where the ashes blew out

later we checked the harbor
to see if it was safe
rather hoping
one had gone astray
and flung itself upon the shore
for all to watch

If I should weep
they would never know

and so I walked
silently
shrugging off hands
in treacherous places
                    wanting to fall

In Williamsburg, Virginia

my uncle
pointed out the Maze
which grew
in the dead
            governor's garden

delighted

I went to it

and stood
poised

inside the
precise
entrance
like a long hallway
the tightly trimmed
bushes
held themselves
pointing each
leaf
and twig
in an unquestioning manner

white gravel
caressed my feet

the sky disappeared
and I

could hear
the sound of water
rushing

I knew each corner
without pausing

Held captive in a cave
Ulysses
sobbed for his wife
who was singing high

melodies
from the center of a
cobweb shawl
of their design

three feathers
I picked
from a stone
in my path

and turning at last
I saw
the speckled bench
and halting fountain
which marked
the end.

                        She

tortures
        the curtains of the window
                    shreds them
                    like some
                                    insane insect

creates a
           demented web
       from the thin folds
       her possessed fingers
           clawing   she
       thrusts them away with
       sharp jabs   of long pins
                       to the walls.

1958

Pan as the Son of Penelope

Refresh my thoughts of Penelope again.

Just HOW
       solitary was her wait?

I notice Someone got to her that

           barrel chested he-goat prancing
           around with his reed pipes

is no fantasy of small talk.
More the result of BIG talk

           and the absence of her husband.

And what a cockeyed lecherous offspring.   What a birth
           THAT must have been.   Did she turn away & sigh?

I believe she dreamed too much.   Falling into her weaving,
           creating herself as a fold in her tapestry.

       a flat dimension character of beauty
       keeping one task in mind and letting nothing HUMAN
                       touch her
—which is pretend.

She knew what she was doing.

OUTSIDE
of that he grabbed her.

Some thing keeps escaping me. Something
about the landing of the husband's boat upon the
shore.

She did not run up and embrace him as I recall.

He came upon her at the house & killed the
suitors.

I choose to think of her waiting for him
concocting his adventures   bringing
the misfortunes to him
—she must have had her hands full.

And where did she hide her impudent monster?

He was acres away by then I suppose in the sunlight leching
at some round breasted sheep
girl.
The cock crowing at dawn never had bigger thoughts
than he did
about waking up the world.

Caption for a Miniature

Outside where the storm goes cracked
he says you can't come in
hold the baby under your sari
and I'm going to sit up here and watch you
in this purple velvet lined tower of
mine, and look at the fruit tree

and watch all the red and yellow pears and
cherries jiggle when it lightnings and
after while maybe I'll have
the chokidar bring up some tea and a plum
and a whole bunch of candy and stuff
and you'd just better stay down there
and get all crummy and muddy.

from The Japan and India Journals

January 7, 1962

Up at 5:15 to see The Mother—stand on balcony.

Meditation last night consisted of middle aged men in blue
shorts and white shirts making a ridiculous spectacle walking
up and down doing exercises. Young men and girls also in uni-
forms. Lights go off. People rise and face map of Mother India.
Seated again, organ music creaks out played (recorded) by the
Mother for 15 minutes. Last 10 minutes or so in silence then
dinner. Curds, vegetables and rice.

I feel constantly to be on the brink—not of understanding—a
much bigger feeling begun on that day when I saw the clouds
break while on the train to Kadoma and thought I am me, here,
now—or more felt a sense of it. And the religiousness of India
seems to bring it out more.

January 8, 1962. Monday

Rise 5:30. The Mother on the balcony. She is in different colors
this morning with white 1920's veil around her head. Yesterday
a green one. Everyone looking up watching her face for 15 min-
utes—enough to make anyone feel strange. She first gazes
slowly all over everyone, then focuses in the distance over their
heads for 10 minutes or less. Then gazes with a smile over
everyone then backs away.

In 1920 the Mother first took management of the Ashram into her hands. She first came to Pondicherry in 1914 with her husband, and left in 1915. Sri Aurobindo died December 5, 1950.

January 10

Sethna visits with Beverly for two hours discussing Sri Aurobindo's philosophy. On November 24, 1926, the *over mind* descended and was planted firmly into Sri Aurobindo. In 1938 he and the mother brought down the *supermind* but were unable to fix it permanently here. In 1956 it descended permanently. The Mother brought it down while she was in the play yard at night meditation. It will work itself out in future evolution to make matter as perfect as the spirit has become under intense meditation. Man will become like an angel here, deathless and not subject to the frailties the human body is now subject to.

January 11, 1962. Thursday

Rise at 4:30 for Tiruvanimalai;—good bus. One pack under seat, one on top of bus. Leaves 5:30. The bus stops. Something has splatted onto the window bars a few seats back of us. A few clumps of dirt have hit the back of my head. Conductor climbs off and lifts with stick a piece of rotting meat off the bars, picked up while passing a tree.

Arrive 10:30. And walked to Osbornes, who had been expecting us later in the evening. House covered with bright bougainvillea. Dry arid countryside with stone hill rising due south. The real heart of India.

They are followers of Sri Ramana Majarshi, whose doctrine is similar to the Zen method, Who am I. Who is it that asks those questions. Preaches loss of ego. They think The Mother a nut who possibly practices black magic of occult type. And Aurobindo very confused in his thinking. Have disdain for the Pondicherry ashram.

But use the same kind of blind enthusiasm for Maharshi as the Pondicherry people do for the Mother and Aurobindo.

The Brahmin School boys sit in front of the Samadhi of Maharshi chanting the Vedas—5 young boys. Their front heads shaved and stripes of ash across their foreheads and arms. Dot of vermillion in the center of their brow. Very rhythmic, almost syncopated chanting. Bored, they squirm around and stare, scratching themselves while they chant.

January 12, 1962. Friday

Gary and I after Tamil breakfast at ashram of sweet milk coffee, two cups in brass containers and a sour rice cake, tasting like slightly soured cream of wheat eaten with a chili powder and a little ghee in it.

Walked up hill behind to where Maharshi meditated in the twenties to a cave house, a spring came out when he was there from the side of the hill.

Lunch at the ashram with the Osbornes on mats of leaves sewed together. He is so tall and white and English with the peculiar pomposity of Englishmen. She is Czech, kind of erratic and volatile, over generous.

Curry and ghee and sauce. And buttermilk in bowl.

After a rest on the roof under bougainvillea, we circumambulate *Arunachala,* the hill, barefoot, from 3:30 to 7:30 PM. Stopping on the way back at the main temple. An enormous construction. In the moonlight feeding the holy elephant bananas in the inner courtyard. He has white ash stripes across his forehead and a vermillion mark. If you give him a coin he will bless you with his trunk—tapping it on your head. It all feels like a movie set.

A wide dry flat plain around the hill—the heart of India—with tall thin palm trees and many old and ruined shrines and temples.

March 1

Rishikesh! Much mail. After early morning fight with Gary, back to bed. Knocked over pail of water. Washed my hair and bathed and washed clothes in stream coming through the woods. The stream from a spring and emptying into the Ganges. A young boy comes by with sheep carried around his neck over his shoulders. Is he whistling to get my attention?

Sivananda from his padded chair directs them to put flower wreath around my neck. And gives us each envelope with Rs 5 in it.

March 2, 1962

Sadhus sitting in meditation, red eyes, matted hair up by the bridge. How can they sit so still says Allen. Gary changes last of my color film exposing by accident last pictures. Losing the following:

1. Portrait of Gary with wet hair, Allen behind in the Ganges.
2. Peter swimming, Allen & Gary bathing.
3. Gary meditating in sand, Allen standing on tall rock in background.
4. Allen, Peter, Gary sitting on bathing steps on Sivananda's side of river.
5. View from lodging across to other side of river from hill where we spent the first night at Rishikesh
6. Gary in front of Agra Fort Pearl Mosque

March 3, 1962

Made Indian style tea on spirit burner—milk, tea, sugar, boiled together, for us all. And rolls with jam and peanut butter. Studying maps. Always windy in the early morning here. And today cloudy and cool. Bird hops through the window looking for crumbs.

Reading Allen's article from *Second Coming*. "When the mode of music changes, the walls of the city shake."

Afternoon all of us on roof on hill. Ganges and small mountains behind us, on the Sivananda side. Swami Sri Lingam doing yoga asanas for us. The eyes, the mouth, being exercised. Great red meaty mouth.

Cows and bulls outside the door, one pins Allen to the gate. Peter pets them.

Chapter II from some book by Tim Leary at Harvard University Center for Research in Personality, who turns everyone onto mushroom pills. Pages peppered with words like: sweet loving guy, sweet new therapy, fine loving afternoon. He says he loves the poets but from the way he writes about them he turns them into unattractive foolish asses, drops just enough phrases through the mouths of others to show how he feels—no baths, big phone bill. Not very bright. Probably wants to write or be spiritual in big way—and envies Burroughs, Ginsberg—who he basically hates—covering it up with gooey admiration. 'Allen Ginsberg, Zen master politician.' Constantly harps on the poorer physical aspects of Allen—thin, glasses, white, stooped shoulders. 'Hung, like me, on doing good.'

March 4, 1962

The rest into Hardwar to see the beginning of Kumba Mela. Terrific wind. Gloomy. Fuzzing of time. I could step back into Brentano's stock room.

Reading *Kim* all day between bouts of laundry. A grey heavy wind dries the clothes on the porch. Lugging buckets from the faucets at the pumps. Soaking the clothes for 30 minutes in the room and back to rinse and bringing back a fresh bucket for new laundry soaking. Sleeping bag liners, shawl, Gary's parka, and on.

April 8

Guided tour bus to Ellora. A young affected guide with an umbrella furled speaks in English but mostly Hindi, constantly urging us to hurry hurry. Completely exhausted, dragging my self through the Buddhist, Brahmin and Jain temples. All of them were painted.

Lunch stop where there is no food to buy.

The Hinayana Buddhas of the Ajanta caves so unrelentingly religious. Puritanical and heavy. No grace at all. Whereas Sanchi had such life. And Ellora (Mahayana) where the Buddhas have a bit more grace—but somehow the caves are over all depressing.

Aurangabad's tomb, a simple plot of ground, covered and surrounded by the English in 1911 with a carved marble screen. Aurangabad, a great and fervent iconoclast sent men out to smash the noses of the Buddhas at Ellora.

Gary leaning, a high tiny speck from the tower at Daultabad Fort.

Come down.

 Then chipmunk approaches
& then runs away. Rats under the toilet pans
  at Ellora
     The flower
  fort.
    Now this path
  the grey lumps, Buddhas

    Pattern following
  the trident of shiva as
   electricity. The
 black Ethiopian. The
   sheep following. Indian
  men tweak each
   other on the ear. Their
 loud voices, flapping
   their hands their English
  another course, about emotion

     Swimming
  up stream against the current.

> Breaking against a
> law,   the muscles on my
>   shoulders always tense.
>
>   Pulling down all the Hindu
> gods, pulling down the
>   green foliage with her
>   hand, the bough
> brings a Buddha. The
>   large round breasts of
> the woman   I envy.

Gary's black cardigan, the one I mended and mended, because it was charcoal grey, for him to get married in, he left on purpose in the Sanchi RR room, holes in the sleeves too thin to be mended, the hot weather at last allowing him to discard it. The station attendant came after us with it. Peter gave it to an old man seated begging at the end of the platform, under a tree. He immediately put it on, examining himself in it. His upper body formerly naked.

Going through the subterranean passageway at the Daultabad Fort, the guide leading the way in close black darkness on either side. Extinguishes his torch. Gary brings out his flashlight. The guide relights the torch. We proceed, squeak of bats.

Occasionally we see a transvestite. A hard face of a man with make up and long hair drawn back in a knot, dressed in a sari.

Auerhahn putting out Lamantia's *Destroyed Works,* an omnibus of Wiener's this spring. Last book was *Dark Brown* of McClure with Fuck Ode and A Garland.

From a letter of Anselm Hollo to Ginsberg . . . "You say you met up with Gary Snyder—he was one of the first new American poets I picked up on five or six years ago—"Riprap"—later his Myths—great clarity *&* humor *&* strength, an un-solemn sage is how I see him in what I've seen of his writings— "Nordice" or something, too, Finn friends of mine dig him. Is he back in Kyoto now? or back to US?"

Vicious, unnecessarily vicious article in 'Time' about Ginsberg, Beats *&* poetry.

April 9

Yesterday we bicycled to Aurangabad caves, easy ride across land that looks like Morocco says Allen. Dry brown desert like land, palm trees, the bluffs in the distance with caves. The first group with a pool or pit at the top, square hole in the rock next to the cave entrance, clear to the bottom and then under rock for seven feet. Allen *&* Peter undress *&* go in *&* then Gary too. I stick my legs in. The second group of caves a mile away across a trail. A fine group of sculptures in good condition inside the Buddha chamber, dancing girls and women musicians. Outside big mother hipped, *&* full breasted Tara figures either side of the door. A tiny swallow has fallen out of his nest, the mother darts anxiously around it, it's too young to fly. Gary, concerned, places it in a more protected niche of rock. Downhill bicycle back, stopping at an ice cream parlor for 1½ bowls of nut ice cream each and an orange drink.

Every night dinner served on the veranda where it's cool. I always take the leftover chappaties to eat the next day with peanut butter and jam. Peter has an omlet since the opium he smoked locked up in the bathroom last night made him sick. Gary *&* I both on hard narrow bed under dusty heavy cotton mosquito net.

April 11, 1962

Letter to Nemi April 10, 1962

Hello Dear Nemi, Yass I got your letter before I left Japan and I bought you a lovely green sari which I will send you later from Japan. Please send me all your paintings in return. I cannot *stand* the Indian mentality, they are very 1930's and vile *&* bad tempered beyond BElief. Allen Ginsberg said he would like to hit his walking stick over the heads of some dirty little boys who were hanging around staring at us in a bus stall the other day. I have reviled them beyond words but unfortunately they don't understand fuck & get your shiteating asshole hands off my luggage & things like that. Actually the heat now makes one more foul. And when they're not trying to shine your shoes as you walk along or stuff a baby in your face through a train window or trample you to death trying to get a train seat before you, they are acting unbearable hoipoloi and asking you what part of the 'States' you're from, and telling you how screwingly SPIRItual they all are, and how they have two transistor radios in their family.

Nemi I do hope my humah was not so heavy handed in my last letter that you misinterpreted my zealous social and political goals. Do not worry. I still hate everybody.

Peter Orlofsky locks himself in the bathroom all night and smokes opium and then vomits all the next morning so we travel slowly.

We met the Dalai Lama last week right after he had been talking with the King of Sikkim, the one who is going to marry an American college girl. The Dal is 27 and lounged on a velvet couch like a gawky adolescent in red robes. I was trying very hard to say witty things to him through the interpreter, but Allen Ginsberg kept hogging the conversation by discribing his experiments on drugs and asking the Dalai Lama if he would like to take some magic mushroom pills and were his drug experiences of a religious nature until Gary said really Allen the inside of your mind is just as boring and just the same as everyone else's is it necessary to go on; and that little trauma was eased over by Gary and the Dalai talking guru to guru like about which positions to take when doing meditation and how to breathe and what to do with your hands, yes yes that's right says the Dalai Lama. And then Allen Ginsberg says to him how many hours do you meditate a day, and he says me? Why I never meditate, I don't have to. Then Ginsberg is very happy because he wants to get instantly enlightened and can't stand sitting down or discipline of the body. He always gobbles down his food before anyone else has started. He came to India to find a spiritual teacher. But I think he actually believes he knows it all, but just wishes he *Felt* better about it.

How is that veterinarian you were going out with. Has his wife had kittens yet/har har. I do think the masses stink, really I do Nemi, don't worry. We are leaving India immediately just as soon as we make ourselves unpopular with some rich girl Allen Ginsberg knows in Bombay who has an air conditioned apartment. If you could just *see* us, our appearance. I try to keep body and gentility together but it is getting spiritless since I have had to wear the same black dress for the last three months (I wear it all day *&* stay up half the night laundering it. I have discovered, by the way, that ironing is not really necessary, you just tell everyone that you just got up from a nap.) But Allen Ginsberg is running around in an unwashed white Indian (grey) pajama outfit with flapping arms *&* legs, or else very short shorts from Israel, and a Greek shirt and red nylon socks. He is balding on top, his curling hair down his neck. But if you think His hair is long, you should see Peter Orlofsky whose hair actually falls over his face to his nose in front (but that's all right because he can take drugs behind it easier) and down to his shoulders in back *&* a tee shirt, that doesn't quite cover 7 inches of his stomach in front and some tennis shoes full of holes without any shoe laces. The Indians for their own perverse reasons seem to adore him. Gary *persists* in wearing one gold earring. Whenever I see any other American tourists I am so embarrassed I could die. You see I am thoroughly middle class at heart and all I want to do is learn how to play bridge. Don Allen took all my poems for his next anthology, then later on asked *Gary* to ask me to send him a short biography, and absolutely no word to me. He's a Grove Press editor. If *someone* doesn't get famous out of my acquaintances my life will be just wrecked because all that bawdiness for no *purpose*. If I don't write a short pure jewel of a novel or get some poems published I'm going to Poison someone. Actually I've sent nothing out because my typing is so poor after working all those years with hangovers at Brentano's. There's no booze in India. I haven't had a drink for 4 months now . . . I dearly hope Time magazine pays no attention to us until I am in the foreground with my smart published novel and nifty green silk toreodor pants and all my jewelry from the Tibetan market. I weight 119 lbs *&* have crows feet at the corners of my lovely beatnik eyes. I am going to try those face recipes for rose petals you sent, very soon. Before its too late. The thing is, I am sounding rather bitter because its been *years* since I've been able to get any wild martini *attention*. All I do is stand around in this black drip dry dress in India.

You'll have to figure out how to wear the sari yourself, or you can make it into a dress or something. Tell me how you've arranged the studio. Have you painted it flat white yet? I am too repelled by the Indian to ask how to drape a sari. Actually the country itself and the things in it are quite lovely oh hell hell. I hope Dave B. doesn't take all of the price of your paintings in commission. Write SOOn. Love Joanne.

October 20, 1962. Saturday

5:15. Uncomfortable: untyped India journal. Things will never be assembled. I can only hope that I will write unceasingly well at certain periods and will be able to discard all those old uncorrected amounts stuck away.

Confused way of turning
   sentence until it changes its intention many times from the beginning and turns itself into a kind of maze. The intention bores me from the outset, turning in the hand like a bauble to catch a light; which way will surprise.

August 16, 1963. Friday

Daimonji night. 8:10. Gary still working. Starting dinner and cleaning up. Make a drink and sip. And go out to find music and singing coming from direction of cemetery. Out the front door into the dark—the four cats after me—into the temple (all shut up dark) and the graveyard. The music and singing loud and rhythmic. Through to the back—its over beyond the bamboo grove. Nansen meows in panic, lost from the rest. The second dai goes up in flames in the hills near us. Fudo, black, slipping in and out the freshly cleaned graves. Its Obon, the summer feast for the dead.

December 19, 1963

Death was a pied piper of multiple men going through a house which was a city. Everyone was waiting for him. I, going to find the best room or section to die. A bar with loud and noisy men. I left. It's not right to die there. Returned to a room which I had passed before, thinking this is the best place, where 3 or 4 young girls and an old woman were laying on quilts and sheets on the floor to wait death. Before, I had gone out into a big kitchen-house and thought to escape out the door and away. In a fenced area I encountered a mad man, bald with a purple-red furious face who was kept there. Let me in let me in, the door wouldn't open. The woman with glasses and grumpy let me back into her kitchen. Who's that I said. It's Khrushchev. Then to the room with quilts. Death with his flute could be heard coming nearer and nearer. I was getting a little nervous and tried to cover myself with a sheet to remain calm. One of the girls, Betty, got up at the last minute, dissarranging the bed and tried to dry a piece of laundry she'd done by waving it in the air. Lay down, the old woman said. It's silly to dry your clothes. You're going to die.

October 29, 1963, Wednesday

In a crowd of people I am suddenly elevated.   No matter that the crowd follows Ginsberg and Snyder, out on a quick demonstration march thru the halls of a tall building out into the gardens, their faces among the trees as little Chinese sages grained into the wood.   White walls, somewhat Grecian, if the fancy takes you.   I AM ELEVATING! from a cross legged position, I rise slowly off the ground in a crowd of people, easy as can be.   ELEVATED!   Mr. Ginsberg and Mr. Snyder frown, not so much?   As they are on their
     busy
way, as groups of people pour their respect and devotion to-wards them.   Pour, pour—they're busy drinking it up all day

in teacups.   Do you think we've sent these young ladies and
gentlemen in the right direction?   That is to say, haven't
we sent them in the right direction though.

                              With my back against a
                                  stone wall
in a courtyard, I am closing my eyes and—Now if you will
just observe me, I will move up off the ground, hopefully
as much as a foot, two feet, grind.   In my Tibetan bathrobe.
Silence.

Philip Whalen's Hat

I woke up about 2:30 this morning and thought about Philip's
hat.
      It is bright lemon yellow, with a little brim
      all the way around, and a lime green hat band, printed
      with tropical plants.
                        It sits on top
      of his shaved head. It upstages every *thing* & every *body*.
He bought it at Walgreen's himself.
I mean it fortunately wasn't a gift from an admirer.
Otherwise he is dressed in soft blues. And in his hands
a long wooden string of Buddhist Rosary beads, which he keeps
moving. I ask him which mantra he is doing—but he tells me
in *Zen,* you don't have to bother with any of that.
You can just *play* with the beads.

It's been a long time

NOTES FROM THE REVOLUTION

During the beat of this story you may find other beats.   I mean
a beat, I mean Cantus, I mean Firm us, I mean paper, I mean in

the Kingdom which is coming, which is here in discovery.

It is also Om Shri Maitreya, you don't go across my vibes,
but with them, losing the pronoun.   It is Thy, it is Three,
it is I, it is me.

Machines are *metal*, they serve us, we take care of them.   This
is to me, and this is to you.   You say you to me, and I say you
to you.   Some machines are very delicate, they are precise,
    they
are not big metal stampers. She made enough poetry to keep
her company.

My Vibes.   You intercepted my vibes.   The long shadows,
the long shadows, the long shadows.   My sweet little tone,
my sweet little tone is my arm.

On what Only: The song that girl sang the song that girl sang

———————————

News bulletin from Keith Lampe

Soon

Little Neural Annie was fined $65 in the Oakland
Traffic Court this season for "driving while in
a state of samadhi." California secular law requires
that all drivers of motor vehicles remain firmly seated
within their bodies while the vehicle is in motion.
This applies to both greater vehicles and lesser
vehicles.

———————————

Every day I burn a stick of incense
                    in front of
Kannon San.   She is Kwan Yin
She is Avalokiteshvara.   This is what
I know about some of her names.
She holds a bottle
in her right hand
by her side and has the other hand
raised up.   This she does
consistently
and without stopping.   I have read
about her but can't remember
it as really important

for how she affects me
as a dark little statue
I make an intelligent
pass at, when I bow
I mean I am hopeful
she evens off the demons.

Oh Holy Mary
how come you come
into my words
I was born with
and on the radio too.
Oh Holy Mary
you'll just say
I'm not a good enough
Christian
to go to heaven &
you look so sad
You are merely human
and wafted above us
the Queen of a big
church who staked out
the real estate
But then again what do I know

of my heart but that it is tight
and wishes to burst
past the wall of my chest

I am depressed, darling
the power of belief
is from me

LEW WELCH

||||||||||||||||||||||||||||||||||||||||||||||||||||||||||||||||||||||||||||||||||||||||||||||||||||||||||||||||||||||||||||||

It has been said that in the sixties you gauged a poet's serious-
ness by the distance Lew Welch's poetry lay from his or her
bed. Lew Welch was born in 1926 in Phoenix, Arizona. Raised
in California, Welch eventually enrolled in College of the Pa-
cific, where he encountered the work of Gertrude Stein. In
1948, he transferred to Reed College, where he roomed with
Gary Snyder and Philip Whalen. Welch studied literature and
calligraphy, and wrote his now-legendary bachelor's thesis on
Stein—recently published as *How I Read Gertrude Stein*. He
completed graduate studies at the University of Chicago and
then spent four years in advertising for Montgomery Ward. He
transferred to Oakland in 1958 and quit his job to resume life
as a poet. He lived in the East-West House, an early San Fran-
cisco experiment in communal living, where both Joanne Kyger
and Philip Whalen also spent time. Much of Welch's life was
devoted to traveling the United States, picking up odd jobs,
backpacking, studying Zen meditation, and trying to find ways
to live in a wilderness hermit's hut and write verse like old Chi-
nese poet-sages. He acquired acclaim as a reader and teacher
during the sixties in San Francisco, supporting himself by long-
shoreman's work on the docks and once with a stint on a fish-
ing boat. Welch's poems are collected in *Ring of Bone: Col-
lected Poems 1950–1971*. His essays are found in *How I Work
as a Poet*. There is also an unfinished novel, *I, Leo*, and his

letters appear in *I Remain: The Letters of Lew Welch with the Correspondence of His Friends.* In spring 1971, he drove to Nevada County to stay on Gary Snyder's land in the Sierra foothills, planning to build the small hermit cottage for which he had searched much of his life. But on May 23, gripped by depression, he took his revolver and vanished into the woods, leaving a brief note of farewell to his friends. His body has never been found. A Zen meditation hall built near Gary Snyder's house in the Sierra Nevada was christened Ring of Bone Zendo after one of Welch's poems.

This Book Is for Magda

What strange pleasure do they get who'd

wipe whole worlds out,

ANYTHING,
to end our lives, our

wild idleness?

But we have charms against their rage—
must go on saying, "Look,
if nobody tried to live this way,
all the work of the world would be in vain."

And now and then a son, a daughter, hears it.

Now and then a son, a daughter

gets away

Chicago Poem

I lived here nearly 5 years before I could
        meet the middle western day with anything approaching
Dignity. It's a place that lets you
        understand why the Bible is the way it is:
Proud people cannot live here.

The land's too flat. Ugly sullen and big it
        pounds men down past humbleness. They
Stoop at 35 possibly cringing from the heavy and
        terrible sky. In country like this there
Can be no God but Jahweh.

In the mills and refineries of its south side Chicago
        passes its natural gas in flames
Bouncing like bunsens from stacks a hundred feet high.
        The stench stabs at your eyeballs.
The whole sky green and yellow backdrop for the skeleton
        steel of a bombed-out town.

Remember the movies in grammar school? The goggled men
        doing strong things in
Showers of steel-spark? The dark screen cracking light
        and the furnace door opening with a
Blast of orange like a sunset? Or an orange?

It was photographed by a fairy, thrilled as a girl, or
        a Nazi who wished there were people
Behind that door (hence the remote beauty), but Sievers,
        whose old man spent most of his life in there,
Remembers a "nigger in a red T-shirt pissing into the
        black sand."

It was 5 years until I could afford to recognize the ferocity.
        Friends helped me. Then I put some

Love into my house. Finally I found some quiet lakes
and a farm where they let me shoot pheasant.

Standing in the boat one night I watched the lake go absolutely
flat. Smaller than raindrops, and only
Here and there, the feeding rings of fish were visible a hundred
yards away—and the Blue Gill caught that afternoon
Lifted from its northern lake like a tropical! Jewel at its ear
Belly gold so bright you'd swear he had a
Light in there. His color faded with his life. A small
green fish . . .

All things considered, it's a gentle and undemanding
planet, even here. Far gentler
Here than any of a dozen other places. The trouble is
always and only with what we build on top of it.

There's nobody else to blame. You can't fix it and you
can't make it go away. It does no good appealing
To some ill-invented Thunderer
Brooding above some unimaginable crag . . .

It's ours. Right down to the last small hinge it
all depends for its existence
Only and utterly upon our sufferance.

Driving back I saw Chicago rising in its gases and I
knew again that never will the
Man be made to stand against this pitiless, unparalleled
monstrocity. It
Snuffles on the beach of its Great Lake like a
blind, red, rhinoceros.
It's already running us down.

You can't fix it. You can't make it go away.
I don't know what you're going to do about it,

But I know what I'm going to do about it. I'm just
    going to walk away from it. Maybe
A small part of it will die if I'm not around

    feeding it anymore.

from Taxi Suite

1. *After Anacreon*

When I drive cab
    I am moved by strange whistles and wear a hat.

When I drive cab
    I am the hunter. My prey leaps out from where it
    hid, beguiling me with gestures.

When I drive cab
    all may command me, yet I am in command of all who do.

When I drive cab
    I am guided by voices descending from the naked air.

When I drive cab
    A revelation of movement comes to me. They wake now.
    Now they want to work or look around. Now they want
    drunkenness and heavy food. Now they contrive to love.

When I drive cab
    I bring the sailor home from the sea. In the back of
    my car he fingers the pelt of his maiden.

When I drive cab
    I watch for stragglers in the urban order of things.

When I drive cab
    I end the only lit and waitful thing in miles of
    darkened houses.

In Answer to a Question From P. W.

In Mexico I'll finish the novel I'll write, rough, while
    fire-watching in Oregon.
The problem is, what kind of typewriter to pack in?

I ought to be able to live 6 months in Mexico on what I
    earn on the Mountain in 4.
They say you can buy dirty books down there.

Since they give you horses to pack things in, how would it
    be if I took in a big old typewriter and left it there?
They don't give you horses to pack things out.

Going to Mexico by motorcycle would be the coolest, but
    Thoreau warns against any undertaking that
    requires new clothes.
Walking is pure, but I haven't achieved simplicity yet.
I'll never willingly hitchhike again.

Next winter I can buy Snyder's Austin for $200, but how
    can I get the money together?
They repossessed my Oldsmobile.
I've never made the foreign-country scene.

Like the sign over the urinal: "You hold your future
    in your hand."
Or what the giant black whore once said, in the back of my
    cab:

> *"Man, you sure do love diggin' at my*
> *titties, now stop that. We get where*
> *we going you can milk me like a*
> *Holstein, but I gotta see your*
> *money first."*

[The Empress Herself Served Tea to Su Tung-po,]

The Empress herself served tea to Su Tung-po,
and ordered him escorted home by
Ladies of the Palace, with torches.

I forgot my flashlight.
Drunk, I'll never get across this
rickety bridge.

Even the Lady in the Sky abandons me.

[Whenever I Make a New Poem,]

Whenever I make a new poem,
the old ones sound like gibberish.
How can they ever make sense in a book?

Let them say:
"He seems to have lived in the mountains.
He traveled now and then.
When he appeared in cities,
he was almost always drunk.

"Most of his poems are lost.
Many of those we have were found in
letters to his friends.

"He had a very large number of friends."

He Thanks His Woodpile

The wood of the madrone burns with a flame at once
lavender and mossy green, a color you sometimes see in a sari.

Oak burns with a peppery smell.

For a really hot fire, use bark.
You can crack your stove with bark.

All winter long I make wood stews:

Poem to stove to woodpile to stove to
typewriter.   woodpile.   stove.

and can't stop peeking at it!
can't stop opening up the door!
can't stop giggling at it

"Shack Simple"

crazy as Han Shan as
Wittgenstein in his German hut, as
all the others ever were and are

             Ancient Order of the Fire Gigglers

who walked away from it, finally,
kicked the habit, finally, of Self, of
man-hooked Man

             (which is not, at last, estrangement)

Sausalito Trash Prayer

Sausalito,
> *Little Willow,*
Perfect Beach by the last Bay in the world,
> *None more beautiful,*

Today we kneel at thy feet
> *And curse the men who have misused you.*

Song of the Turkey Buzzard

> *For Rock Scully*
> *who heard it*
> *the first*
> *time*

Praises, Tamalpais,
> *Perfect in Wisdom and Beauty,*
She of the Wheeling Birds

I

The rider riddle is easy to ask,
but the answer might surprise you.

How desperately I wanted Cougar
(I, Leo, etc.)
> brilliant proofs: terrain,
color, food, all.
nonsense. All made up.

> *They were always there, the*
> *laziest high-flyers, bronze-winged,*
> *the silent ones*

"A cunning man always laughs and smiles,
          even if he's desperately hungry,
while a good bird always flies like a vulture,
          even if it is starving."

                    (Milarepa sang)

Over and over again, that sign:

I hit once, with a .22
heard the "flak" and a feather flew off, he
flapped his wings just once and
went on sailing. Bronze

(when seen from above)

                    as I have seen them, all day sitting
                    on a cliff so steep they
                    circled below me, in the up-draft
                    passed so close I could see his
                    eye.

   Praises Tamalpais,
      Perfect in Wisdom and Beauty,
   She of the Wheeling Birds

Another time the vision was so clear another saw it, too.

Wet, a hatching bird, the shell of the egg streaked with dry
scum, exhausted, wet, too weak to move the shriveled wings,
fierce sun-heat, sand. Twitching, as with elbows (we all have
the same parts). Beak open, neck stretched, gasping for air. O
how we want to live!

"Poor little bird," she said, "he'll never make it."

   Praises, Tamalpais,
      Perfect in Wisdom & Beauty,
   She of the Wheeling Birds

Even so, I didn't get it for a long long while. It finally came
in a trance, a coma, half in sleep and half in fever-mind. A
Turkey Buzzard, wounded, found by a rock on the mountain.
He wanted to die alone. I had never seen one, wild, so close.
When I reached out, he sidled away, head drooping, as dizzy as
I was. I put my hands on his wing-shoulders and lifted him. He
tried, feebly, to tear at my hands with his beak. He tore my
flesh too slightly to make any difference. Then he tried to heave
his great wings. Weak as he was, I could barely hold him.

A drunken veterinarian found a festering bullet in his side,
a .22 that slid between the great bronze scales his feathers were.
We removed it and cleansed the wound.

Finally he ate the rotten gophers I trapped and prepared
for him. Even at first, he drank a lot of water. My dog seemed
frightened of him.

> They smell sweet
> meat is dry on their talons
>
> The very opposite of
> death
>
> bird of re-birth
> Buzzard
>
> meat is rotten meat made
> sweet again and
>
> lean, unkillable, wing-locked
> soarer till he's but a
>
> speck in the highest sky
> infallible
>
> eye finds Feast! on
> baked concrete

free!

squashed rabbit ripened:
    our good cheese

(to keep the highways clean, and bother no Being)

II

Praises Gentle Tamalpais
Perfect in Wisdom and Beauty of the
sweetest water
and the soaring birds

great seas at the feet of thy cliffs

Hear my last Will & Testament:

Among my friends there shall always be
one with proper instructions
for my continuance.

Let no one grieve.
I shall have used it all up
used up every bit of it.

What an extravagance!
What a relief!

On a marked rock, following his orders,
place my meat.

All care must be taken not to
frighten the natives of this
barbarous land, who
will not let us die, even,
as we wish.

With proper ceremony disembowel what I
no longer need, that it might more quickly
rot and tempt

my new form

*

NOT THE BRONZE CASKET BUT THE BRAZEN WING

SOARING FOREVER ABOVE THEE O PERFECT

O SWEETEST WATER O GLORIOUS

WHEELING

BIRD

[The Image, As in a Hexagram:]

The image, as in a Hexagram:

The hermit locks his door against the blizzard.
He keeps the cabin warm.

All winter long he sorts out all he has.
What was well started shall be finished.
What was not, should be thrown away.

In spring he emerges with one garment
and a single book.

The cabin is very clean.

Except for that, you'd never guess
anyone lived there.

[I Saw Myself]

I saw myself
a ring of bone
in the clear stream
of all of it

and vowed,
always to be open to it
that all of it
might flow through

and then heard
"ring of bone" where
ring is what a

bell does

LENORE KANDEL

||||||||||||||||||||||||||||||||||||||||||||||||||||||||||||||||||||||||||||||||||||||||||||||||||||||||||||

LENORE KANDEL was a legendary presence in San Francisco in the fifties and sixties and the author of several volumes of poetry, including *The Love Book* and *Word Alchemy*. In 1967 she wrote of herself, "I was born under the sign of Capricorn, originally in New York City and later in Pennsylvania, Los Angeles, San Francisco, and other occasions. I am no longer a professional belly-dancer, school-bus driver, or choir singer. I stand witness for the divine animal and the possibility of the ecstatic access of enlightenment." *The Love Book*, a celebration of sexuality and the divine that the San Francisco old-boy mentality wasn't ready for, provoked an obscenity trial. Poets, publishers, and college professors testified on her behalf, and her work was eventually exonerated. Out of that experience came "Poetry Is Never Compromise," which served as the introduction to *Word Alchemy* and was reprinted in *Poetics of the New American Poetry*, edited by Donald Allen and Warren Tallman. Kerouac based the character Romona Swartz in his novel *Big Sur* on Lenore Kandel. A re-issue of *The Love Book* was published by Superstition Street Press in 2003.

"Poetry Is Never Compromise"

Poetry is never compromise. It is the manifestation/translation of a vision, an illumination, an experience. If you compromise your vision you become a blind prophet.

There is no point today in that poetry which exists mainly as an exercise in dexterity. Craft is valuable insofar as it serves as a brilliant midwife for clarity, beauty, vision; when it becomes enamored of itself it produces word masturbation.

The poems I write are concerned with all aspects of the creature and of that total universe through which he moves. The aim is toward the increase of awareness. It may be awareness of the way a bird shatters the sky with his flight or awareness of the difficulty and necessity of trust or awareness of the desire for awareness and also the fear of awareness. This may work through beauty or shock or laughter but the direction is always toward clear sight, both interior and exterior.

This demands honesty within the poet and the poem. An honesty sometimes joyful and sometimes painful, whether to the poet or the reader or both. Two poems of mine, published as a small book, deal with physical love and the invocation, recognition, and acceptance of the divinity in man through the medium of physical love. In other words, it feels good. It feels so good that you can step outside your private ego and share the grace of the universe. This simple and rather self-evident statement, enlarged and exampled poetically, raised a furor difficult to believe. A large part of the furor was caused by the poetic usage of certain four letter words of Anglo-Saxon origin instead of the substitution of gentle euphemisms.

This brings up the question of poetic language. Whatever is language is poetic language and if the word required by the poet does not exist in his known language then it is up to him to discover it. The only proviso can be that the word be the correct word as demanded by the poem and only the poet can be the ultimate judge of that.

Euphemisms chosen by fear are a covenant with hypocrisy

and will immediately destroy the poem and eventually destroy the poet.

Any form of censorship, whether mental, moral, emotional, or physical, whether from the inside out or the outside in, is a barrier against self-awareness.

Poetry is alive because it is a medium of vision and experience.

It is not necessarily comfortable.

It is not necessarily safe.

Poetry has moved out of the classroom and into the street and thus brought about a flow of cross-pollination, many of the fruits of which are viable in both mediums. Academia tended to breed the fear of offense, i.e. that which might offend someone. Visions and language both were often dwarfed and muted, the poem too often becoming a vehicle for literary gymnastics.

Street poetry avoids the fear-trap, but too often loses its visions through a lack of clarity, through sloppiness, through a lack of the art of the craft.

Poetry as poetry has no need to be classified in either of the above pigeon-holes nor in any other. It exists. It can not exist in the company of censorship.

When a poet censors his vision he no longer tells the truth as he sees it. When he censors the language of the poem he does not use those words which, to him, are the most perfect words to be used. This self-stunting results in an artificial limitation imposed on an art whose direction is beyond the limits of the conceivable. There are no barriers to poetry or prophecy; by their nature they are barrier-breakers, bursts of perception, lines into infinity. If a poet lies about his vision he lies about himself and in himself; this produces a true barrier. When a poet through fearful expediency uses language other than that which is perfect to the poem he becomes a person of fearful expediency.

When an outside agency takes it upon itself to attempt the censorship of poetry it is censoring the acceptance of truth and the leap toward revelation.

When a society becomes afraid of its poets, it is afraid of itself. A society afraid of itself stands as another definition of hell. A poem that is written and published becomes available to those who choose to read it. This seems to me to imply one primary responsibility on the part of the poet—that he tell the truth as he sees it. That he tell it as beautifully, as amazingly, as he can; that he ignite his own sense of wonder; that he work alchemy within the language—these are the form and existence of poetry itself.

A good part of the audience for modern poetry is young. We move in a world where the polarities and possibilities of life and death exist as a constant consciousness. Once the concept and availability of overkill was made public knowledge the aura of the possibility of cosmic death became visible. There have been eras when the young could slip softly into their elders' lives, when if they wanted to ignore the deeper issues of humanity, of man's relationship to man, it was made easy for them. This is not such a time and the choices of the young are deep and hard. At eighteen the young men must decide whether they will enter into the national pastime of death. A great many of the young are choosing to manifest a different way of life, one motivated toward pleasure, toward enlightenment, and toward mutual concern, instead of accepting the world of war and personal despair which has been offered them by the majority of their elders.

There are heavy choices to make and there is no avoidance possible.

Those who read modern poetry do so for pleasure, for insight, sometimes for counsel. The least they can expect is that the poet who shares his visions and experiences with them do so with no hypocrisy. To compromise poetry through fear is to atrophy the psyche. To compromise poetry through expediency is the soft, small murder of the soul.

[1967]

First They Slaughtered the Angels

I

First they slaughtered the angels
tying their thin white legs with wire cords
and
opening their silk throats with icy knives
They died fluttering their wings like chickens
and their immortal blood wet the burning earth

we watched from underground
from the gravestones, the crypts
chewing our bony fingers
and
shivering in our piss-stained winding sheets
The seraphs and the cherubim are gone
they have eaten them and cracked their bones for marrow
they have wiped their asses on angel feathers
and now they walk the rubbled streets with
eyes like fire pits

II

who finked on the angels?
who stole the holy grail and hocked it for a jug of wine?
who fucked up Gabriel's golden horn?
            was it an inside job?

who barbecued the lamb of god?
who flushed St. Peter's keys down the mouth of a
North Beach toilet?

who raped St. Mary with a plastic dildo stamped with the
Good Housekeeping seal of approval?
            was it an outside job?

where are our weapons?
where are our bludgeons, our flame throwers, our poison

gas, our hand grenades?
we fumble for our guns and our knees sprout credit cards,
we vomit canceled checks
standing spreadlegged with open sphincters weeping soap suds
from our radioactive eyes
and screaming
for the ultimate rifle
the messianic cannon
the paschal bomb

the bellies of women split open and children rip their
way out with bayonets
spitting blood in the eyes of blind midwives
before impaling themselves on their own swords

the penises of men are become blue steel machine guns,
they ejaculate bullets, they spread death as an orgasm

lovers roll in the bushes tearing at each other's genitals
with iron fingernails

fresh blood is served at health food bars in germ free
paper cups
gulped down by syphilitic club women
in papier-mâché masks
each one the same hand-painted face of Hamlet's mother
at the age of ten
we watch from underground
our eyes like periscopes
flinging our fingers to the dogs for candy bars
in an effort to still their barking
in an effort to keep the peace
in an effort to make friends and influence people

III

we have collapsed our collapsible bomb shelters
we have folded our folding life rafts
and at the count of twelve

they have all disintegrated into piles of rat shit
nourishing the growth of poison flowers
and venus pitcher plants

we huddle underground
hugging our porous chests with mildewed arms
listening to the slow blood drip from our severed veins
lifting the tops of our zippered skulls
to ventilate our brains
        they have murdered our angels

we have sold our bodies and our hours to the curious
we have paid off our childhood in dishwashers and miltown
and rubbed salt upon our bleeding nerves
in the course of searching
        and they have shit upon the open mouth of god
they have hung the saints in straitjackets and they have
tranquilized the prophets
they have denied both christ and cock
and diagnosed buddha as catatonic
they have emasculated the priests and the holy men and
censored even the words of love
    Lobotomy for every man!
and they have nominated a eunuch for president
    Lobotomy for the housewife!
    Lobotomy for the business man!
    Lobotomy for the nursery schools!
and they have murdered the angels

    IV

now in the alleyways the androgynes gather swinging their
lepers' bells like censers as they prepare the ritual
rape of god
    the grease that shines their lips is the fat of angels
    the blood that cakes their claws is the blood of angels

they are gathering in the streets and playing dice with
angel eyes
they are casting the last lots of armageddon

V

now in the aftermath of morning
we are rolling away the stones from underground, from the
caves
we have widened our peyote-visioned eyes
and rinsed our mouths with last night's wine
we have caulked the holes in our arms with dust and flung
libations at each other's feet

and we shall enter into the streets and walk among them and
do battle
holding our lean and empty hands upraised
we shall pass among the strangers of the world like a
bitter wind

and our blood will melt iron
and our breath will melt steel
we shall stare face to face with naked eyes
and our tears will make earthquakes
and our wailing will cause mountains to rise and the sun to
    halt

THEY SHALL MURDER NO MORE ANGELS!
        not even us

Spring 61

    country?   have lost our pride
as nationals   no man can die for billboards
        as have for freedom
who froze his balls at Valley Forge
(14° below) pissed blood and wept in pain
(wept) wept a man willfully engaged
to fight for certain rights

My brother (34 years old)
drinks chocolate flavored metrecal
writing TV scripts
My lover (34 years old) catches fine fish
but cannot fill out forms
in triplicate
(Alaska is not for all of us)
he can barely buy brandy to blur his impotence
he is a man breaking his pride against

What Were Your Earnings Last Year
    and
How Long Have You Lived At This Address
    and
Are You Now

these men of Gloucester fought arm's length with whales
(the smell, they say, it never did wear off—
the reek of such huge dying)
    why be   half safe

yesterday we went to the ocean and prised mussels
from low-tide rocks
cooked them with onion   carrots   celery seed
    (delicious)
cut fingers healed in sea water

there is a pride in handknit sweaters
    unknown
to knitting machines and
        other robots

Gettysburg was not an outing
Bull Run, Appomattox, anywhere
and dance hall girls came high

Fort Sumter   Bunker Hill

THIS IS A NATIONAL MONUMENT

this African student, the other night
    at a party
My people are dying, he said
yaws . . . fevers . . . things like that
I'd like to stay here, he said
direct plays . . .
I must go home and lead my people

PHILIP WHALEN

||||||||||||||||||||||||||||||||||||||||||||||||||||||||||||||||||||||||||||||||||||||||||||||||||||||||||||||||||||||||||||||||||

PHILIP WHALEN was born in Portland, Oregon, in 1923. He enlisted in the U.S. Army Air Force and served from 1943 to 1946 as a radio operator and mechanics instructor, while experimenting with novels in the style of Thomas Wolfe. From 1946 to 1951, Whalen studied at Reed College on the G.I. Bill, rooming in a house with Gary Snyder and Lew Welch. While at Reed, he discovered the writings of D. T. Suzuki and developed a lifetime interest in Asian religions, particularly Zen Buddhism. After receiving a B.A. in literature and languages in 1951, Whalen took up residence in San Francisco, where he joined Snyder, Allen Ginsberg, Michael McClure, and others for the famous Six Gallery reading on October 6, 1955. In 1967 and again from 1969 to 1971, he lived in Kyoto, where he wrote *Scenes of Life at the Capital*. Back in the United States, Whalen moved into the San Francisco Zen Center in 1972, and on February 3, 1973, was ordained *Unsui*, Zen Buddhist monk, with the Dharma name *Zenshin Ryufu*. In 1975, he served as head monk at the Tassajara retreat center. He was a regular visiting faculty member at Naropa University during the seventies and eighties. Though he never sought or achieved popular acclaim, a range of young poets have consistently turned to his writings for inspiration and guidance. Whalen's books include *Heavy Breathing, Off the Wall* (interviews), two novels, and the out-of-print but indispensable *On Bear's Head*.

On September 14, 1991, Philip Whalen was installed as abbot of the Hartford Street Zen Center, San Francisco. He died June 26, 2002. A major selection of his poetry, *Overtime,* was issued as a part of the Penguin Poets series in 1999.

Further Notice

I can't live in this world
And I refuse to kill myself
Or let you kill me

The dill plant lives, the airplane
My alarm clock, this ink
I won't go away

I shall be myself—
Free, a genius, an embarrassment
Like the Indian, the buffalo

Like Yellowstone National Park.

22:ix:56

Sourdough Mountain Lookout

Tsung Ping (375–443): "Now I am old and infirm. I fear I shall no more be able to roam among the beautiful mountains. Clarifying my mind, I meditate on the mountain trails and wander about only in dreams."
   —in THE SPIRIT OF THE BRUSH, tr. by Shio Sakanishi, p. 34.

FOR KENNETH REXROTH

I always say I won't go back to the mountains
I am too old and fat there are bugs mean mules
And pancakes every morning of the world

Mr. Edward Wyman (63)
Steams along the trail ahead of us all
Moaning, "My poor old feet ache, my back
Is tired and I've got a stiff prick"
Uprooting alder shoots in the rain

Then I'm alone in a glass house on a ridge
Encircled by chiming mountains
With one sun roaring through the house all day
& the others crashing through the glass all night
Conscious even while sleeping

    Morning fog in the southern gorge
    Gleaming foam restoring the old sea-level
    The lakes in two lights green soap and indigo
    The high cirque-lake black half-open eye

Ptarmigan hunt for bugs in the snow
Bear peers through the wall at noon
Deer crowd up to see the lamp
A mouse nearly drowns in the honey
I see my bootprints mingle with deer-foot
Bear-paw mule-shoe in the dusty path to the privy

Much later I write down:
    "raging. Viking sunrise
    The gorgeous death of summer in the east"
(Influence of a Byronic landscape—
Bent pages exhibiting depravity of style.)

Outside the lookout I lay nude on the granite
Mountain hot September sun but inside my head
Calm dark night with all the other stars

HERACLITUS: "The waking have one common world
But the sleeping turn aside
Each into a world of his own."

I keep telling myself what I really like
Are music, books, certain land and sea-scapes
The way light falls across them, diffusion of
Light through agate, light itself . . . I suppose
I'm still afraid of the dark

       "Remember smart-guy there's something
       Bigger something smarter than you."
       Ireland's fear of unknown holies drives
       My father's voice (a country neither he
       Nor his great-grandfather ever saw)

       A sparkly tomb a plated grave
       A holy thumb beneath a wave

Everything else they hauled across Atlantic
Scattered and lost in the buffalo plains
Among these trees and mountains
From Duns Scotus to this page
A thousand years

       (". . . a dog walking on his hind legs—
       not that he does it well but that he
         does it at all.")

Virtually a blank except for the hypothesis
That there is more to a man
Than the contents of his jock-strap

EMPEDOCLES: "At one time all the limbs
Which are the body's portion are brought together
By Love in blooming life's high season; at another
Severed by cruel Strife, they wander each alone
By the breakers of life's sea."

Fire and pressure from the sun bear down
Bear down centipede shadow of palm-frond
A limestone lithograph—oysters and clams of stone

Half a black rock bomb displaying brilliant crystals
Fire and pressure Love and Strive bear down
Brontosaurus, look away

My sweat runs down the rock

HERACLITUS: "The transformations of fire
are, first of all, sea; and half of the sea
is earth, half whirlwind. . . .
It scatters and it gathers; it advances
and retires."

I move out of a sweaty pool
         (The sea!)
And sit up higher on the rock

Is anything burning?

The sun itself! Dying
Pooping out, exhausted
Having produced brontosaurus, Heraclitus
This rock, me,
To no purpose
I tell you anyway (as a kind of loving) . . .
Flies & other insects come from miles around
To listen
I also address the rock, the heather,
The alpine fir

BUDDHA: "All the constituents of being are
Transitory: Work out your salvation with diligence."

(And everything, as one eminent disciple of that master
Pointed out, has been tediously complex ever since.)

There was a bird
Lived in an egg
And by ingenious chemistry

Wrought molecules of albumen
To beak and eye
Gizzard and craw
Feather and claw

My grandmother said:
"Look at them poor bed-
raggled pigeons!"

And the sign in McAlister Street:

"IF YOU CAN'T COME IN
SMILE AS YOU GO BY
L♡VE
THE BUTCHER"

I destroy myself, the universe (an egg)
And time—to get an answer:
There are a smiler, a sleeper and a dancer

We repeat our conversation in the glittering dark
Floating beside the sleeper.
The child remarks, "You knew it all the time."
I: "I keep forgetting that the smiler is
Sleeping; the sleeper, dancing."

From Sauk Lookout two years before
Some of the view was down the Skagit
To Puget Sound: From above the lower ranges,
Deep in forest—lighthouses on clear nights.

This year's rock is a spur from the main range
Cuts the valley in two and is broken
By the river; Ross Dam repairs the break,
Makes trolley buses run
Through the streets of dim Seattle far away.

I'm surrounded by mountains here
A circle of 108 beads, originally seeds
   of *ficus religiosa*
       Bo-Tree
A circle, continuous, one odd bead
Larger than the rest and bearing
A tassel (hair-tuft) (the man who sat
       under the tree)
In the center of the circle,
A void, an empty figure containing
All that's multiplied;
Each bead a repetition, a world
Of ignorance and sleep.

Today is the day the goose gets cooked
Day of liberation for the crumbling flower
Knobcone pinecone in the flames
Brandy in the sun

Which, as I said, will disappear
Anyway it'll be invisible soon
Exchanging places with stars now in my head
To be growing rice in China through the night.

Magnetic storms across the solar plains
Make Aurora Borealis shimmy bright
Beyond the mountains to the north.

Closing the lookout in the morning
Thick ice on the shutters
Coyote almost whistling on a nearby ridge
The mountain is THERE (between two lakes)
I brought back a piece of its rock
Heavy dark-honey color
With a seam of crystal, some of the quartz
Stained by its matrix
Practically indestructible
A shift from opacity to brilliance

(The Zenbos say, "Lightning-flash & flint-spark")
Like the mountains where it was made

What we see of the world is the mind's
Invention and the mind
Though stained by it, becoming
Rivers, sun, mule-dung, flies—
Can shift instantly
A dirty bird in a square time

Gone
Gone
REALLY gone
Into the cool
O MAMA!

Like they say, "Four times up,
Three times down." I'm still on the mountain.

Sourdough Mountain 15:viii:55
Berkeley 27–28:viii:56

[The quotes of Empedocles and Heraclitus are from John Burnet's
Early Greek Philosophy, Meridian Books, New York.]

Hymnus Ad Patrem Sinensis

I praise those ancient Chinamen
Who left me a few words,
Usually a pointless joke or a silly question
A line of poetry drunkenly scrawled on the margin of a quick
              splashed picture—bug, leaf,
              caricature of Teacher
      on paper held together now by little more than ink
      & their own strength brushed momentarily over it
Their world & several others since
Gone to hell in a handbasket, they knew it—

Cheered as it whizzed by—
& conked out among the busted spring rain cherryblossom
     winejars
Happy to have saved us all.

                                                    31:viii:58

Complaint: To the Muse

You do understand I've waited long enough
There's nobody else that interests me more than a minute
I've got no more ambition to shop around for poems or love
Come back!
             or at least answer your telephone
I'm nowhere without you

     This is the greatest possible drag
     Slower than the speed of light or always
     A little less than critical mass

     The energy the steam the poop is here
     Everything is (by Nature) Energy, I myself
     A natural thing & certainly massive enough

     A block of lead (the end of all radiation)
     I don't even reflect much daylight, not to speak of
              glowing in the dark
     I'll never get it off the ground

This room is full of 1 fly & an alarmclock
It is uninhabitable

If I wasn't drunk & blowing wine-fumes & peanut breath in
     your face
Maybe you'd be nice to me.

You do understand
I'd much rather listen, Lady
Than go on babbling this way, O rare gentle
& wise, it isn't enough that your face, your body
Are uniquely beautiful—I must hear you tell me
       about the weather
We might even quarrel if nothing else
You know the answer & don't, won't quit kidding me along
Hanging me up like Sir John Suckling
       in a tag of lace or muslin

I can see right through all those veils
But you can run fast & I've got a bum knee

& you been a long time gone

11-12:ix:58

"Never Apologize; Never Explain"

A pair of strange new birds in the maple tree
Peer through the windows,
Mother and father visiting me:
      "You are unmarried,
      No child begot
      Now we are birds, now you've
         forgotten us
      Although in dreams we visit you
         in human shape"

They speak Homer's language
Sing like Aeschylus

The life of a poet: less than $\frac{2}{3}$ds of a second

18:II:67

Regalia in Immediate Demand!

Necklace of human bones
Cup a silver-mounted cranium
Thigh-bone trumpets
A skull drum

Dear President Nixon, you are welcome in Lhasa!
And where is dear Mr Edgar Hoover?

                                        19:IV:67

International Date Line,
Monday/Monday 27:XI:67

Here it comes again, imagination of myself
Someplace in Oregon woods I sit on short
Wide unpainted wooden cabin steps
Bare feet wiggle toes in dirt and moss and duff
The sun shines on me, I'm thinking about all of us
How we have and haven't survived but curiously famous
Alive or dead—X has become a great man, Y very nearly
Greater, perhaps in some other dimension, Z apparently
Still in a frenzy pursuit of universal admiration, fame & love

And there's LeRoi seated in TIME magazine wheelchair
Head bashed in under hospital bandage
Blood all running down the side of his face

Walking beside the Kamogawa, Remembering Nansen and Fudo and Gary's Poem

Here are two half-grown black cats perched on a
       lump of old teakettle brick plastic garbage
         ten feet from the west bank of the River.
I won't save them. Right here Gary sat with dying Nansen,
The broken cat, warped and sick every day of its life,
Puke & drool on the *tatami* for Gary to wipe up & scold,
"If you get any worse I'm going to have you put away!"
The vet injected an overdose of nemby and for half an hour
Nansen was comfortable.

How can we do this, how can we live and die?
How does anybody choose for somebody else.
How dare we appear in this Hell-mouth weeping tears,
Busting our heads in ten fragments making vows &
       promises?

Suzuki Roshi said, "If I die, it's all right. If I should
live, it's all right. Sun-face Buddha, Moon-face Buddha."
Why do I always fall for that old line?

We don't treat each other any better. When will I
Stop writing it down.

Kyoto 14:IV:69

Postscript, 17:IV:69 (from De Visser, Vol. I, pp. 197–198), 20th Commandment of the *Brahmajala Sutra* (Nanjo 1087): ". . . always practise liberation of living beings (*hō jō,* 放 生)."

Chanson d'Outre Tombe

They said we was nowhere
Actually we are beautifully embalmed
        in Pennsylvania
They said we wanted too much.
Gave too little, a swift hand-job
        no vaseline.
We were geniuses with all kinds
        embarrassing limitations
O if only we would realize our potential
O if only that awful self-indulgence
& that shoddy politics of irresponsibility
O if only we would grow up, shut up, die
& so we did & do & chant beyond
        the cut-rate grave digged by
                indignant reviewers
O if we would only lay down & stay
        THERE—In California, Pennsylvania
Where we keep leaking our nasty radioactive
        waste like old plutonium factory
Wrecking your white expensive world

                    Tassajara, 27:III:1979

from The Diamond Noodle

Or passing a hedge, I see between the stems that make a thick
bushy wall, that screened summerhouse with an almost Chi-
nese roof, was it a birdcage, originally? a wonder! I found all
artificial waters—birdbaths, fishponds, fountains—rich and
magnificent outside of time: Eternal summer light and heat,
jewels and gold beyond eye-corner, the Princess, the Genii: si-
lence in which my slightest movement or the sudden flick of

bird, leaf, bug, admitted quick inaudible progression of chords from invisible distant orchestra which I knew had been playing continuously but required some visible motion to bring my attention back to it, my delight . . . gone, forgotten a moment later, I'm concentrating on some single flower or fish, then again something (flick!) short and quick beyond eye-shot, and I hear the music again, a wink of time: after a series of nearly snowless winters, a heavy pack of dry snow at last, eight or ten inches of it, Trevitt Street becomes a mountain of pleasure, our sleds ("flexible Flyer") zooming down fifteen blocks of steep hill in and out of the streetlights in night so black it's thick, the air clean but soft, nothing like the paralyzing, antihuman cold of the Middle West or Colorado. The cops blocked traffic off the hills that we used for coasting. Summer again, the Dip is open, a float moored near the riverbank, a few blocks east of the ferry slip which was, in its turn, built on an historical site: the longest mahogany bar in the world had stood there in the old Umatilla House, the hotel where General Grant had stayed). On the Dip was a tall tin slide with a water pump at the top to sluice you down the trough into the river, an enormous (we said "five hundred foot") diving tower, tall chair and shack for the lifeguard, there was a smelly board bathhouse on the beach where we could dress. Summer spent walking up & down the hills of the town, chestnut locust sycamore shade past the stores and banks are scary one brick building block of Chinatown and railroad and over the bank to the bathhouse. Columbia green water unless gangs of little kids roiled up sand near the shore. While swimming under water I hear metal "chung" of the ferry boat engine as it loops across the water to Washington, probably my father's on board, sitting in his car, he's on his way to Goldendale, blue eyes watching the line of hills ahead, the mountains downriver, no doubt worrying about my mother, my sister & me, remembering his own childhood poverty and loss of mother, brother, childhood horror . . . now stuck with job of hustling for devalued money (what is this Roosevelt fellow going to do?) to pay the rent, buy gas, feed everybody, Depression.

A List

a) the world of common experience wherein reign the clock, the schedules based on the existence of an ideal clock, which lends money its value, pays the police, the world of "strangers," "the public": that world in which I am an object

b) the world of the past, composed of my own recollections and what I choose to accept as "history"

c) the world of phantasy, active daydream in which I write or not

d) quasi-trance succeeding upon meditation, experienced while walking about in World a) above

e) the world of nature as I see it when I'm alone in the woods or on the beach

> 1) this is the world that more or less matches with descriptions in textbooks on geology, botany, biology &c.
>
> 2) it is this world which, according to one scientific theory, has produced my physical person: I am a collection of cells which are governed by inherited genes and the metabolism of goody inside these minute, &, hopefully, continuously cooperating independent organisms.

f) trance and supersensory condition, ecstasy, rapture, etc.

g) dream

> 1) conscious dreaming, during light sleep
>
> 2) vivid dreaming in which the dream is all of reality I'm at that moment aware of

h) total unconsciousness produced by deep sleep, anaesthesia or accidental "knockout" (hit by automobile, for example)

i) drunkenness

j) illness (fever dream/hallucination, &c.)

k) drug worlds

> 1) hospital medication
>
> 2) peyotl world, "total vision," paradigm of *samadhi*
>
> 3) cannabis, producing audio/visual transformations without loss of immediate contact with World a)
>
> 3.1) hashish, also overindulgence in cannabis produces total awareness of World a) while at the same time producing a paralysis of the private will

4) heroin: euphoria, "soul security", the World a) seems to become civilized and charming

l) world of conscious composition—interior direct report of internally heard speech (thought) . . . as now—as if another person were listening to me, as the Freudian analyst is popularly imagined as doing: listening impartially, imperturbably, alert, paying close attention, not replying, but it is understood that he's interested in having me continue . . . these words being the mirror in which I am at the moment admiring myself—feelings of excitement, pleasure, release, self-importance, the idea that this activity is meaningful and valuable. Something like this also happens when I'm concentrating on reading music while playing the piano. (add: feeling of conscious thought or calculation)

m) World of sexual congress, wherein is simply pleasure and communication, wherein it opens into quasi-trance or small *samadhi,* or (the worst) wherein a total break of communication occurs, total separation suddenly happens, each party suddenly experiencing total isolation

n) World of traveling: something of what Burroughs has described as "Interzone": insubstantiality of scene, meetings with uprooted "outrageous" persons (angry ghosts &c.), profound insecurity takes, paranoia scenes (distinguished from travel in company with one or more persons, also modes of travel)

o) World of complete emotional entanglement, upset, involvement causing complete abstraction from it (combines with World b) above) yet causing "withdrawal" from World a), distorting and loading all perceptions, tending to falsify all other worlds, including b), e.g. I become cut off from my past knowledge of how to cope with immediate problems

p) World of conscious silent contemplation of objects, of art, of literature, of nature as in e) above

q) World of other persons (as distinguished from "strangers" or "the public" as in World a))

    1) family—which partly overlaps with World b) and with several other worlds—family as Culture, as Authority, and as separate interesting human persons whom I love and hate

2) friends and acquaintances
3) teachers, employers, fellow workers
4) audience: those who read me but don't ever meet me, and those who hear me read to them, and those who read or see me and who also have met me, talked with me once, for a few minutes

r) World of business, jobs &c—although this happens within World a) and deals more or less exclusively with it, it is an abstract world of its own, yet it tries to deal with persons. It sees persons as "roles" in which they are useful and manageable. There are hopefully "controlled" emotional involvements, but they must be governed by the general rule, that "Business is Business"

s) World of the Academy

t) The Army

u) World of Letters (editing & publishing, criticism, journalism, all the public and annoying side of writing)

v) Art World, i.e. the mechanical, public side of it: the gallery, theater, the concert hall, &c.

w) World as a particular age-group or "generation"

Distinguish between worlds where I am object—for example, in a) and j) (wherein I am patient of doctor, dentist &c) or r) wherein I am an employee, s) where I am a student or teacher, t) where I was an enlisted man, u), v) and w) wherein I am an audience, the subject of a painting, where I am onstage, i) where I am drunk, &c. &c. &c.

Distinguish at last between illusion and reality. Oh boy. And act as occasion requires, immediately, direct from center of absolute enlightenment (nobody like "I" or "me") . . . I get this idea from a number of sources, most particularly from books, introspection, and the example of a few extraordinary men I've known. I must take care to react only to the substantial, the actual even situation that is NOW, and to recognize them for the illusory things that they are, all the scares, worries, warped recollections, prejudices, misinterpretations, hopes and wishes ABOUT the world I'm dealing with. The most important and substantial world to be in is that of other persons. Most of them seem to see themselves as locked into a single world or at least a very restricted number of worlds—action outside of these worlds doesn't seem possible to these people, other worlds make no sense to them. The reality of their impressions, the reality of their suffering is absolutely real to me, but ordinary pity, insofar as it leads to a smug patronizing attitude on my part, is useless and ugly. I must see them with a combination of love, understanding & detachment—in a word, with compassion. Action from that center alone can be of any use to others. If I act distractedly, ignorantly, I create a tangle of "bad" consequences—if not "bad" ones, they are certainly unnecessary ones which confuse and vitiate my own mind and feelings. There's a complete paradox if it is all stated grammatically: "complete responsibility is complete freedom." These are false terms, too, for what have notions of "completeness" and "totality" to do with a temporary and constantly changing world/person I call "me"? And its imaginations about "virtue" or "correctness" &c. I stop again. Cold hands. Noise in the street. Red carpet blue and yellow design. A shelf made of boards, books, a chair, a map a wall two doors. Light is on, as it is night. Purposely I break here, I make myself stop.

BOB KAUFMAN

||||||||||||||||||||||||||||||||||||||||||||||||||||||||||||||||||||||||||||||||||||||||||||||||||||||||||||||||||||||

BOB KAUFMAN was born in New Orleans in 1925. His mother was a Catholic from Martinique, his father an Orthodox Jew. He joined the U.S. Merchant Marine at age thirteen, served for twenty years, and then settled in San Francisco. A regular of North Beach in the late fifties and early sixties, he ran a series of poetry readings at the Co-Existence Bagel Shop and other cafés. Kaufman's poetry was rigorously honest, and picked up on jazz rhythms and street speech—he was the quintessential urban Beat poet. His insistence on free speech got him into trouble with the San Francisco police on a number of occasions. In 1959, he joined Allen Ginsberg and other poets to found *Beatitude,* a poetry journal that took its name from Jack Kerouac's etymological riffing on the term *beat.* Kaufman was politically active but fell into despair at times: on hearing that John F. Kennedy was killed, he undertook a vow of silence that lasted twelve years. His first book of poetry was published in 1965, and two years later Ferlinghetti's City Lights issued his *Golden Sardine.* Other books include *Solitudes Crowded with Loneliness* and many translations into French. Since Kaufman's death in San Francisco on January 12, 1986, he has come into a new reputation as an important voice in African-American poetry. Coffee House Press published a collection of his work, *Cranial Guitar,* in 1996.

Blues Note

Ray Charles is the black wind of Kilimanjaro,
Screaming up-and-down blues,
Moaning happy on all the elevators of my time.

Smiling into the camera, with an African symphony
Hidden in his throat, and (*I Got a Woman*) wails, too.

He burst from Bessie's crushed black skull
One cold night outside of Nashville, shouting,
And grows bluer from memory, glowing bluer, still.

At certain times you can see the moon
Balanced on his head.

From his mouth he hurls chunks of raw soul.
He separated the sea of polluted sounds
And led the blues into the Promised Land.

Ray Charles is a dangerous man ('way cross town),
And I love him.

for Ray Charles's birthday
N.Y.C./1961

Abomunist Manifesto

ABOMUNISTS JOIN NOTHING BUT THEIR HANDS OR LEGS,
OR OTHER SAME.

ABOMUNISTS SPIT ANTI-POETRY FOR POETIC REASONS
AND FRINK.

ABOMUNISTS DO NOT LOOK AT PICTURES PAINTED
BY PRESIDENTS AND UNEMPLOYED PRIME MINISTERS.

IN TIMES OF NATIONAL PERIL, ABOMUNISTS, AS REALITY
AMERICANS, STAND READY TO DRINK THEMSELVES
TO DEATH FOR THEIR COUNTRY.

ABOMUNISTS DO NOT FEEL PAIN, NO MATTER HOW MUCH
IT HURTS.

ABOMUNISTS DO NOT USE THE WORD SQUARE EXCEPT WHEN
TALKING TO SQUARES.

ABOMUNISTS READ NEWSPAPERS ONLY TO ASCERTAIN THEIR
ABOMINUBILITY.

ABOMUNISTS NEVER CARRY MORE THAN FIFTY DOLLARS
IN DEBTS ON THEM.

ABOMUNISTS BELIEVE THAT THE SOLUTION OF PROBLEMS
OF RELIGIOUS BIGOTRY IS, TO HAVE A CATHOLIC
CANDIDATE FOR PRESIDENT AND A PROTESTANT
CANDIDATE FOR POPE.

ABOMUNISTS DO NOT WRITE FOR MONEY; THEY WRITE
THE MONEY ITSELF.

ABOMUNISTS BELIEVE ONLY WHAT THEY DREAM ONLY
AFTER IT COMES TRUE.

ABOMUNIST CHILDREN MUST BE REARED ABOMUNIBLY.

ABOMUNIST POETS, CONFIDENT THAT THE NEW LITERARY
FORM "FOOT-PRINTISM" HAS FREED THE ARTIST
OF OUTMODED RESTRICTIONS, SUCH AS: THE ABILITY TO
READ AND WRITE, OR THE DESIRE TO COMMUNICATE,
MUST BE PREPARED TO READ THEIR WORK AT DENTAL
COLLEGES, EMBALMING SCHOOLS, HOMES FOR UNWED
MOTHERS, HOMES FOR WED MOTHERS, INSANE ASYLUMS,
USO CANTEENS, KINDERGARTENS, AND COUNTY JAILS.
ABOMUNISTS NEVER COMPROMISE THEIR REJECTIONARY
PHILOSOPHY.

ABOMUNISTS REJECT EVERYTHING EXCEPT SNOWMEN.

Notes Dis- and Re- Garding Abomunism

Abomunism was founded by Barabbas, inspired by his dying
    words: "I wanted to be in the middle, but I went too
    far out."
Abomunism's main function is to unite the soul with oatmeal
    cookies.
Abomunists love love, hate hate, drink drinks, smoke smokes,
    live lives, die deaths.
Abomunist writers write writing, or nothing at all.
Abomunist poetry, in order to be compleatly (Eng. sp.)
    understood, should be eaten . . . except on fast days,
    slow days, and mornings of executions.
Abomunists, could they be a color, would be green,
    and tell everyone to go.
Uncrazy Abomunists crazy unAbomunists by proxy kicky
    tricks, as follows:
  By telling psychometric poets two heads are better
    than none.
  By selling middle names to impotent personnel managers.
  By giving children brightly wrapped candy fathers.
  By biting their own hands after feeding themselves.
  By calling taxis dirty names, while ordering fifths
    of milk.
  By walking across hills, ignoring up and down.
  By giving telescopes to peeping Toms.
  By using real names at false hotels.
Abomunists who feel their faith weakening will have to
    spend two weeks in Los Angeles.
When attacked, Abomunists think positive, repeating over
    and under: "If I were a crime, I'd want to be
    committed . . .
            No! . . . Wait!"

Further Notes

  (taken from "Abomunismus und Religion" by Tom Man)
Krishnamurti can relax the muscles of your soul,
Free your aching jawbone from the chewinggum habit.

Ouspensky can churn your illusions into butter and
Give you circles to carry them in, around your head.
Subud can lock you in strange rooms with vocal balms
And make your ignorant clothing understand you.
Zen can cause changes in the texture of your hair,
Removing you from the clutches of sexy barbers.
Edgar Cayce can locate your gallstones, other organs,
On the anarchistic rockpiles of Sacramento.
Voodoo Marie can give you Loas, abstract horses,
Snorting guides to tar-baby black masses.
Billy can plug you into the Christ machine. Mail in your
Mind today. Hurry, bargain God week, lasts one week only.

$$ Abomunus Craxioms $$

Egyptian mummies are lousy dancers.
    Alcoholics cannot make it on root beer.
Jazz never made it back down the river.
    Licking postage stamps depletes the body fluids.
Fat automobiles laugh more than others, and frink.
    Men who die in wars become seagulls and fly.
Roaches have a rough time of it from birth.
    People who read are not happy.
People who do not read are not happy.
    People are not very happy.
These days people get sicker quicker.
    The sky is less crowded in the West.
Psychiatrists pretend not to know everything.
    Way out people know the way out.
Laughter sounds orange at night, because
    reality is unrealizable while it exists.
Abomunists knew it all along,
    but couldn't get the butterscotch down.

Excerpts From the Lexicon Abomunon

*At election time, Abomunists frink more, and naturally, as
hard-core Abo's, we feel the need to express ourselves some-
what more abomunably than others. We do this simply by not*

expressing ourselves (abomunization). We do not express ourselves in the following terms:

Abommunity: n. Grant Avenue & other frinky places.

Abomunarcosis: n. Addiction to oatmeal cookies & liverwurst.

Abomunasium: n. Place in which abomunastics occur, such as bars, coffee shops, USO's, juvenile homes, pads, etc.

Abomunastics: n. Physical Abomunism.

Abomunate, The: n. The apolitical CORPUS ABOMUNISMUS.

Abomunette: n. Female type Abomunist (rare).

Abomunibble: v. 1. To bite a daisy. 2. How poets eat.

Abomunicate: v. To dig. (Slang: to frink.)

Abomunics: n. Abomunistic techniques.

Abomunificance: n. The façade behind the reality of double-talking billboards.

Abomunify: v. To (censored) with an Abomunette, or vice versa.

Abomunik: n. Square abomuflack.

Abomunism: n. Footprintism. A rejectory philosophy founded by Barabbas and dedicated to the proposition that the essence of existence is reality essential and neither four-sided nor frinky, but not non-frinky either.

Abomunist: n. One who avows Abomunism, disavowing almost everything else, especially butterscotch.

Abomunitions: n. Love, commonly found in the plural state, very.

Abomunity: n. A by-product of abomunarcosis, also obtained by frinking. (Thus: Frinkism.)

Abomunize: v. To carefully disorganize—usually associated with frinking.

Abomunoid: adj. Having some Abomunistic qualities such as tragictories, pail faces, or night vision.

Abomunology: n. The systematic study of Abomunism; classes every other Frinksday, 2 a.m.

Abomunosis: n. Sweet breath.

Abomunosophy: n. Theoretical Abomunism.

Abomunull: n. 1. They. 2. One who is not quite *here.*

Abomusical: adj. Diggable sounds.

Abomutiny: n. Regimentation. v. To impose organization from without, i.e., without oatmeal cookies.

Frink: v. To (censored). n. (censored) and (censored).

Frinkism: n. A sub-cult of Abomunism, not authorized nor given abomunitude by Bomkauf.

Frinky: adj. Like (censored).

—Compiled by BIMGO

Abomunist Election Manifesto

1. Abomunists vote against everyone by not voting for anyone.
2. The only proposition Abomunists support are those made to members of the opposite sex.
3. Abomunists demand the abolition of Oakland.
4. Abomunists demand low-cost housing for homosexuals.
5. Abomunists demand suppression of illegal milk traffic.
6. Abomunists demand statehood for North Beach.
7. The only office Abomunists run for is the unemployment office.
8. Abomunists support universal frinkage.
9. Abomunists demand split-level ranch-type phonebooths.
10. Abomunists demand the reestablishment of the government in its rightful home at ?

Still Further Notes Dis- & Re- Garding Abomunism

The following translation is the first publication of the Live Sea Scrolls, found by an old Arab oilwell driller. He first saw them on the dead beds of the live sea. Thinking they were ancient bubblegum wrappers he took them to town to trade in for hashish coupons. As chance would have it, the hashish pipes were in the hands of a visiting American relief official, who reluctantly surrendered them in return for two villages and a canal. We developed the cunic script by smearing it with tanfastic sun lotion, after which we took it down to the laundromat and placed it in the dryer for two hours ($1.20). We then ate four pounds of garlic bread & frinked; then we translated *this diary. We feel this is one of the oldest Abomunist documents yet discovered.*

MONDAY—B.C.—minus 4—10 o'sun, a.m.

Nazareth getting too hot, fuzz broke up two of my poetry readings last night. Beat vagrancy charge by carrying my toolbox to court—carpenters O.K. Splitting to Jeru. as soon as I get wheels.

TUESDAY—B.C.—minus 3—8 o'sun, p.m.

Jeru. cool, Roman fuzz busy having a ball, never bother you unless someone complains. Had a ball this morning, eighty-sixed some square bankers from the Temple, read long poem on revolt. Noticed cats taking notes, maybe they are publisher's agents, hope so, it would be crazy to publish with one of those big Roman firms.

WEDNESDAY—B.C.—minus 2—11 o'sun, a.m.

Local poets and literary people throwing a big dinner for me tonight, which should be a gas. Most of the cats here real cool, writing real far out—only cat bugs me is this Judas, got shook up when I refused to loan him thirty pieces of silver, he seems to be hung on loot, must be a lush.

THURSDAY—B.C.—minus 1—10 o'sun, p.m.

I am writing this in my cell. I was framed. How can they give the death sentence on charges of disorderly conduct and having public readings without a permit? It's beyond me. Oh well, there's always hope. Maybe that lawyer Judas is getting me can swing it. If he can't, God help me.

FRIDAY—Neutral—5 o'sun, a.m.

Roman turnkey was around passing out crosses. The two thieves have good connections so they got first crack at them—I got stuck with the biggest one. One of the guards doesn't dig my beard and sandals—taunted me all night. I'm going to be cool now, but tomorrow I'll tell him to go to hell, and what's so groovy is: he will. . . . somebody coming. I feel sort of abomunable. Barabbas gets a suspended sentence and I make the hill. What a drag. Well, that's poetry, and I've got to split now.

Boms

1.   Stashed in his minaret, towering
     Over the hashish wells, Caliph
     Ralph inventoried his popcorn hoard
     While nutty eunuchs conced his concubines.

2.   Movies about inventors' lives and glass-encased
        historical documents do not move me as much as
        drinking or hiccupping in the bathtub.

3.   Filled with green courage we sneezed political,
     Coughing our dirty fingernails for President.

4.   Ageless brilliant colored spiders webbing eternally,
     Instead of taking showers under the fire hydrants
        in summer.

5.   Unruly hairs in the noses of statues in public gardens
     Were placed there by God in a fit of insane jealousy.

6.   Single-breasted suits, dancing in the air,
     Turned up their cuffs at double-breasted suits
     Plodding down the street.

7.   Greedy burglars stole my mother and father,
     And gave me a free pass to the circus and I like stripes.

8.   Misty-eyed, knee-quaking me, gazing on the family
        Home,
     Realizing that I was about to burn it down.

9.   Waterspouts, concealed in pig knuckle barrels, rumbled,
     As tired storms whispered encouragement.

10.   Angry motives scrambled for seating space,

Shaking their fist at the moon.

11. Liver salesmen door to doored back pats,
    Disturbing chimneysweeps sleeping on roofs.

12. Daily papers suicided from tree tops,
    Purpling the lawn with blueprints.

13. Caribou pranced in suburban carports,
    Hoofmarking the auto-suggestions.

14. Pentagonal merit badges flowed
    Gracefully over the male nurses' heads.

15. Disordered aquariums, dressed in shredded wheat,
    Delivered bibles to pickles crying in confessionals.

Abomunist Rational Anthem

(to be sung before and after frinking)

Derrat slegelations, flo goof babereo
Sorash sho dubies, wago, wailo, wailo.

Geed bop nava glid, nava glied, nava
Speerieder, huyedist, hedacaz, ax, O, O.

Deeredition, Boomedition, squom, squom, squom,
Dee beetstrawist, wapago, wapago, loco,
        locoro, locoest
Voometeyereepetiop, bob, bop, bop, whipop.

Dearat, shloho, kurritip, plog, mangi, squom pot,
Clopo jago, bree, bree, asloopered, akingo labiop,
Engpop, engpop, boint plolo, plolo, bop bop.

(Music composed by Schroeder.)

Abomunist Documents

(discovered during ceremonies at the Tomb of the Unknown Draftdodger)

Boston, December 1773

Dear Adams:

I am down to my last can of tea, and cannot afford to score for more as the British Pushers have stamped a new tax on the Stuff, I know that many Colony Cats are as hung as I am, so why don't we get together on the Night of the Sixteenth and Go down to the Wharf and swing with a few Pounds. I think it will be cooler if we make the Scene dressed as Indians, the British Fuzz, will not know who the Tea-Heads are, it will be very dark so we will have to carry torches, tell the Cats not to goof with the torches and start a Fire, that would ruin the whole Scene.

Later,
HANCOCK

West Point, December 1778

Dear Wife:

I am trying my best to raise the Money for the Rent, but the Army has no funds for Personal Hardships, I sounded George about Promotion, but the Virginia Crowd seems to be in Control so even my hero status can't be any good. Met a very nice English Cat named André, and he has offered to see if he can swing a Loan for me, I don't know where he can get so much money, but since he has been so nice, it would be traitorous to ask.

P.S. He was telling me how much cheaper it is to live in England. Maybe when this is over we can settle there. I have been doing a lot of drawing in my spare time, and tonight I promised to show André some of my sketches, if I can find them, they are all mixed up with my defense plans and I've broken my glasses.

Have to close now. I can hear André sneaking in, the chances
he takes. He really loves Art.

Yours, faithfully,

BENEDICT

Abomnewscast . . . on the Hour . . .

America collides with iceberg piloted by Lindbergh baby. . . .
Aimee Semple Macpherson, former dictator of California, dis-
covered in voodoo nunnery disguised as Moby Dick. . . . New
hit song sweeping the country, the Leopold & Loeb Cha-cha-
cha. . . . Pontius Pilate loses no-hitter on an error, league split
over scorer's decision, Hebrew fireballer out for season with
injured hands. . . . Civilian Defense Headquarters unveils new
bomb shelter with two-car garage, complete with indoor patio
and barbecue unit that operates on radioactivity, comes in dec-
orator colors, no down payment for vets, to be sold only to
those willing to sign loyalty oath. . . . Forest Lawn Cemetery
opens new subdivision of split-level tombs for middle-income
group. . . . President inaugurates new policy of aggressive lead-
ership, declares December 25th Christmas Day. . . . Pope may
allow priests to marry, said to be aiming at one big holy family.
. . . Norman Rockwell cover, "The Lynching Bee" from "Post"
Americana series, wins D.A.R. Americanism award. . . . Rus-
sians said to be copying TV format with frontier epic filmed in
Berlin, nuclear Wagon Train features Moiseyev Dancers. . . .
Red China cuts birthrate drastically, blessed events plummet to
two hundred million a year. . . . Cubans seize Cuba, outraged
U.S. acts quickly, cuts off tourist quota, administration intro-
duces measure to confine all rhumba bands to detention camps
during emergency. . . . Both sides in Cold War stockpiling
atomic missiles to preserve peace, end of mankind seen if peace
is declared, UN sees encouraging sign in small war policy,
works quietly for wider participation among backward na-
tions. . . . End of news. . . . Remember your national emergency
signal, when you see one small mushroom cloud and three large
ones, it is not a drill, turn the TV off and get under it. . . .
Foregoing sponsored by your friendly neighborhood Abomu-
nist. . . . Tune in next world. . . .

MICHAEL MCCLURE

||||||||||||||||||||||||||||||||||||||||||||||||||||||||||||||||||||||||||||||||||||||||||||||||||||||||||||||||||||||||||

MICHAEL MCCLURE was born in 1932 in Marysville, Kansas. In 1954 he attended art classes at San Francisco State College and took a poetry workshop given by Robert Duncan in the mid-1950s and performed in a reading of Duncan's play *Faust Foutu*. In 1955, McClure joined Gary Snyder, Philip Whalen, Allen Ginsberg, and the San Francisco surrealist Philip Lamantia at the historic Six Gallery reading. McClure's early experimental writings included "Peyote Poem," written while on the sacramental peyote plant, and "Dark Brown," a wildly erotic sexual vision. His book *Ghost Tantras* restored what he called "beast language" to poetry—growls, moans, coos, whimpers, and roars intermingling with prayer and celebration in lexically recognizable human speech. He achieved underground fame through a succession of plays, including the sexy, terrifying "The Beard." McClure's poetry remains grounded in a biological and spiritual sensibility ("Consciousness is a real thing like the hoof of a deer . . ."). McClure is also a chronicler of the innovative and liberating poetries of the fifties and sixties—his *Scratching the Beat Surface* is a book-length account of the period written by one of its active members. His ecological activism is expressed in poems like the angry "For the Death of 100 Whales," and his appearance with Gary Snyder at the U.N. Environmental Conference in Stockholm in 1972. He has published more than twenty books, including *Rain Mirror: New*

Poems and *Plum Stones: Cartoons of No Heaven*. He has also
worked extensively with Ray Manzarek, the Doors' keyboard-
ist, and with the experimental composer and musician Terry
Riley.

———————

from **Dark Brown**

(Fuck Ode)

THE HUGE FIGURES FUCKING THE HUGE FIGURES
                                        FUCKING
THE HUGE FIGURES FUCKING ON THE CLIFFS ON THE
                        BANKS IN THE BLACK RIVER
    in with the fields without proportion, the black clover
      grown meadows. THERE IS NO SIZE! Undreaming and
      vast as a dream. This is love INVENTED. The huge
                        COCK
      slipping in the soft dream. Not dream. In the cunt,
      THERE! In the mouth. The slipping of figures upon
        the other. The rocking, the hugging swaying,
                        HOLDING.
THE FIGURES JOIN THEIR BODIES TO THEIR BODIES,
            the skin walls are joined! Arm of arm
    held to arm. The huge faces and behemoth legs,
      the round arms of love made anew. We slip
    down into the black clover. I/slide into the
    scented grass I sing in your ear. My song is nothing
        but the sounds of my feeling. Music is ugly. My
          song is the same as yours holding me.
ALL IS QUIET BUT MY SONG TO ME, YOUR SONG
            to you. This is our touching. This
        is the vast hall that we inhabit. Coiling,
      standing. Cock into rose-black meat. Tongue
        into rose meat. Come upon your breasts, Come
            upon your tongue, come in your burrow
          Cavern love snail breath strange arm line

OH SLEEP SLEEP NOT. OH STRENGTH BODY
LOVE
There are no lies in your face your eyes
I see in darkness. There is a golden
casket hanging there over our heads,
Silver, Silver Carafe, No!
!A SIGHT, SIGHT!
THE VOID OF OUR SENSES ETERNAL THE COCK!!!!
My cock is blue and pink in the vast
night. Night? In the vast. OH
ever undreaming I feel you/ I, you
are my body as I claim it. This is not
Nothing. Oh Ever ever!! Oh not chalice but
body. Oh tongue lined
sweetness of buttock and tight sleekness of
asshole. Oh mount of meat fur
coated, hand brushed. Huge Figures, Fucking,
perfumes eternal called perfumes. Remembrances
of this ever moment. Oh MEADOWS MEADOWS
MEADOWS MEADOWS MEADOWS MEADOWS MEADOWS
MEADOWS MEADOWS MEADOWS
MEADOWS OF THIS, tracery orange black in my closed eye
touch
of clover, of all soft and destroyed body-crushed flowers
IN THE BANKS ON THE BLACK RIVERS I REPRIEVE
MYSELF
from the false-to-you/myself. From the false to myself
creating moments. Each moment the last each the new
Invention. Each the last protection and attack

AND NOT THAT BUT THE BREATHING LAST. THE HARD-
ON THE FEEL-UP
The stretched cock plunging you. The Oh Not Dream, HOLDING
THE
grasp of myself by myself. The body known at last!!!
!AT LAST!

YOUR HAIR IS A BLOND FIELD AND A MEADOW IN
                                         BLACKNESS.
THE CLOVER THE SIZE OF MY LEG! THERE IS NO SKY
eyes closed or open. Oh Love Love Already recaptured and
lost. Each instant of stone, basalt and huge each a
square boulder among the figures not lost on the eye!
THE JERT JERT JERT OF THE COME INTO THE HEAT
of my inside-cock. Burning. The tube of
myself. Oh mangled line! Oh burning beauty!
COMED EYE SOBBING AND TEARS OF LAUGHTER, OH
breathing. Oh false explanations. Freed

Of all lies the face is pure. The gestures are imm-
ortal. THE FIRE IS FIRE CONFUSIONS BURNT IN
upon themselves. What is speed? Oh false
to myself uncovered! Oh come in your pink-rose
cunt and on your tongue tip. Breast. NO!! Shoulder
in my mouth. Bite on your buttock. Ass kissed
BEATENED AND FRESHENED NOT LOVE NO BUT
new.
OH FEAR FEAR FEAR TORN AND GONE. OH HUGE
                                      FIGURES, BREATH.
OH CLOVER CLOVER CLOVER AND NOT MUSIC OH
                                      HUGE UGLINESS

that is beauty! OH beauty that is huge ugliness. Oh
vast halls of meadows and blackness. Dark
water. Oh who has been here before I
raise me in Seraph-hood! I say it risen from fear I
expand the face arm nerve muscle of myself to
include myself. The step to fill it is easy. Oh all
unsimple. Simple. Oh beatened darkness huge and whole.
MY COCK YOUR HAND OUR MOUTHS YOUR MEAT
                                      CUNT MY SIZE

BLACK LIGHT BLACK LIGHT BLACK LIGHT BLACK LIGHT

and meat beast creatures turning huge. Light
clover cool in your hug of me of my hug.
NOT MUSIC!!!

OH BEGONIA PETAL ON THE PAGE, Worm within. NOT
MUSIC!
My arms huge cradles on the clover. My back a block.
Your/my pant in pleasure and shriek of coming. The
waves of it and toe-twists. The muscles revolt
each seeks to become a lover. OH STOP STOP.
((Pride, liberty, love, have one meaning—Invention.))
I, my body, I, I, I, I, I, buckle!
The instant test.
NOT NOT MUSIC.
I BUCKLE FROM ONE VISION, SIGHT, FROM THE
CLOVER.

(THIS IS THE CAVE OF THE VOID OF OUR SENSES. THIS IS
ALL OPEN.
Open your mouth to me You/I. Let me lay the huge head of my
cock
on your tongue again in blackness. Swell til it comes white spurts
in blackness. Let your breasts stretch as they do. What color I
see
them what shape they are, solid figure. Spread your legs. The
shape
you make them/I/for me. I feel the hair with my tongue my
cock as I enter. Oh past, past. There is one tense. There is
one.
I/ HUGE FIGURE FUCKING IN BLACKNESS,
moistness of clover warm/cool. Wet of tongue and meat-cunt
cool/warm. Bèige taste in blackness. As you sink to my knees
and fall to grasp you/I. Come drop on your shoulder.
THIS IS THE DARKNESS IN BLACK LIGHT THIS IS THE
CLOVER THIS
is the valley and black river. Carafe again, no

the found hunt. Not the Chase, the all moment. The whole
blossom,
not the ion exchanged. The come shot and huge
slipping
BLACK WATER IN BLACKNESS WATER CASCADING
on the cliffs and the banks and the meadow.))

NO LIMIT TO THIS NO MEDALLION NO MOVED WITHIN
BUT
all blackness and meadow, river, clover, bulks
fucking. You/I suck come from me in huge motions of mouth
blossom/ cunt/ arm round but. I slip down to cover
you forever. Not I outspoken but all others inspoken. Oh bright
dark I/you/I.

OH D. H. LAWRENCE LAWRENCE LAWRENCE I AM
WHOLE AS IS JOHN WEBSTER
his huge body there on the bank-tips, cliff-edge joined
his desire-love with his body. Oh see him there!!!!!!!!

WOMAN WOMAN WOMAN WOMAN WOMAN WOMAN

I-You/I, now
FOREVER!!!

(A Garland)

OH LET LOVE OH ME LOVE OH LET LOVE YOUR SWEET
BONES AND BREASTS
sweet slim round arms and firm ass. Touch you
where you swell. Kiss your soft flesh. Make meat
of you and bite your pale lips. Push my finger
in you, BODY, warm where. Oh let me lick. I kiss
your slim fingers. Kiss you in your hair and bite
your waist. Feel the skin of you like lace moved and
torn by the touch of what I make to you. And press
your shoulder. Hug your back

to me. And slip my dry cock under your moist ass,
and bite you on the neck. Rub your
belly with my hand and finger your lips
and hole. OH LET LOVE OH ME.
I want it.

OH LIE OH LET LOVE DOWN BEFORE ME SPREAD YOUR
HAIR LONG
on the pillow. Black pantied, no naked! Open
your eyes and mouth wide. Your dark eyes and hair
over the pillow. Leave your long white-pink open
spread before me. With a picture of Jesus beside
on the bedstead. And mouth open smile, I
climb and hunch over your face. Fondle my cock
and lick my balls beneath your chin! No
I hurry. Open your mouth wide your
red mouth, your white teeth the pink roof
of your throat. Your long hair spread
on the pillow.

SMIRKING SMILE OH OH MURKY HOLE BE GONE BE
LOVE
invented. Be enormous as a fuck. Fucked arm,
fucked mouth and ass. Let me lick salty
water from your belly. Let me run my stiff
cock between your breasts, beneath your arm.
I suck your tits and ears. Tongue your
clitoris. Dream and lie upon your belly, push
my fingers in your hole and feel your ass,
and you lick and suck my
soft cock to make it hard again.
!THIS IS A CLASP!
Hold my balls in your mouth and breathe
upon my ass. Lick come from my fingers. Jack
me off. Smell yourself upon my hands
and prick. I bite the arm you slip beneath
my back.
I plunge within the hole you open

there before me. Feel your cunt pull open
wide.
SMIRKING SMILE OH OH MURKY HOLE BE GONE BE
LOVE

LET OH LIE LOVE SLIP DOWN ON YOUR KNEES AND
BLOW ME
See your mouth pushed opened spread with the size
of the thing in it. See your lovely face mis-
shapen into new beauty. Feel the hard slick thing
in it. Feel the pink head of it
back in your throat! Down on your knees
before me. Hands held to your cheeks and ears,
your long soft legs folded under you. Only
warm damp wet moist mouth hot hot with my cock
in it. Working to make me come, eyes flashing
upward. Seeing the arms held to your cheeks to feel
the cock pushing inside them. Seeing
my face above. Hearing the groan. Catching
the shot splash of come on your tongue.

LIE OH HUNCH OH LOVE CLIMB OVER ME PUT YOUR
ASS OVER
my face put your mouth over my cock. I look up
into your asshole and hole! I feel your lips and teeth
on my cock. Tongue I put against your asshole,
your sweet asscheeks I spread with my hands. Tip
tongue I move over the crease circled hole, feel
you relax and slip it inside. And feel your tense
of shame. Sleek clean inner asshole. Put my tongue
to your cunt and lick upward, the whole crease.
Tongue over hole tongue over asshole. One hand knead-
ing your breast. Feeling your hair
and breath on my toes.

For the Death of 100 Whales

(American GI's stationed in Iceland murdered one hundred killer whales with machine guns, 1954.)

Hung midsea
Like a boat mid-air
The Liners boiled their pastures:
The Liners of flesh,
The Arctic steamers.

Brains the size of a football
Mouths the size of a door.

The sleek wolves
Mowers and reapers of sea kine.
THE GIANT TADPOLES
(Meat their algae)
Lept
Like sheep or children.
Shot from the sea's bore.

Turned and twisted
(Goya!!)
Flung blood and sperm.
Incense.
Gnashed at their tails and brothers,
Cursed Christ of mammals,
Snapped at the sun,
Ran for the sea's floor.

Goya! Goya!
Oh Lawrence
No angels dance those bridges.
OH GUN! OH BOW!
There are no churches in the waves,
No holiness,
No passages or crossings
From the beasts' wet shore.

from Peyote Poem

Clear—the senses bright—sitting in the black chair—Rocker—
     the white walls reflecting the color of clouds
     moving over the sun. Intimacies! The rooms

          not important—but like divisions of all space
               of all hideousness and beauty. I hear
               the music of myself and write it down

I read the meanings of scratched walls and cracked ceilings.

     I am separate. I close my eyes in divinity and pain.

          I blink in solemnity and unsolemn joy.

     I smile at myself in my movements. Walking
          I step higher in carefulness. I fill

     space with myself. I see the secret and distinct
          patterns of smoke from my mouth

          I am without care part of all. Distinct.
     I am separate from gloom and beauty. I see all.

(SPACIOUSNESS

And grim intensity—close within myself. No longer
               a cloud
          but flesh real as rock. Like Herakles

          of primordial substance and vitality.
     And not even afraid of the thing shorn of glamor

but accepting.
The beautiful things are not of ourselves

but I watch them. Among them.

———————————————

And the Indian thing. It is true!
Here in my Apartment I think tribal thoughts.)

———————————————

STOMACHE!!!

There is no time. I am visited by a man
who is the god of foxes
there is dirt under the nails of his paw
fresh from his den.
We smile at one another in recognition.

I am free from Time. I accept it without triumph

—a fact.

Closing my eyes there are flashes of light.

My eyes won't focus but leap. I see that I have three feet.
I see seven places at once!
The floor slants—the room slopes
things melt
into each other. Flashes
of light

and meldings. I wait

seeing the physical thing pass.

I am on a mesa of time and space.

!STOM-ACHE!

Writing the music of life
in words.

Hearing the round sounds of the guitar
as colors.
Feeling the touch of flesh.

Seeing the loose chaos of words
on the page.
(ultimate grace)
(Sweet Yeats and his ball of hashish.)

My belly and I are two individuals
joined together
in life.

THIS IS THE POWERFUL KNOWLEDGE
we smile with it.

At the window I look into the blue-gray
gloom of dreariness.
I am warm. Into the dragon of space.
I stare into clouds seeing
their misty convolutions.

The whirls of vapor

I will small clouds out of existence.

They become fish devouring each other.

And change like Dante's holy spirits

becoming an osprey frozen skyhigh

to challenge me.

from Ghost Tantras

2

PLEASURE FEARS ME, FOOT ROSE, FOOT BREATH,
BY BLAHHR MOKGROOOOOOO TARRR
nowp tytath brooooooooooooooooooooo

———

In the middle of the night I dreamed I was a creature
like the great Tibetan Yogi Milarepa.
I sang a song beginning:
"Home lies in front of you not in the past.
Follow your nose
to it."
It had great mystic import, both apparent and hidden.
I was pleased with it.
GOOOOOOOOOOR!
GROOOOOOOOOOOOOOOOOOOOH!
GOOOOOOOO.
ROOOOOOOOOOOOH!
POWFF! RAHH! BLAHHR!

4

DOORWAYS ARE BARE GARDENS OF COOL
SHADOWS!
ENTRANCEWAYS ARE GARDENS OF FUTURITY!
GAHROOOOOOOOOOOOOOOOOOOOOOOOOH!
GAHROOOOOOOOOOOOOOOOOOOOOOOOOOOH!
We memorized the remembrances of our sexuality
—holding hands with our heads in the opposite directions.
All of our dearness returned.
We are youthful again
and liberated! LIBERATED!
In the morn I saw the coold doorways & entrances
through the colorful real true myth of the night.
KROOOOOOOOOOOOL-MRIST,

grooooooooooorfreeeeeeeeeee
above greye-kra!
Sweeting. Sweetling!

23

NOH VISION I WANT BUT THE FLESH
OF ME BRINGING THEE-THOU
tooorm now bye-tha being two loves together mrahh
of our grooh thowmm narg froooo byme
NAKRAYOTHBAHKTA GRITOOORM BLIST.
MOORBWAH! TOWM!
Woman holding a child who is a woman
holding a child. GREE HANT
shawl of holding el coolorrs.
Thy in and about brooo nah mooom
bweeth. Mahkeeng oon eer gant. SEE!
Woman holding a child who is a wooman
holding gree-hant a child.
THHAHHRNOOM GRAHHHHH.
Modest. Modest. Modest holding a suckling.
THY BABE.

39

MARILYN MONROE, TODAY THOU HAST PASSED
THE DARK BARRIER
—diving in a swirl of golden hair.
I hope you have entered a sacred paradise for full
warm bodies, full lips, full hips, and laughing eyes!
AHH GHROOOR. ROOOHR. NOH THAT OHH!
OOOH . . .
Farewell perfect mammal.
Fare thee well from thy silken couch and dark day!
AHH GRHHROOOR! AHH ROOOOH. GARR
nah ooth eeze farewell. Moor droon fahra rahoor
rahoor, rahoor. Thee ahhh-oh oh thahrr
noh grooh rahhr.

(August 6, 1962)

51

I LOVE TO THINK OF THE RED PURPLE ROSE
IN THE DARKNESS COOLED BY THE NIGHT
We are served by machines making satins
of sounds.
Each blot of sound is a bud or a stahr.
Body eats bouquets of the ear's vista.
Gahhhrrr boody eers noze eyes deem thou.
NOH. NAH-OHH
hrooor. VOOOR-NAH! GAHROOOOO ME.
Nah droooooh seerch. NAH THEE!
The machines are too dull when we
are lion-poems that move & breathe.
WHAN WE GROOOOOOOOOOOOOOOR
hann dree myketoth sharoo sree thah noh deeeeeemed ez.
Whan eeeethoooze hrohh.

Song: Vietnam

Platinum fur and brass revolver shine
Love Lion, Lioness are dead
And the U.S. ground is red
And everything is going fine
With platinum fur and brass revolver shine
—with sweet dust of gun and white neck

It's time, it's time, I know it's time
To tell that Love Lion, Lioness
are alive!
With platinum fur and brass revolver shine
—with sweet dust of gun and white neck

People say, "Don't get out of line
Love Lion, Lioness are dead"
And the U.S. ground is red
with Oriental blood

Platinum fur and brass revolver shine
—with sweet dust of gun and white neck

With lace and fur and sugared blood
With fur and leather whirr and creak
Till they learn how to speak
—Love Lion, Lioness
are alive!
—with sweet dust of gun and white neck

Mad Sonnet: Fame

OH HOW I WANT THEE FAME!
FAME, THOU VIOLET LAOCOÖN OF TOILING BRAWN
and writhing snakes enwreathed on upturned
GRIEVED FACES.
Oil and sweat shake from the locks of the famous,
and though they moan they are stoic as a tree.
Fame loops out fat coils like a half-forgotten dream
and binds men's wrists in their romantic agony.

Fame, you are a rotten plum!
I wipe you from my fingers
with a rosy napkin.

LET ME SEE THE LOVE TENDRILS
of woman and child!
AWAY FAME!

My spirit is not trapped by love of fame.

I am not hungry for death's attitudes.

BLESS NIGHT.

Mad Sonnet: Grace

I LOVE SEAHORSES, TEDDYBEARS, AFRICAN VIOLETS,
MICROSCOPES
AND AXES but I will not be ashamed!
I am the graceful man of my era.
I LOVE
Killer Whales, and the spiral galaxies,
and Keats, and viruses, and anti-particles,
and the dainty and dark perversity of lovely women
with hooked noses and black hair—or blond and plump
with slim ankles—Brahms,
MELVILLE, AND MARX (Harpo), REICH, FREUD,
and the juvenile delusions of Einstein.
I like fat and muscle, sweet and bitter,
and all of the Comedy of Glory.

AND I SAY,
if the last vast natural philosopher
vanishes—the grizzly bear from the peak—
or the soft hallucinatory moth
from the cactus blossom . . .

WATCH OUT!
They are not replaceable
by robots

Reading Frank O'Hara in a Mexican Rainstorm

"THE ENORMOUS BLISS of American death,"
is not so huge here, Frank,
where the rain has fallen for twelve hours
into the blue pool
in the patio
where it rises

nearing the point where it will flood the house.
The sound of the beat on the roof
resembles the dream of a hive of bees.

Somewhere a little boy stands under
    an old tin roof.
There is a postcard of Art Blakey tacked
    to the white plaster wall
and muddy shoes grow warm in front of the fire.

I remember your broken nose, Frank,
and the Gauloise that hangs
            from your mouth.

Somewhere a little boy stands under
    an old tin roof
and he takes off his straw hat
and he scratches his hair.

Senate Hearings

IT IS ALMOST BEAUTIFUL when fraud and hypocrisy
        reach this peak and become exquisite,
        exquisite in contempt for intelligence.
    With black faces or white faces
            we are always
            this way

        as
        if

        Freud
        and
        Whitehead

had never been born!
    —As if our most contemptible
or laughable lies
are the mountain tops of our aspirations.

We are always this way but these early years
of the nineties make me feel creepy
as if I live in a movie
with spittle-spewing, sneering, sullen,
    snide, plotting figures
from the caricatures of Daumier

    and the nightmares of Goya!

GARY SNYDER

||||||||||||||||||||||||||||||||||||||||||||||||||||||||||||||||||||||||||||||||||||||||||||||||||||||||||||||||||||||||||||||

GARY SNYDER was born in 1930 in San Francisco and raised in the Pacific Northwest. He spent his childhood on a farm. As a teenager, he lived alone and by his wits on the streets of Portland, Oregon. He entered Reed College, where he housed with Lew Welch and Philip Whalen, and graduated in anthropology. Snyder did graduate work in anthropology at University of Indiana but transferred to the University of California at Berkeley to study classical Chinese and pursue Zen Buddhist practice. He worked several summers with the U.S. Forest Service until he was dismissed for affiliations with leftist groups. He became friends with Kenneth Rexroth. (It was Rexroth who urged Allen Ginsberg to seek Snyder out.) Snyder joined Michael Mc-Clure, Allen Ginsberg, and Philip Whalen for the Six Gallery reading. Kerouac's novel *The Dharma Bums* memoralizes the Kerouac-Snyder friendship; the two lived together briefly in Snyder's Marin County cabin. Snyder received a scholarship from the First Zen Institute, which led to nearly fifteen years in Japan, studying Oriental and Zen poetry, writing essays and poems, and keeping journals. Snyder's first book, *Riprap*, was published in Japan by the poet Cid Corman. Snyder married Joanne Kyger and the two traveled to India, meeting up with Ginsberg and Peter Orlovsky. Together they met the Dalai Lama and sought out various Hindu and Buddhist teachers. Snyder returned in the early seventies to the North American continent—which he called Turtle Island, honoring the Native American presence—and raised two sons with Masa Uehara, in the Sierra Nevada foothills. Snyder continues to live in the Sierra Nevadas where he works on bioregionalist issues, and did so for many years with his wife, Carole Koda, who passed away in 2006. He is an esteemed scholar of Chinese poetry and culture, and a philosopher of wilderness, language, biology, and poetics in the lineage of Henry David Thoreau and John Muir. His poetry books include *Myths and Texts,* and the thirty-year-long poem project *Mountains and Rivers without End,* published in 1997. Collections of essays and journals include *Earth House Hold.*

Milton by Firelight

Piute Creek, August 1955

"O hell, what do mine eyes
        with grief behold?"
Working with an old
Singlejack miner, who can sense
The vein and cleavage
In the very guts of rock, can
Blast granite, build
Switchbacks that last for years
Under the beat of snow, thaw, mule-hooves.
What use, Milton, a silly story
Of our lost general parents,
        eaters of fruit?

The Indian, the chainsaw boy,
And a string of six mules
Came riding down to camp
Hungry for tomatoes and green apples.
Sleeping in saddle-blankets
Under a bright night-sky

Han River slantwise by morning.
Jays squall
Coffee boils

In ten thousand years the Sierras
Will be dry and dead, home of the scorpion.
Ice-scratched slabs and bent trees.
No paradise, no fall,
Only the weathering land
The wheeling sky,
Man, with his Satan
Scouring the chaos of the mind.
Oh Hell!

Fire down
Too dark to read, miles from a road
The bell-mare clangs in the meadow
That packed dirt for a fill-in
Scrambling through loose rocks
On an old trail
All of a summer's day.

Hay for the Horses

He had driven half the night
From far down San Joaquin
Through Mariposa, up the
Dangerous mountain roads,
And pulled in at eight a.m.
With his big truckload of hay
          behind the barn.
With winch and ropes and hooks
We stacked the bales up clean
To splintery redwood rafters
High in the dark, flecks of alfalfa
Whirling through shingle-cracks of light,

Itch of haydust in the
      sweaty shirt and shoes.
At lunchtime under Black oak
Out in the hot corral,
—The old mare nosing lunchpails,
Grasshoppers crackling in the weeds—
"I'm sixty-eight" he said,
"I first bucked hay when I was seventeen.
I thought, that day I started,
I sure would hate to do this all my life.
And dammit, that's just what
I've gone and done."

Cartagena

Rain and thunder beat down and flooded the streets
We danced with Indian girls in a bar,
      water half-way to our knees,
The youngest one slipped down her dress and danced
      bare to the waist,
The big negro deckhand made out with his girl on his lap
      in a chair her dress over her eyes
Coca-cola and rum, and rainwater all over the floor.
In the glittering light I got drunk and reeled through
      the rooms,
And cried, "Cartagena! swamp of unholy loves!"
And wept for the Indian whores who were younger than me,
      and I was eighteen,
And splashed after the crew down the streets wearing
      sandals bought at a stall
And got back to the ship, dawn came,
      we were far out at sea.

Colombia 1948—Arabia 1958

from Cold Mountain Poems

> Kanzan, or Han-shan, "Cold Mountain" takes his name from where he lived. He is a mountain madman in an old Chinese line of ragged hermits. When he talks about Cold Mountain he means himself, his home, his state of mind. He lived in the T'ang dynasty—traditionally A.D. 627–650, although Hu Shih dates him 700–780. This makes him roughly contemporary with Tu Fu, Li Po, Wang Wei, and Po Chü-i. His poems, of which three hundred survive, are written in T'ang colloquial: rough and fresh. The ideas are Taoist, Buddhist, Zen. He and his sidekick Shih-te (Jittoku in Japanese) became great favorites with Zen painters of later days—the scroll, the broom, the wild hair and laughter. They became Immortals and you sometimes run onto them today in the skidrows, orchards, hobo jungles, and logging camps of America.

1

The path to Han-shan's place is laughable,
A path, but no sign of cart or horse.
Converging gorges—hard to trace their twists
Jumbled cliffs—unbelievably rugged.
A thousand grasses bend with dew,
A hill of pines hums in the wind.
And now I've lost the shortcut home,
Body asking shadow, how do you keep up?

2

In a tangle of cliffs I chose a place—
Bird-paths, but no trails for men.
What's beyond the yard?
White clouds clinging to vague rocks.
Now I've lived here—how many years—
Again and again, spring and winter pass.
Go tell families with silverware and cars
"What's the use of all that noise and money?"

10

I have lived at Cold Mountain
These thirty long years.
Yesterday I called on friends and family:
More than half had gone to the Yellow Springs.
Slowly consumed, like fire down a candle;
Forever flowing, like a passing river.
Now, morning, I face my lone shadow:
Suddenly my eyes are bleared with tears.

12

In my first thirty years of life
I roamed hundreds and thousands of miles.
Walked by rivers through deep green grass
Entered cities of boiling red dust.
Tried drugs, but couldn't make Immortal;
Read books and wrote poems on history.
Today I'm back at Cold Mountain:
I'll sleep by the creek and purify my ears.

13

I can't stand these bird-songs
Now I'll go rest in my straw shack.
The cherry flowers out scarlet
The willow shoots up feathery.
Morning sun drives over blue peaks
Bright clouds wash green ponds.
Who knows that I'm out of the dusty world
Climbing the southern slope of Cold Mountain?

15

There's a naked bug at Cold Mountain
With a white body and a black head.
His hand holds two book-scrolls,
One the Way and one its Power.
His shack's got no pots or oven,

He goes for a walk with his shirt and pants askew.
But he always carries the sword of wisdom:
He means to cut down senseless craving.

16

Cold Mountain is a house
Without beams or walls.
The six doors left and right are open
The hall is blue sky.
The rooms all vacant and vague
The cast wall beats on the west wall
At the center nothing.

Borrowers don't bother me
In the cold I build a little fire
When I'm hungry I boil up some greens.
I've got no use for the kulak
With his big barn and pasture—
He just sets up a prison for himself.
Once in he can't get out.
Think it over—
You know it might happen to you.

20

Some critic tried to put me down—
"Your poems lack the Basic Truth of Tao"
And I recall the old-timers
Who were poor and didn't care.
I have to laugh at him,
He misses the point entirely,
Men like that
Ought to stick to making money.

23

My home was at Cold Mountain from the start,
Rambling among the hills, far from trouble.

Gone, and a million things leave no trace
Loosed, and it flows through the galaxies
A fountain of light, into the very mind—
Not a thing, and yet it appears before me:
Now I know the pearl of the Buddha-nature
Know its use: a boundless perfect sphere.

24

When men see Han-shan
They all say he's crazy
And not much to look at
Dressed in rags and hides.
They don't get what I say
& I don't talk their language.
All I can say to those I meet:
"Try and make it to Cold Mountain."

For a Far-out Friend

Because I once beat you up
Drunk, stung with weeks of torment
And saw you no more,
And you had calm talk for me today
            I now suppose
I was less sane than you,
You hung on dago red,
            me hooked on books,
You once ran naked toward me
Knee deep in cold March surf
On a tricky beach between two
            pounding seastacks—

I saw you as a Hindu Deva-girl
Light legs dancing in the waves,
Breasts like dream-breasts
Of sea, and child, and astral

Venus-spurting milk.
And traded our salt lips.

Visions of your body
Kept me high for weeks, I even had
           a sort of trance for you
A day in a dentist's chair.
I found you again, gone stone,
In Zimmer's book of Indian Art:
Dancing in that life with
Grace and love, with rings
And a little golden belt, just above
           your naked snatch
And I thought—more grace and love
In that wild Deva life where you belong
Than in this dress-and-girdle life
You'll ever give
Or get.

For the Boy Who Was Dodger Point Lookout
Fifteen Years Ago

[On a backpacking trip with my first wife in the Olympic moun-
tains, having crossed over from the Dosewallips drainage, de-
scended to and forded the Elwha and the Goldie, and climbed
again to the high country. Hiking alone down the Elwha from
Queets basin, these years later, brings it back.]

The thin blue smoke of our campfire
down in the grassy, flowery,
heather meadow
two miles from your perch.
The snowmelt pond, and Alison,
half-stoopt bathing like
Swan Maiden, lovely naked,
ringed with Alpine fir and
gleaming snowy peaks. We

had come miles without trails,
you had been long alone.
We talked for half an hour up
there above the foaming creeks
and forest valleys, in our
world of snow and flowers.

I don't know where she is now;
I never asked your name.
In this burning, muddy, lying,
blood-drenched world
that quiet meeting in the mountains
cool and gentle as the muzzles of
three elk, helps keep me sane.

Four Poems for Robin

Siwashing it out once in Siuslaw Forest

I slept under   rhododendron
All night   blossoms fell
Shivering on   a sheet of cardboard
Feet stuck   in my pack
Hands deep   in my pockets
Barely   able   to   sleep.
I remembered   when we were in school
Sleeping together   in a big warm bed
We were   the youngest lovers
When we broke up   we were still nineteen.
Now our   friends are married
You teach   school back east
I dont mind   living this way
Green hills   the long blue beach
But sometimes   sleeping in the open
I think back   when I had you.

A spring night in Shokoku-ji

Eight years ago this May
We walked under cherry blossoms
At night in an orchard in Oregon.
All that I wanted then
Is forgotten now, but you.
Here in the night
In a garden of the old capital
I feel the trembling ghost of Yugao
I remember your cool body
Naked under a summer cotton dress.

An autumn morning in Shokoku-ji

Last night watching the Pleiades,
Breath smoking in the moonlight,
Bitter memory like vomit
Choked my throat.
I unrolled a sleeping bag
On mats on the porch
Under thick autumn stars.
In dream you appeared
(Three times in nine years)
Wild, cold, and accusing.
I woke shamed and angry:
The pointless wars of the heart.
Almost dawn. Venus and Jupiter.
The first time I have
Ever seen them close.

December at Yase

You said, that October,
In the tall dry grass by the orchard
When you chose to be free,
"Again someday, maybe ten years."

After college I saw you
One time. You were strange.
And I was obsessed with a plan.

Now ten years and more have
Gone by: I've always known
      where you were—
I might have gone to you
Hoping to win your love back.
You still are single.

I didn't.
I thought I must make it alone. I
Have done that.

Only in dream, like this dawn,
Does the grave, awed intensity
Of our young love
Return to my mind, to my flesh.

We had what the others
All crave and seek for;
We left it behind at nineteen.

I feel ancient, as though I had
Lived many lives.

And may never now know
If I am a fool
Or have done what my
    karma demands.

Nansen

I found you on a rainy morning
After a typhoon
In a bamboo grove at Daitoku-ji.
Tiny wet rag with a
Huge voice, you crawled under the fence
To my hand. Left to die.

I carried you home in my raincoat.
"Nansen, cheese!" you'd shout an answer
And come running.
But you never got big,
Bandy-legged bright little dwarf—
Sometimes not eating, often coughing
Mewing bitterly at inner twinge.

Now, thin and older, you won't eat
But milk and cheese. Sitting on a pole
In the sun. Hardy with resigned
Discontent.
You just weren't made right. I saved you,
And your three-year life has been full
Of mild, steady pain.

For a Stone Girl at Sanchi

half asleep on the cold grass
        night rain flicking the maples
under a black bowl upside-down
on a flat land
        on a wobbling speck
smaller than stars,
                space,
the size of a seed,
        hollow as bird skulls.
light flies across it.
        —never is seen.

a big rock weathered funny,
old tree trunks turnd stone,
        split rocks and find clams.
                all that time
loving;
two flesh persons changing,

clung to, doorframes
        notions, spear-hafts
in a rubble of years.
                touching,
this dream pops. it was real:
        and it lasted forever.

Circumambulating Arunachala

for centuries sadhus live and die
in dolmen rock-slab huts near
        Arunachala

Small girls with gaudy flowers
flash down the bare walk road,
        the weight, the power,
the full warm brilliance of the human mind
        behind their eyes:
                they die or sicken in a year.

Below the hill—
wells, ponds, spiky trees,
carvd fragments of soft bodies,
        female bellies,
                centuries old.

Through the Smoke Hole

for Don Allen

I

There is another world above this one; or outside of this one;
        the way to it is thru the smoke of this one, & the hole that
        smoke goes through. The ladder is the way through the

smoke hole; the ladder holds up, some say, the world above; it might have been a tree or pole; I think it is merely a way.

Fire is at the foot of the ladder. The fire is in the center. The walls are round. There is also another world below or inside this one. The way there is down thru smoke. It is not necessary to think of a series.

Raven and Magpie do not need the ladder. They fly thru the smoke holes shrieking and stealing. Coyote falls thru; we recognize him only as a clumsy relative, a father in old clothes we don't wish to see with our friends.

It is possible to cultivate the fields of our own world without much thought for the others. When men emerge from below we see them as the masked dancers of our magic dreams. When men disappear down, we see them as plain men going somewhere else. When men disappear up we see them as great heroes shining through the smoke. When men come back from above they fall thru and tumble; we don't really know them; Coyote, as mentioned before.

II

Out of the kiva come
masked dancers or
plain men.
          plain men go into the ground.

out there out side all the chores
        wood and water, dirt,
wind, the view across the flat,
here, in the round
                        no corners
head is full of magic figures—
woman your secrets aren't my secrets
what I cant say I wont
walk round

put my hand flat down.
you in the round too.
gourd vine blossom.
walls and houses drawn up
from the same soft soil.
thirty million years gone
                    drifting sand.
   cool rooms pink stone
worn down fort floor, slat sighting
   heat shine on jumna river

dry wash, truck tracks in the riverbed
coild sand pinyon.

                    seabottom
                    riverbank
                    sand dunes
the floor of a sea once again.

                    human fertilizer
                    underground water tunnels
                    skinny dirt gods
                    grandmother berries
                                        out
through the smoke hole.
          (for childhood and youth *are* vanity)

a Permian reef of algae,

out through the smoke hole
swallowd sand
                salt mud
swum bodies,   flap
to the limestone blanket—

lizzard tongue,   lizzard tongue

          wha, wha, wha   flying
in and *out* thru the smoke hole

> plain men
> come out of the ground.

As for Poets

As for poets
The Earth Poets
Who write small poems,
Need help from no man.

The Air Poets
Play out the swiftest gales
And sometimes loll in the eddies.
Poem after poem,
Curling back on the same thrust.

At fifty below
Fuel oil won't flow
And propane stays in the tank.
Fire Poets
Burn at absolute zero
Fossil love pumped back up.

The first
Water Poet
Stayed down six years.
He was covered with seaweed.
The life in his poem
Left millions of tiny
Different tracks
Criss-crossing through the mud.

With the Sun and Moon
In his belly,
The Space Poet
Sleeps.

No end to the sky—
But his poems,
Like wild geese,
Fly off the edge.

A Mind Poet
Stays in the house.
The house is empty
And it has no walls.
The poem
Is seen from all sides,
Everywhere,
At once.

No Shoes No Shirt No Service

Padding down the street, the
Bushmen, the Paiute, the Cintas Largas
        are refused.
The queens of Crete,
The waiting-ladies of the King of Bundelkhand.
Tārā is kept out,
Bare-breasted on her lotus throne.

        (officially, no one goes through
        unofficially, horses go through,
        carriages go through—)

The barefoot shepherds, the bare-chested warriors

        (what is this gate,
        wide as a highway
        that only mice can enter?)

The cow passed through the window nicely—
Only the tail got stuck,

And the soils of this region will be fertile again
After another round of volcanoes
Nutrient ash—
    Shiva's dancing feet
    (No shoes)

Old Woman Nature

Old Woman Nature
naturally has a bag of bones
    tucked away somewhere.
    a whole room full of bones!

A scattering of hair and cartilage
    bits in the woods.

A fox scat with hair and a tooth in it.
    a shellmound
        a bone flake in a streambank.

A purring cat, crunching
    the mouse head first,
        eating on down toward the tail—

The sweet old woman
    calmly gathering firewood in the
        moon . . .

Don't be shocked,
She's heating you some soup.

*VII 81, Seeing Ichikawa Ennosuke
in "Kurozuka"—"Demoness"—at the
Kabuki-za in Tokyo*

Building

We started our house midway through the Cultural Revolution,
The Vietnam war, Cambodia, in our ears,
    tear gas in Berkeley,
Boys in overalls with frightened eyes, long matted hair, ran
    from the police.
We peeled trees, drilled boulders, dug sumps, took sweat baths
    together.
That house finished we went on
Built a schoolhouse, with a hundred wheelbarrows,
    held seminars on California paleo-indians during lunch.
We brazed the Chou dynasty form of the character "Mu"
    on the blacksmithed brackets of the ceiling of the lodge,
Buried a five-prong vajra between the schoolbuildings
    while praying and offering tobacco.
Those buildings were destroyed by a fire, a pale copy rebuilt
    by insurance.

Ten years later we gathered at the edge of a meadow.
The cultural revolution is over, hair is short,
    the industry calls the shots in the Peoples Forests,
Single mothers go back to college to become lawyers.

Blowing the conch, shaking the staff-rings
    we opened work on a Hall.
Forty people, women carpenters, child labor, pounding nails,
Screw down the corten roofing and shape the beams
    with a planer,
The building is done in three weeks.
We fill it with flowers and friends and open it up.

Now in the year of the Persian Gulf,
Of Lies and Crimes in the Government held up as Virtues,
    this dance with Matter
Goes on: our buildings are solid, to live, to teach, to sit,
To sit, to know for sure the sound of a bell—

This is history. This is outside of history.
Buildings are built in the moment,
   they are constantly wet from the pool
     that renews all things
    naked and gleaming.

The moon moves
Through her twenty-eight nights.
Wet years and dry years pass;
Sharp tools, good design.

Word Basket Woman

Years after surviving
the Warsaw uprising,
she wrote the poems of ordinary people
building barricades while being shot at,
small poems were all
that could hold so much
close to death   life
without making it false.

Robinson Jeffers, his tall cold view
quite true in a way, but why did he say it
as though he alone
stood above our delusions, he also
feared death, insignificance,
and was not quite up to the inhuman beauty
of parsnips or diapers, the deathless
nobility   at the core of all ordinary things

I dwell
in a house on the long west slope
of Sierra Nevada, two hundred mile
swell of granite,
bones of the Ancient Buddha,

miles back from the seacoast
on a line of fiery chakras
in the deep nerve web of the land,

Europe forgotten now, almost a dream—
but our writing
is sidewise and roman, and the language
a compote of old wars and tribes from some
place overseas. Here
at the rim of the world
where the *panaka* calls in the *chá*—the heart
words are Pomo, Miwok, Nisenan,
and the small poem word baskets
stretch to the heft of their burden.

I came this far to tell
of the grave of my great-
grandmother Harriet Callicotte
by itself on a low ridge in Kansas.
The sandstone tumbled,
her name almost eaten away,
where I found it in rain drenched grass
on my knees, closed my eyes
and swooped under the earth
to that loam dark, holding her emptiness
and placed one cool kiss
on the arch of her white
pubic bone.

VI 85, Carneiro Kansas
XII 87, Kitkitdizze

A Literary Guide to Beat Places

||||||||||||||||||||||||||||||||||||||||||||||||||||||||||||||||||||||||||||||||||||||||||||||||||||||||||||||||||||||||||||||||

Berkeley

At Kenneth Rexroth's urging, Allen Ginsberg knocked on the door of Gary Snyder's Berkeley cottage in 1955. Ginsberg and Jack Kerouac were to join Snyder in Berkeley, Ginsberg taking a cottage on Milvia Street. Philip Whalen also lived in Berkeley and washed test tubes at the University of California to support his poetry writing. Kerouac's *The Dharma Bums* sets the Berkeley scene—wine, marijuana, Buddhism, mystical sex, suicidal young women, wild writing. Most of the cottages have been replaced by wasteful and indecorous apartment buildings, but Berkeley's ambience of cafes, bookshops, and leftist politics remains. An early inspiration for Beat poets was Berkeley's connection to anthropology and research into the primitive— Jaime de Angulo (an early representative of Bohemianism), the great anthropologists Paul Radin, Alfred Kroeber, Edward Sapir, and the geologist Carl Sauer all had taught at the University. In 1965, the University hosted the Berkeley Poetry Conference. Snyder, Ginsberg, Charles Olson, Jack Spicer, LeRoi Jones, Robert Duncan, and countless other poets congregated for the first big poetry festival in the United States, climaxing with proto-Beat Charles Olson presiding "in all his sodden brilliance" over a methedrine evening of talk and verse (see Charles Olson's *Reading at Berkeley*).

Big Sur

Big Sur, California, was an early haven for hobos, poets, anthropologists, musicians, recluses, and writers like Henry Miller, Robinson Jeffers, Jaime de Angulo, Harry Partch. Lawrence Ferlinghetti's cabin at Bixby Canyon, where numerous parties and retreats took place, figures mythically in writings by Kerouac, Ginsberg, and Lew Welch. See Kerouac's *Big Sur* (in which a particularly onomatopoeic, rapturous passage captures the ebb and tide and crash of the ocean) as well as Ginsberg's poem "Bixby Canyon" and the letters of Lew Welch gathered in *I Remain*. See also Richard Brautigan, *A Confederate General from Big Sur.*

Bubb's Creek

Bubb's Creek, in King's Canyon National Park, Southern Sierras, California, was the site of a long rucksack and poetry trip by foot, à la Bashō, into the Sierra Nevada wilderness by Gary Snyder and Allen Ginsberg. Snyder's "Bubb's Creek Haircut" memorializes the journey—full of loggers, trail crews, mosquitoes, as well as hitchhike journeys and Salvation Army store supply posts. Today, one of King's Canyon's popular backpack trails winds its way up Bubb's Creek.

Denver

Denver was the birthplace of Neal Cassady and a gathering place for Cassady, Ginsberg, and Kerouac on their coast-to-coast jaunts. Larimer Street bars were the scene. Though Larimer is much gentrified today, bartenders still swear that "Jack Kerouac sat on that barstool!" Kerouac's *Visions of Cody* depicts Cassady's early life in speakeasies and alleyways of Denver.

India

In 1962–63, India was a place of pilgrimage for Allen Ginsberg and Peter Orlovsky. They were joined there by Joanne Kyger and Gary Snyder from January to April, 1962. There were visits to the Dalai Lama, various Hindu swamis, and the German writer Lama Govinda, and a rigorous examination of culture, archaeological sites, ashrams, and opium dens. Ginsberg and Orlovsky lived in both Banaras and Calcutta, where Ginsberg smoked *ganja* with *sadhus* and meditated on smoldering corpses at Nimtala Ghat. See Allen Ginsberg's *Indian Journals;* Peter Orlovsky's *Leper's Cry;* Gary Snyder's *Passage through India* and his "Kali" section of *The Back Country;* Joanne Kyger's *Japan and India Journals.* India, original home of Buddhism and site of countless artistic and spiritual practices, wild literatures, street musicians, and festivals, continues to draw poets.

Kyoto

Kyoto, Japan, was the residence of many expatriate American poets and Zen students in the 1950s and 1960s. Initially, the draw was the First Zen Institute, run at Daitokuji Temple by Ruth Fuller Sasaki, which brought Gary Snyder as a Zen student to Kyoto on a scholarship in 1956. Snyder and Joanne Kyger were married and lived there, first in the nearby village of Yasé and then in Kyoto proper. The poet Cid Corman has made Kyoto his home since the 1950s, when he sat every day in a local coffee shop meeting with poets and editing issues of *Origin* magazine. Corman published Snyder's first book, *Riprap.* Ten years after the war, Kyoto attracted many Beat writers with its fresh and lively arts scene, numerous potters in town studying on Fulbrights, and a brisk flavor of dharma. The city is strewn with Zen temples and rock gardens. Buddhist scholar Burton Watson lived there. Short-term residents and visitors included Alan Watts, Clayton Eshleman, Daniel Ellsberg, and many other writers, famous and obscure. Philip Whalen lived there in the late 1960s and wrote *Scenes of Life at the Capital.* See Kyger's *Japan and India Journals,* Snyder's essay "Spring Sesshin at Daitokuji" in *Earth House Hold,* and various poems from *The Back Country.*

Lowell

Lowell, Massachusetts, was the birthplace and childhood town of Jack Kerouac, who was also buried there after his death in 1968. It now offers a Kerouac memorial with big monoliths along the Merrimack River inscribed with passages from his novels. Various of Kerouac's childhood houses and hangout joints can be seen in town (use Barry Gifford's *Kerouac's Town* as a guide). Lowell was the site of several "Duluoz Mythology" books by Kerouac, including *The Town and the City, Dr. Sax, Vanity of Duluoz,* and *Visions of Gerard.* There is a scene in Bob Dylan's film *Renaldo and Clara* with Dylan and Allen Ginsberg at the Lowell cemetery at the gravesite of Jack Kerouac.

Marin County

There are Beat sites all over Marin County, California. Mount Tamalpais, "The Sleeping Lady," dominates the landscape. On her flanks sits the town of Mill Valley, where Snyder lived in a cottage he named Marin-an. Kerouac stayed with him for a while and wrote *Old Angel Midnight* while sitting in a window of the cabin. Local parties drew huge Beat crowds. Inspired by Japanese and Tibetan pilgrims, poets circumambulated Mount Tamalpais intoning traditional and newly devised Buddhist chants. Nearby, Muir and Stinson beaches were scenes of clam digs and barbecues. Lew Welch, inspired by one massive offshore rock, wrote his poem "Wobbly Rock." The hidden coastal town of Bolinas became a residence for many writers. Philip Whalen, Robert Creeley, Bobbie Louise Hawkins, Robert Grenier, Tom Clark, Aram Saroyan, Bill Berkson, and others have lived there. Richard Brautigan shot himself there. Joanne Kyger still lives in Bolinas, helps edit the *Bolinas Hearsay News,* and is herself a compendium of the lore, magic, and literary history of the place.

Mexico City

William Burroughs and his wife, Jean Vollmer, began a peripatetic life in places where drugs were easily obtainable. They lived in New Orleans and Texas, but by 1950 they had moved to Mexico City, where Burroughs wrote *Junk,* a factual book about his drug experiences begun as a "memory exercise." It was published in 1953 as a pulp paperback titled *Junky* under the pseudonym "William Lee." On September 6th, 1951, Burroughs accidentally killed his wife and was charged in Mexico City with criminal imprudence. Released on bail, Burroughs went on to South America in quest of *yage*, a powerful hallucinogen. Jack Kerouac spent the summer of 1955 in Mexico City, where he composed the highly experimental, spontaneous *Mexico City Blues*, a poem of 242 choruses influenced by jazz rhythms. Also see his novel *Tristessa*, an account of a love affair set in Mexico City.

Naropa University: The Jack Kerouac School of Disembodied Poetics

Naropa University, in Boulder, Colorado, was founded by Chögyam Trungpa Rinpoche, a poet, calligrapher, and lineage holder of the Kargyu, or "crazy wisdom" school of Tibetan Buddhism. A refugee from Tibet, Trungpa had come to America (after spending time at Oxford University) "looking for the poets." At an historic gathering in the summer of 1974, which included Gregory Bateson, John Cage, Allen Ginsberg, Diane di Prima, Anne Waldman, Jackson MacLow, and others—with the notion that Naropa was "a hundred year project at least"—Ginsberg and Waldman founded the Jack Kerouac School of Disembodied Poetics. Naropa was also to house a Buddhist studies program, contemplative psychotherapy, and music and dance programs. Since then, the poetics school, which offers accredited B.A. and (residential and low-residency) M.F.A. degrees in writing and poetics, has been a stronghold of the "outrider" tradition in American poetry. A month-long summer program hosts writers from all over the world and has organized major conferences, such as the *On the Road* Conference, Beats and Other Rebel Angels Conference, and many others. The Naropa Audio Archive, which has received several federal and private preservation grants, is one of the world's largest audio collections of post-World War II American poetry. Some of the Archive's estimated 5,000 hours of audio material (and growing) are available online. See *Talking*

Poetics (Vols. 1 and 2), *Disembodied Poetics: Annals of the Jack Kerouac School,* and *Civil Disobediences: Poetics and Politics in Action.* Allen Ginsberg, Peter Orlovsky, William Burroughs, Gregory Corso, Philip Whalen, Gary Snyder, Amiri Baraka, Joanne Kyger, Diane di Prima, Michael Mclure, and Lawrence Ferlinghetti have all served on the faculty.

New York City

Greenwich Village

Greenwich Village gained renown as the home and workshop of artists and freethinkers, folk such as anarchist Alexander Berkman and literary innovator Alfred Kreymborg. Barns, stables, and houses along the crooked, crowded streets were converted into studios, eating establishments, nightclubs, theaters, and shops, and the Village developed a reputation for Bohemianism. Maxwell Bodenheim, the novelist and poet, was for many years a fixture on the bohemian scene, epitomizing the reigning free spirit. Poets Marianne Moore and Mina Loy, novelist Djuna Barnes, and many others lived there in the twenties and beyond. In a Greenwich Village bar in 1950, Allen Ginsberg met Gregory Corso, a twenty-year-old "jail kid." Corso then lived on Bleecker Street. The Village's heyday as a center for radical literary and political activity had passed in 1940 with the area's increasing gentrification, although many writers and artists continued to meet at bars like the San Remo and jazz clubs such as the Village Vanguard and the Village Gate. The sixties saw a rebirth of some magnitude with the increase of folk clubs for performers like Dave Van Ronk and Bob Dylan. Israel Young's Folklore Center had a regular poetry reading series in the sixties and early seventies.

The Lower East Side, the East Village

The Lower East Side of Manhattan is generally associated with inexpensive housing and thus has been a haven for waves of immigrants over the years. Today, it is an area of tremendous ethnic diversity whose boundaries have shifted away from its original locus around Delancey Street. The Lower East was, by the 1920s, a hotbed of political activity and intellectual life. Various East Coast Beat writers lived in the Village from time to time. Diane di Prima resided for a while at the Albert Hotel. Allen Ginsberg lived in an apartment on East Twelfth Street and was an active member of the East Village community for many decades.

St. Mark's Place, in the East Village, was the main street for the counterculture in the 1960s, as waves of hippies descended into this area attracted by the cheap rents, tolerant radical politics, and the ambience of the lifestyle. Ed Sanders had his Peace Eye Book Shop there. Tompkins Square Park has in recent years been at the center of a bitter dispute over rights of the homeless. Many poets and artists affiliated with the Poetry Project at St. Mark's Church In-the-Bowery reside there as well.

The Poetry Project at St. Mark's Church In-the-Bowery

Part of an original arts project that included film and theater, the Poetry Project was founded in 1966 with a grant from President Lyndon Johnson's Office of Economic Opportunity, the mandate being "to work with alienated youth on the Lower East Side." Poets meeting regularly at the Cafe Metro then moved to the St. Mark's parish hall. St. Mark's—former Dutch Reformed Church (the second oldest church site in New York City), now Episcopal—has had a long and interesting "outrider" history: Isadora Duncan danced among the pews, Houdini performed feats of magic, Frank Lloyd Wright lectured there. After it became home to the Poetry Project, Paul Blackburn, with his huge Wollensack tape recorder, dutifully recorded the myriad bardic voices and became the spiritual "Daddy" for the Project, with Joel Oppenheimer as its first director. Since then, the Poetry Project has been a venue for public literary events, memorial readings, and marathon New Year all-day events, as well as serving as an ongoing haven and resource center for writers—offering workshops, a lecture series, publications, annual symposia, art auctions, and a quarterly newsletter. The Poetry Project archives house over 1,700 tapes and continues to grow under a new generation of leadership.

The historic graveyard has trees planted in memory of Allen Ginsberg, Frank O'Hara, Ted Berrigan and others. See *All Poets Welcome* and *The Angel Hair Anthology.*

The Bowery Poetry Club, Study Abroad on the Bowery

Founded by poet Bob Holman, The Bowery Poetry Club is a major performance venue and force on the music and poetry scene. It hosts round the clock events and performance from many different poetry "zones" and has one of the most diverse audiences in the country. Evenings honoring Gregory Corso's poem "Bomb" and Ginsberg's *Howl* are legendary.

A maverick pedagogical program entitled Study Abroad on the Bowery offers classes in writing, performance, and activism, providing a Certificate in Applied Poetics to students. The program seeks to preserve and enhance the oral tradition of poetry and to restore poetry to a central position in the culture.

Chelsea Hotel

Located at 222 West Twenty-third Street, the Chelsea Hotel was built in 1882 as the first cooperative apartment building in New York City and became a hotel in 1905. Celebrated literary guests and tenants over the years have included Mark Twain, O. Henry, Thomas Wolfe, Edgar Lee Masters, Dylan Thomas, William S. Burroughs, Herbert Huncke, Harry Smith, Gregory Corso, and James Schuyler. Andy Warhol's *Chelsea Girls* was filmed there. Many of the Beat writers lived in the Chelsea area in the fifties. Kerouac was writing *On the Road* while living on East Twenty-first Street. In 1958 and 1959 LeRoi Jones (Amiri Baraka) and Hettie Jones had their salon on Twentieth Street near Ninth Avenue. Harry Smith—archivist, anthropologist, and mystic extraordinaire—had his vast tape archive project housed at the Chelsea ("Materials for the Study of Religion and Culture") and recorded Allen Ginsberg's "First Blues" for Folkways Records. See Hettie Jones's memoir *How I Became Hettie Jones,* particularly the section "Twentieth Street."

Columbia University

Allen Ginsberg began studying at Columbia in 1943 while on a scholarship from the Paterson, New Jersey, YMCA, thinking he wanted to become a labor lawyer. He and Lucien Carr (now a journalist), also an undergraduate at Columbia, were looking for a "New Vision" in literature. They first lived in the Second Avenue dormitory at the Theological Seminary. Within a short time the two met up with William Burroughs and Jack Kerouac. Kerouac had originally come to New York from Lowell in 1939 at the age of seventeen to Horace Mann School and Columbia on a football scholarship. With the onset of World War II, he dropped out of Columbia to enlist in the Navy. He returned after a discharge (for "indifferent character") and a stint through the war as a merchant marine seaman. He complained about his Columbia friends' "tedious intellectualness." Burroughs introduced the others to Herbert Huncke, a Times Square hustler who introduced them to the word "beat" and the vivid haunts of Times Square. Neal Cassady showed up in 1946, a Denver acquaintance of one of Ginsberg's friends at Columbia. The opening pages of Kerouac's *On the Road* describe Cassady's impact on the Columbia group. Allen Ginsberg was expelled from Columbia twice, once after writing "Butler has no balls" (a reference to Columbia President Nicholas Murray Butler) and letting Kerouac sleep in his room overnight, and a second time after letting Huncke store stolen loot in his apartment. Ginsberg spent time in Presbyterian Hospital after the second episode. The West End Bar near Columbia was a gathering place for these early "outriders" along with writers Louis Simpson, John Hollander, and Richard Howard. Seminal teachers at Columbia included Raymond Weaver (first biographer of Melville and discoverer of the manuscript of *Billy Budd*, who taught Zen koans in his English 13 communication class), Lionel Trilling, Jacques Barzun, Meyer Shapiro, and F. W. Dupee.

Paris

Paris was the home of many heroes of the Beats—Dadaists, Surrealists, and Cubists, as well as Céline, Michaux, and Duchamp, the three elders whom Ginsberg and Corso sought out as "great masters." At the Père-Lachaise cemetery is Apollinaire's grave, another scene of pilgrimage, which occasioned a fine Ginsberg poem, "At Apollinaire's Grave."

On the Left Bank, around the corner from Place St. Michel at 9 rue Git-le-Coeur stood the unnamed hotel later dubbed the "Beat Hotel." Run by a Madame Rachou, it had a clientele of junkies, jazz musicians, prostitutes, artists, writers. In October, 1957, Allen Ginsberg and Peter Orlovsky took up residence there, and were shortly joined by Burroughs and Corso. This was the site of the final arranging of *Naked Lunch,* a long collaborative effort by Burroughs and his friends, which was first published by Olympia Press. Brion Gysin moved into the hotel; one day, cutting out a picture frame on a pile of newspapers, he discovered the "cut-up method" of writing. When challenged in the 1960s by Tristan Tzara as to why the Americans were doing what the Dadaists had invented decades before, he answered, "Because you did not do it well enough."

Reed College

Gary Snyder, Lew Welch, and Philip Whalen went to Reed College in Portland, Oregon. They shared a house, recognized one another as poets, and developed ongoing interests in Hindu and Buddhist ideas. Snyder found R. H. Blyth's volumes on haiku, which led them to D. T. Suzuki and into the literature of Zen. Snyder's graduating thesis, *He Who Hunted Bear in His Father's Village,* was published by Four Seasons in 1982. For years young writers made pilgrimages to Reed's library to read Welch's thesis, "How I Read Gertrude Stein," which Four Seasons Publications issued in 1996.

San Francisco

Gary Snyder's essay "North Beach" memorializes the early days in San Francisco. When the Beat poets arrived, there was already an active poetry scene meeting in local bars and apartments—the San Francisco Renaissance. Kenneth Rexroth, Jack Spicer, Robert Duncan, and Joanne Kyger met regularly, as well as many lesser-known political activists, painters, novelists, and journalists. In 1953 Lawrence Ferlinghetti opened City Lights Bookstore, the first bookshop in the United States devoted entirely to paperbacks. City Lights published Ginsburg's

Howl and Other Poems, which sparked off an historic obscenity trial against the publisher that ended in October 1957 with the acquittal of the defendants. Other City Lights authors include Bob Kaufman, Gregory Corso, Gary Snyder, Kenneth Rexroth, Paul Blackburn, Paul Bowles, Jaime de Angulo, and Philip Lamantia, as well as a constant infusion of writers from European, South American, Central American, and Mexican backgrounds. Across Jack Kerouac Alley from City Lights is Vesuvio's, scene of much drinking and conversation. Most of the jazz clubs Kerouac wrote about are gone, but the Cafe Trieste remains, and Chinatown sprawls out behind City Lights.

Across town at 300 Page Street is the San Francisco Zen Center, founded by students of Suzuki Roshi. The Center has for years been friendly to poets and students of Buddhism. Philip Whalen lived and wrote at the Page Street Center for years; in 1991 he was inducted abbot of the Hartford Street Zen Center in the Castro district, which houses an AIDS hospice.

Sourdough Mountain

Gary Snyder and Philip Whalen served summers as fire watchers on the summit of this isolated peak in the Cascades. Jack Kerouac served a summer on nearby Desolation Peak. See Whalen's poem "Sourdough Mountain," sections from his *Diamond Noodle,* Kerouac's *Desolation Angels,* Gary Snyder's "Lookout's Journal," and various poems.

Tangier

Tangier, Morocco, was the longtime residence of Paul Bowles, who helped establish the city as an expatriate haven. Poet and cut-up artist Brion Gysin ran a restaurant there from 1950 to 1958 but quit when his business partners, musicians from the Akl Sharif hill tribe, left a hidden amulet to drive him off. Burroughs wrote long letters from Tangier to Allen Ginsberg; parts of those letters became *Naked Lunch.* In the spring of 1957 Kerouac, then Ginsberg and Orlovsky, arrived with the express purpose of putting a book together from Burroughs's many scattered sheets of writing. See Regina Weinrich's movie *Paul Bowles: The Complete Outsider.*

Bibliography

||||||||||||||||||||||||||||||||||||||||||||||||||||||||||||||||||||||||||||||||||||||||||||||||||||||||||

Primary Sources

Baraka, Amiri. *Dutchman and the Slave.* New York: William Morrow, 1971.

———. *The Autobiography of LeRoi Jones/Amiri Baraka.* New York: Freundlich Books, 1984.

———. *The LeRoi Jones/Amiri Baraka Reader,* 2nd ed. Edited by William J. Harris. New York: Thunder's Mouth, 1999.

———. *Transbluesency: Selected Poems 1961–1995.* New York: Marsilio, 1995.

Burroughs, William S. *The Western Lands.* New York: Viking Penguin, 1988.

———. *Naked Scientology, Ali's Smile.* New York: Left Bank, 1991.

———. *Nova Express.* New York: Grove-Atlantic, 1992.

———. *Port of Saints.* Berkeley, Calif.: Blue Wind, 1992.

———. *The Soft Machine.* New York: Grove-Atlantic, 1992.

———. *The Wild Boys: A Book of the Dead.* New York: Grove-Atlantic, 1992.

———. *My Education: A Book of Dreams.* New York: Viking, 1995.

———. *The Ticket That Exploded.* New York: Grove-Atlantic, n.d.

Burroughs, William S., and Allen Ginsberg and Oliver Harris, ed. *The Yage Letters Redux.* San Francisco: City Lights, 2006.

Burroughs, William S., and James Grauerholz and Barry Miles, eds. *Naked Lunch: The Restored Text.* New York: Grove Press, 2004.

Burroughs, William S., and Oliver Harris, ed. *Junky,* 50th Anniversary Edition. New York: Penguin, 2003.

Cassady, Neal. *The First Third.* San Francisco: City Lights, 1971.

Corso, Gregory. *Gasoline, The Vestal Lady on Brattle and Other Poems.* Pocket Poets Series no. 8. San Francisco: City Lights, 1981.

————. *Long Live Man*. New York: New Directions, 1962.

————. *Herald of the Autochthonous Spirit*. New York: New Directions, 1981.

————. *Mindfield, New and Selected Poems,* 2nd ed. New York: Thunder's Mouth, 1998.

————. *An Accidental Autobiography*. New York: New Directions, 2003.

di Prima, Diane. *Memoirs of a Beatnik*. New York: Penguin, 1998.

————. *Revolutionary Letters*. San Francisco: City Lights, 1971.

————. *Loba*. New York: Penguin, 1998.

————. *Selected Poems: 1956–1975*. Plainfield, Vermont: North Atlantic, 1975.

————. *Pieces of a Song: Selected Poems*. San Francisco: City Lights, 1990.

————. *Recollections of My Life as a Woman*. New York: Penguin, 2002.

Ferlinghetti, Lawrence. *A Coney Island of the Mind*. New York: New Directions, 1968.

————. *These Are My Rivers: New and Selected Poems 1955–1993*. New York: New Directions, 1993.

————. *Americus, Book 1*. New York: New Directions, 2005.

Ginsberg, Allen. *Howl and Other Poems*. San Francisco: City Lights, 1956.

————. *Collected Poems 1947–1980*. New York: Harper & Row, 1985.

————. *Howl: Original Draft Facsimile, Transcript and Variant Versions*. Edited by Barry Miles. New York: Harper & Row, 1986.

————. *Cosmopolitan Greetings, Poems 1986–1992*. New York: HarperCollins, 1994.

————. *Death and Fame: Last Poems 1993–1997*. New York: Harper Perennial, 2000.

————. *Deliberate Prose: Selected Essays 1952–1995*. New York: Harper Perennial, 2001.

————. *Selected Poems: 1947–1995*. New York: Harper Perennial, 2001.

————. *Collected Poems 1947–1997*. New York: HarperCollins, 2006.

Kandel, Lenore. *The Love Book*. Oakland, Calif.: Superstition Street Press, 2003.

————. *Word Alchemy*. New York: Grove, 1967.

Kaufman, Bob. *Abomunist Manifesto*. San Francisco: City Lights, 1959.

————. *Solitudes Crowded with Loneliness*. New York: New Directions, 1965.

————. *Golden Sardine*. Pocket Poets Series no. 21. San Francisco: City Lights, 1967.

————. *The Ancient Rain: Poems 1956–1978*. Edited by Raymond Foye. New York: New Directions, 1981.

————. *Cranial Guitar*. Minneapolis: Coffee House, 1996.

Kerouac, Jack. *Mexico City Blues*. New York: Grove, 1959.

————. *The Town and the City*. San Diego: Harcourt Brace, 1970.

————. *The Dharma Bums*. New York: Viking Penguin, 1971.

————. *Desolation Angels*. New York: Perigee, 1978.

————. *Visions of Gerard*. New York: McGraw-Hill, 1990.

————. *On the Road*. New York: Viking Penguin, 2002.

————. *Big Sur*. New York: Viking Penguin, 1992.

————. *Visions of Cody*. New York: Viking Penguin, 1993.

————. *Vanity of Duluoz*. New York: Viking Penguin, 1994.

————. *The Scripture of the Golden Eternity*. San Francisco: City Lights, 1994.

————. *Some of the Dharma*. New York: Penguin, 1999.

Kerouac, Jack, and Douglas Brinkley, ed. *Windblown World: The Journals of Jack Kerouac 1947–1954*. New York: Penguin, 2006.

Kyger, Joanne. *The Tapestry and the Web*. San Francisco: Four Seasons Foundation, 1965.

————. *Places To Go*. Los Angeles: Black Sparrow, 1970.

————. *All This Every Day*. Berkeley, Calif.: Big Sky, 1975.

————. *The Wonderful Focus of You*. Calais, Vermont: Z Press, 1980.

————. *Just Space: Poems 1979–1989*. Santa Rosa, Calif.: Black Sparrow, 1991.

————. *Again: Poems 1989–2000*. Albuquerque: La Alameda Press, 2001.

————. *As Ever: Selected Poems*. New York: Penguin, 2002.

————. *Strange Big Moon: The Japan and India Journals, 1960–1964*. Berkeley, Calif.: North Atlantic Books, 2000.

McClure, Michael. *Meat Science Essays*. San Francisco: City Lights, 1963.

————. *Ghost Tantras*. San Francisco: Four Seasons Foundation, 1969.

————. *Antechamber and Other Poems*. New York: New Directions, 1978.

————. *Selected Poems*. New York: New Directions, 1986.

————. *Rebel Lions*. New York: New Directions, 1991.

————. *Huge Dreams: San Francisco and Beat Poems*. New York: Penguin, 1998.

————. *Scratching the Beat Surface*. New York: Penguin, 1995.

————. *Touching the Edge*. Boston: Shambhala, 1999.

Orlovsky, Peter. *Leper's Cry*. New York: Phoenix Bookshop, 1982.

————. *Clean Asshole Poems and Smiling Vegetable Songs, Poems 1957–1977*. Pocket Poets Series no. 37. San Francisco: City Lights, 1978. Reprint. Orono, Maine: Northern Lights, 1993.

Snyder, Gary. *Riprap*. Kyoto: Origin, 1959.

———. *The Back Country*. New York: New Directions, 1968.

———. *Earth House Hold: Technical Notes and Queries to Fellow Dharma Revolutionaries*. New York: New Directions, 1969.

———. *Mountains and Rivers Without End*. New York: Counterpoint, 1997.

———. *Axe Handles*, Reprint ed. Emeryville, Calif.: Shoemaker and Hoard, 2005.

———. *Left Out in the Rain*. Berkeley, Calif.: North Point, 1986.

———. *No Nature: New and Selected Poems*. New York: Pantheon, 1992.

———. *The Gary Snyder Reader*. New York: Counterpoint, 2000.

———. *The Practice of the Wild*. Emeryville, Calif.: Shoemaker & Hoard, 2004.

Wieners, John. *The Hotel Wentley Poems*. San Francisco: Averhahn, 1958; rev. ed., San Francisco: Dave Haselwood, 1965.

———. *Selected Poems, 1958–1984*. Santa Barbara: Black Sparrow, 1986.

———. *Cultural Affairs in Boston*. Santa Rosa, Calif.: Black Sparrow, 1988.

Welch, Lew. *I, Leo: An Unfinished Novel*. San Francisco: Grey Fox, 1977.

———. *Ring of Bone: Collected Poems 1950–1971*. San Francisco: Grey Fox, 1979.

Whalen, Philip. *On Bear's Head*. New York: Harcourt, Brace and World, 1964.

———. *The Diamond Noodle*. Berkeley, Calif.: Poltroon, 1980.

———. *Heavy Breathing: Poems 1967–1983*. San Francisco: Four Seasons Foundation, 1980.

———. *Overtime: Selected Poems*. New York: Penguin, 1999.

Anthologies

Allen, Donald, ed. *The New American Poetry 1945–1960*. New York: Grove, 1960.

Allen, Donald, and George Butterick. *The Post-Moderns: The New American Poetry Revised*. New York: Grove, 1982.

Charters, Ann, ed. *The Portable Beat Reader*. New York: Viking Penguin, 1992.

Clay, Steven, and Rodney Phillips. *A Secret Location on the Lower East Side: Adventures in Writing, 1960–1980*. New York: Granary Books, 1998.

Johnson, Kent, and Greg Paulenich, eds. *Beneath a Single Moon: Buddhism in Contemporary American Poetry*. Boston: Shambhala Publications, 1991.

Knight, Arthur, and Kit Knight, eds. *The Beat Vision*. New York: Paragon, 1987.

———. *Kerouac and the Beats*. New York: Paragon, 1988.

Knight, Brenda, ed. *Women of the Beat Generation*. Berkeley, Calif.: Conari Press, 1996.

McDarrah, Fred, ed. and photographer. *Kerouac and Friends, A Beat Generation Album*. New York: William Morrow, 1985.

Peabody, Richard. *A Different Beat: Writing by Women of the Beat Generation*. London: Serpent's Tail, 1997.

Tonkinson, Carole, ed. *Big Sky Mind: Buddhism and the Beat Generation*. New York: Riverhead, 1995.

Waldman, Anne, ed. *Out of This World: An Anthology of Writing from the St. Mark's Poetry Project 1966–1991*. New York: Crown, 1992.

Waldman, Anne, and Lisa Birman, eds. *Civil Disobediences*. Minneapolis: Coffee House Press, 2004.

Interviews, Journals, Letters, Essays

Allen, Donald, ed. *Off the Wall: Interviews with Philip Whalen*. Bolinas, Calif.: Four Seasons Foundation, 1978.

Burroughs, William S. *Letters to Allen Ginsberg 1953–57*. New York: Full Court, 1982.

Burroughs, William S., with Daniel Odier. *The Job: Writings and Interviews*. London: Calder, 1984.

Charters, Ann, ed. *Jack Kerouac: Selected Letters 1940–1956*. New York: Viking Penguin, 1995.

Ginsberg, Allen. *Indian Journals*. San Francisco: City Lights, 1970.

———. *Allen Verbatim: Lectures on Poetry, Politics, Consciousness*. New York: McGraw-Hill, 1974.

———. *As Ever: The Collected Correspondence of Allen Ginsberg and Neal Cassady*. Berkeley, Calif.: Creative Arts, 1977.

———. *Composed on the Tongue: Literary Conversations 1967–1977*. Bolinas, Calif.: Grey Fox, 1980.

———. *Journals Mid-Fifties 1954–1958*. Edited by Gordon Ball. New York: HarperCollins, 1995.

Ginsberg, Allen, and William S. Burroughs. *The Yage Letters*. San Francisco: City Lights, 1963.

Harris, Oliver, ed. *The Letters of William Burroughs 1945–1959*. New York: Viking Penguin, 1993.

McClure, Michael. *Scratching the Beat Surface: Essays on New Vision from Blake to Kerouac*. New York: Penguin, 1994.

Snyder, Gary. *The Real Work: Interviews and Talks 1964–1979*. New York: New Directions, 1980.

———. *Passage through India*. San Francisco: Grey Fox Press, 1984.

————. *The Practice of the Wild.* New York: Farrar, Straus & Giroux Inc., 1990.

————. *A Place in Space.* Washington, D.C.: Counterpoint, 1995.

Welch, Lew. *How I Work as a Poet and Other Essays.* San Francisco: Grey Fox, 1973.

————. *I Remain: The Letters of Lew Welch and the Correspondence of His Friends.* 2 vols. San Francisco: Grey Fox, 1980.

Biographies

Charters, Ann. *Kerouac: A Biography.* San Francisco: Straight Arrow, 1973.

————. ed. *The Beats: Literary Bohemians in Postwar America.* Vol. 16, Parts 1 and 2 of *Dictionary of Literary Biography.* Detroit: Gale Research, 1983.

Gifford, Barry, and Lawrence Lee. *Jack's Book: An Oral Biography of Jack Kerouac.* New York: Penguin, 1979.

Halper, Jon, ed. *Gary Snyder: Dimensions of a Life.* San Francisco: Sierra Club Books, 1991.

McNally, Dennis. *Desolate Angel: Jack Kerouac, The Beat Generation and America.* New York: Delta Books, 1979.

Miles, Barry. *Ginsberg: A Biography.* New York: Simon & Schuster, 1989.

————. *William Burroughs: El Hombre Invisible, A Portrait.* New York: Hyperion, 1992.

Morgan, Bill. *I Celebrate Myself: The Somewhat Private Life of Allen Ginsberg.* New York: Viking, 2006.

Morgan, Ted. *Literary Outlaw, The Life and Times of William S. Burroughs.* New York: Henry Holt, 1988.

Mottram, Eric. *William Burroughs: The Algebra of Need.* London: Marion Boyars, 1977.

Nicosia, Gerald. *Memory Babe: A Critical Biography of Jack Kerouac.* New York: Grove, 1985.

Saroyan, Aram. *Genesis Angels: The Saga of Lew Welch and the Beat Generation.* New York: William Morrow, 1979.

Schumacher, Michael. *Dharma Lion: A Biography of Allen Ginsberg.* New York: St. Martin's, 1992.

Silesky, Barry. *Ferlinghetti: The Artist in His Time.* New York: Warner, 1990.

Skerl, Jennie. *William S. Burroughs.* Boston: Twayne, 1985.

Related Texts

Cassady, Carolyn. *Off The Road, My Years with Cassady, Kerouac and Ginsberg.* New York: Morrow, 1990.

————. *Heart Beat, My Life with Jack and Neal.* Berkeley, Calif.: Creative Arts, 1976.

Charters, Ann, photographs and text. *Beats & Company,* Portrait of a Literary Generation. New York: Dolphin Doubleday, 1986.

Davidson, Michael. *The San Francisco Renaissance, Poetics and Community at Mid-Century.* New York: Cambridge University Press, 1989.

Ferlinghetti, Lawrence, and Nancy J. Peters. *Literary San Francisco.* New York: Harper & Row, 1980.

Fields, Rick. *How the Swans Came to the Lake: A Narrative History of Buddhism in America,* Third Edition. Boston: Shambhala Publications, 1992.

Gifford, Barry. *Kerouac's Town.* Santa Barbara, Calif.: Capra, 1973.

Goddard, Dwight. *A Buddhist Bible.* Boston: Beacon, 1994.

Gysin, Brion. *The Third Mind,* with William S. Burroughs. New York: Seaver Books, 1987.

Holmes, John Clellon. *Go.* New York: Ace, 1952.

Huncke, Herbert. *The Evening Sun Turned Crimson.* New York: Cherry Valley, 1980.

Johnson, Joyce. *Minor Characters.* New York: Houghton Mifflin, 1983.

Jones, Hettie. *How I Became Hettie Jones.* New York: Penguin, 1990.

Kerouac, Jack. *Reads On The Road.* Beverly, Mass.: Rykodisc, 1999.

Lee, A. Robert. *The Beat Generation Writers.* East Haven, Conn.: Pluto Press, 1996.

Meltzer, David. *The San Francisco Poets.* New York: Ballantine Books, 1971.

Morgan, Bill. *Howl on Trial: The Battle for Free Expression.* San Francisco: City Lights, 2006.

Norse, Harold. *Beat Hotel.* San Diego: Atticus, 1983.

Olson, Charles. *Reading at Berkeley.* Berkeley, Calif.: Small Press Distribution, 1966.

Rexroth, Kenneth. *The Collected Shorter Poems.* New York: New Directions, 1966.

————. *The Collected Longer Poems.* New York: New Directions, 1968.

Sanders, Ed. *Tales of Beatnik Glory.* New York: Carol Publishing Group, 1990.

Suzuki, Daisetz Teitaro. *Essays in Zen Buddhism.* New York: Grove-Atlantic, 1989.

Suzuki, Shunryu. *Zen Mind Beginner's Mind.* New York: John Weatherhill, 1970.

Trungpa, Chögyam. *The Myth of Freedom: And the Way of Meditation.* Boston: Shambhala Publications, 1988.

Tytell, John. *Naked Angels: The Lives and Literature of the Beat Generation.* New York: McGraw-Hill, 1976.

Films

Fried Shoes, Cooked Diamonds. With Gregory Corso, William Burroughs, Allen Ginsberg, Timothy Leary, Peter Orlovsky, Anne Waldman. Directed by Constanzo Allione. New York: Mystic Fire Video, n.d.

It Don't Pay To Be An Honest Citizen. With bit parts by Allen Ginsberg and William S. Burroughs. New York: Object Productions/ Jacob Burkhardt, 1984.

The Life and Times of Allen Ginsberg. Directed by Jerry Aronson. New York: First Run Features, 1992.

Poetry In Motion. Produced by Ron Mann Sphinx Productions. New York: Giorno Poetry Systems, n.d.

Pull My Daisy. Narrated by Jack Kerouac, with Gregory Corso, Peter Orlovsky, Larry Rivers, and David Amram. Directed by Robert Frank and A. Leslie. Houston: Houston Museum of Art, 1958.

What Happened to Kerouac. Directed by Richard Lerner and Lewis MacAdams. New York: New Yorker Films, 1985.

Audio Recordings

The Beat Generation. Santa Monica, Calif.: Rhino/Word Beat, 1992.

Burroughs, William S. *Call Me Burroughs.* Santa Monica, Calif.: Rhino/Word Beat, 1994.

Burroughs, William, et al. *First Thought, Best Thought.* Boulder, Colorado: Sounds True, 2004.

Ginsberg, Allen. *Holy Soul Jelly Roll: Poems and Songs 1949–1993.* Santa Monica, Calif.: Rhino/Word Beat, 1994.

———. *Howl and Other Poems.* Berkeley, Calif.: Fantasy Rerelease, 1998.

Kerouac, Jack. *The Jack Kerouac Collection.* Santa Monica, Calif.: Rhino/Word Beat, 1993.

Web Sites

Allen Ginsberg: Trust www.allenginsberg.org
Amiri Baraka: www.amiribaraka.com
City Lights Bookstore: www.citylights.com
Diane di Prima: dianediprima.com
Jacket Magazine: jacketmagazine.com
John Wieners: tomraworth.com/wieners.html
Modern American Poetry: www.english.uiuc.edu/maps/index.htm
Museum of American Poets: www.poetspath.com
Naropa Audio Archive: www.naropa.edu/audioarchive/
PennSound: www.writing.upenn.edu/pennsound
Philip Whalen: epc.buffalo.edu/authors/whalen/index.html
The Beat Museum: www.Kerouac.com or info@kerouac.com

Credits